T5-BAR-990

THE ECONOMICS OF SMALL FIRMS

A EUROPEAN CHALLENGE

Studies in Industrial Organization

Volume 11

The Economics of Small Firms

A European Challenge

edited by

ZOLTAN J. ACS

Merrick School of Business, University of Baltimore, Baltimore, U.S.A.

and

DAVID B. AUDRETSCH

Wissenschaftszentrum Berlin für Sozialforschung, Berlin, F.R.G.

KLUWER ACADEMIC PUBLISHERS

DORDRECHT / BOSTON / LONDON

Library of Congress Cataloging-in-Publication Data

The Economics of small firms : a European challenge / edited by Zoltan J. Acs and David B. Audretsch.
p. cm. -- (Studies in industrial organization ; 11)
ISBN 0-7923-0484-5 (U.S.)
1. Small business--Congresses. I. Ács, Zoltán J. II. Audretsch, David B. III. Series: Studies in industrial organization ; v. 11.
HD2341.E255 1990
338.6'42--dc20 89-38742
CIP

Published by Kluwer Academic Publishers,
P.O. Box 17, 3300 AA Dordrecht, The Netherlands

Sold and distributed in the U.S.A. and Canada
by Kluwer Academic Publishers,
101 Philip Drive, Norwell, MA 02061, U.S.A.

In all other countries, sold and distributed
by Kluwer Academic Publishers Group,
P.O. Box 322, 3300 AH Dordrecht, The Netherlands

Printed on acid-free paper.

PRINTED IN THE NETHERLANDS

Table of Contents

List of Tables

List of Figures

List of Figures

Chapter 2

2.1 [illegible] Rates, Controlled by Human [illegible]

Chapter 3

3.1 [illegible] of Innovations and [illegible] Large and Small Firms

Chapter 4

4.1 The Potential Relation between Growth and Capital [illegible]

Chapter 5

5.1 [illegible]

Chapter 6

6.1 [illegible]

Chapter 7

7.1 [illegible]

Chapter 8

8.1 [illegible]

Chapter 9

9.1 [illegible] of Machine [illegible]

Acknowledgements

On November 17–18, 1988, an international conference was held in West Berlin at the Wissenschaftszentrum Berlin für Sozialforschung (WZB). The purpose of the conference was to examine the increasing importance of small firms in national economies. It was Joachim Schwalbach who first suggested the idea of holding a conference on the subject. It goes without saying that an international conference of this dimension could not have been held without significant support. We are grateful to the WZB for financial support and to Manfred Fleischer for institutional guidance.

We would like to thank all of the participants for the time and effort they put into the conference and their papers. Their willingness to rewrite to our exacting specifications is greatly appreciated. Special thanks go to Bruce Kirchhoff of Fairleigh Dickinson University and David J. Storey of the University of Warwick for their efforts at helping to organize the conference at various stages. David S. Evans, Joachim Schwalbach, David J. Storey and Bo Carlsson read the introduction and made many helpful suggestions.

Special thanks go to Linda Cieminski, Christian Loycke de Roux and Hannelore Trautmann for organizing the day-to-day activities of the conference. Their painstaking support made the conference a pleasure for participants and organizers alike. We thank the *AER* for permission to reprint chapter six.

1. Small Firms in the 1990s*

ZOLTAN J. ACS and DAVID B. AUDRETSCH

I. Introduction

In the Fall of 1988 an international conference was held at the Wissenschaftszentrum Berlin für Sozialforschung (WZB). This was the first conference devoted entirely to the subject of Small Business Economics. The present volume which is an outgrowth of that conference contains revised versions of papers which were presented at that conference. Most of the papers in this book grew out of research projects examining the role of small firms in national economies. We include papers from six countries exploiting twelve rich databases.

The major themes of research in the field of small business economics are not new. Many of these questions have been touched upon previously by A. Marshall (1920) who analysed the process of industry evolution, F. Knight's (1921) discussion of the characteristics of the entrepreneur, and J. Schumpeter's (1934) examination of the role of the entrepreneur in economic development are classics. However, despite the increased importance of small firms and their growing contribution to advanced economies, most of the literature in economics concerned with firm size has focused on the role of large firms. The purpose of this conference was to examine the increasing importance of small firms in the economy today.

The volume before us does not cover the whole field of small business economics.[1] It examines few issues of methodology on what constitutes a small firm, and it does not include the rich literature on financing small business (Horowitz and Pettit, 1984, and Evans and Jovanovic, 1989). The question of job generation and public policy, which has been examined in great detail (Storey and Johnson, 1987), is only touched upon here. Also, issues of regulation and deregulation (Brock and Evans, 1986), as well as issues of regional development (Florida and Kenney, 1988) are excluded. The focus of this volume is much narrower. Most of the papers deal with fundamental questions, some of which have not been systematically examined before an international context: firm growth, entrepreneurship, technology, employment.

We feel that projects in international comparative research offer an enormous potential for insight, comprehension, and learning, not only for the community of scholars, but for policy analysis as well. Creating networks of researchers, and thus expanding the scope for theorizing beyond national boundaries is natural in a world that is increasingly characterized by the internationalization of markets. To be sure, comparative international research poses formal barriers of language, information gathering, and interpretation. To this challenge we rise.

Our plan in this introductory chapter is as follows. In the second section we present evidence on the emergence of small firms in the U.S. which has resulted in a fundamental shift in the size distribution of firms. The reasons for this shift are examined in the third section.

Z.J. Acs and D.B. Audretsch (eds.), The Economics of Small Firms: A European Challenge. 1–22.

In the fourth section we turn to the question of small-firm growth. Small-firm growth is a different and more complex question than commonly understood. This leads to the discussion of entrepreneurship in the fifth section. The sixth section examines the role of technological change and its impact on small firms. The seventh section examines the question of job generation, while the penultimate section considers arguments why Europeans should abandon their unquestionable faith in economies of scale for support of small firms.

II. The Emergence of Small Firms

Our story begins in the U.S.[2] It was in the area of job generation that the recent emergence of small firms was first identified. In 1981 David Birch revealed the startling findings from his long-term study of U.S. job generation. Despite the prevailing conventional wisdom at the time, Birch (1981, p. 8) found that, "... whatever else they are doing, large firms are no longer the major providers of new jobs for Americans." Instead, he discovered that most new jobs emanated from small firms. While his exact methodology and application of the underlying data have been a source of considerable controversy (Storey and Johnson, 1987; and Armington and Odle, 1982), as well as the exact quantitative estimates, his qualitative conclusion that the bulk of new jobs have emanated from small enterprises has been largely substantiated (Acs and Audretsch, 1989a). Of course, as a number of critics have pointed out (see FitzRoy, 1989a), the entire notion and measure of job generation is elusive, because no information is gained about the extent to which the generated jobs subsequently disappear. This qualification also applies to the observation that the number of new U.S. businesses has been drastically increasing over time. Still, in 1976 there were 376,000 new firms started, while in 1986 there were 703,000 new businesses. This 87 percent increase was more than twice as great as the 39 percent increase in Gross National Product which occurred over the same period (Brock and Evans, 1989) What is perhaps more striking is that average real GNP-per-firm increased by nearly two-thirds between 1947 and 1980, from $ 150,000 to $ 250,000. However, within the next seven years it had fallen by about 14 percent to $ 210,000.

This emergence of small firms has not escaped the attention of the popular press. For example, *The Economist* reports, "Despite ever-larger and noisier mergers, the biggest change coming over the world of business is that firms are getting smaller. The trend of a century is being reversed. Until the mid-1970s the size of firms everywhere grew; the numbers of self-employed fell. Ford and General Motors replaced the carriage-maker's atelier; McDonald's Safeway and W.H. Smith supplanted the corner shop. No longer. Now it is the big firms that are shrinking and small ones that are on the rise. The trend is unmistakable – and businessmen and policy-makers will ignore it at their peril".[3]

Of course, there is a temptation to attribute this relative increase in the number of small firms and in small-firm employment to the obvious long-term transition of employment into services and out of the manufacturing sector. That is, employment in U.S. manufacturing fell from 40 percent of the total work force in 1959 to 27.7 percent of the work force in 1984. In fact, as we will shortly show, the shift in economic activity from large to small firms has been even greater in manufacturing than in services or finance.

Until recently it was virtually impossible to measure U.S. economic activity for small firms as well as for large firms, and to make comparisons over time. As a result of this lack of information about small firms, and in order to understand the economic impact of small business in the economy, the U.S. Congress passed the Economic Policy Act of 1980, which commissioned the U.S. Small Business Administration to create the Small Business Data Base. We use this data base here to measure the extent to which small firms have emerged as a driving force in the U.S. economy. More complete explanations of the data can be found in Acs and Audretsch (1989a) and Phillips and Kirchhoff (1989), and Brown and Phillips (1989).

Table 1.1 shows the percentage of net employment growth between 1976 and 1986 according to five firm-size categories. What is perhaps most surprising is that large firms, defined as firms with at least 500 employees, experienced negative growth in manufacturing, while they accounted for nearly half of the employee growth in the service and finance sectors. As Table 1.2 indicates, overall employment for the economy grew during this period by about one-third. However, small firms, defined as those with fewer than 500 employees, accounted for well over one-half of this growth. An implication from Tables 1.1 and 1.2 is that, had there not been a shift in employment out of manufacturing and into services and the finance sector, the emergence of small firms in the U.S. economy would have been even greater. This is because new jobs have been consistently generated by small firms at a *higher* rate in manufacturing than in either services or the finance sector.

That a sizeable restructuring of American manufacturing markets has occurred is evident in Fig. 1.1, which compares the share of manufacturing sales accounted for by small firms between 1976 and 1986. In 1976 firms with fewer than 100 employees accounted for 11.6 percent of sales in manufacturing. By 1986 their share of manufacturing sales had risen by more than one-quarter, to nearly 15 percent. Similarly, the share of sales accounted for by U.S. firms with fewer than 500 employees rose from 20.4 percent in 1976 to 25.8 percent in 1986. It is clear from Tables 1.1-2 that a fundamental shift in the size distribution of firms has occurred. Small firms are playing an increasingly important role in the U.S. economy, and particularly in the manufacturing sector.

Table 1.1. Employment growth and small-firm share of growth by sector, 1976–1986.[a]

	Employment growth rate (%)	Small-firm share (%)
Aggregate	32.36	57.23
Manufacturing	6.00	110.00
Service	69.09	53.75
Finance	71.15	51.74

[a] A small firm is defined as an enterprise with fewer than 500 employees. The small-firm share is the percentage of new jobs accounted for by small firms.

Source: U.S. Small Business Administration, Office of Advocacy, Small Business Database, USELM file, V.9, December 1987 (Table prepared August 1988).

Table 1.2. Percentage of employment growth by size of firm, 1976–1986.

Number of employees in firm	Percentage of employment growth			
	Aggregate 1976–1986	Manufacturing 1976–1986	Services 1976–1986	Finance 1976–1986
1–19	26.23	64.85	20.76	21.24
20–99	17.43	41.46	15.93	16.15
100–499	13.57	4.60	17.06	14.35
500 +	42.77	– 10.91	46.25	48.26
Total	100.00	100.00	100.00	100.00

Source: U.S. Small Business Administration, Office of Advocacy, Small Business Database, USELM file, V.9, December 1987 (Table prepared August 1988).

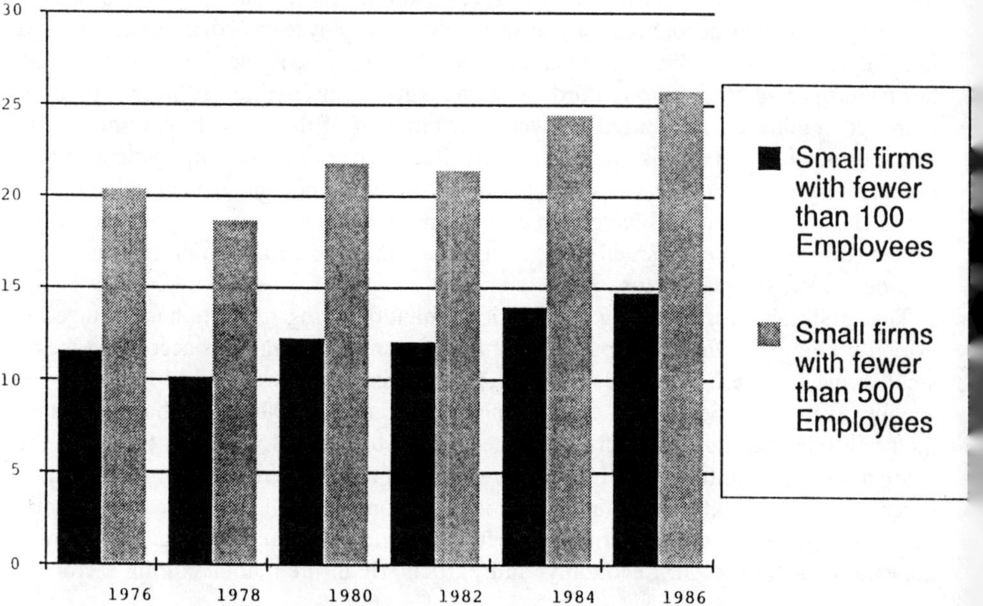

Fig. 1.1. Percentage of sales contributed by small manufacturing firms, 1976–1986. *Source*: U.S. Establishment and Enterprise Microdata File, April 1988.

III. Shift in the Firm-Size Distribution

There are at least six major factors underlying the shift in the firm size distribution, which was documented in the previous section. These are: (1) the implementation of new flexible technologies; (2) the increased globalization of American markets; (3) a changing composition of the labor force; (4) the proliferation of consumer demand, away from standardized mass-produced goods and towards stylized and personalized products; (5) government deregulation in numerous markets; and (6) a period of "creative destruction", in the Schumpeterian (1934) sense, is currently ongoing, whereby a cluster of innovations, in the sense that Mensch (1979) introduced, are reshaping industries, just as entrepreneurs developing new products and processes are displacing existing entrenched firms and institutions. While the evidence is still inconclusive, we believe that the most *decisive* factor contributing to the emergence of small firms has been a fundamental shift in the underlying technology.

Throughout most of this century, industrial technology favored mass production, or the application of special purpose machines to produce standardized products. Inherent in this technology is inflexibility and a bias towards large firms over small firms. However, more recently manufacturing technology "... has been revolutionized by the cost reduction of small-scale production relative to large-scale and the degree of flexibility offered by the technology" (Carlsson, 1984). Piore and Sabel (1984) suggest that the emergence of this new flexible technology represents, in fact, an "industrial divide" where firms and society are confronted with a choice of technological modes. In referring to the Italian example, where an increased reliance on small-scale production has resulted from underlying technological and institutional changes, Piore and Sable (1983) argue that flexible production will tend to promote the relative viability of small firms.

Increased globalization has rendered U.S. markets more subject to volatility, as a result of both competition from a greater number of foreign competitors as well as from exchange rate fluctuations. Thus, organizational and productive flexibility, which tend to be more within the domain of small firms than in that of their larger counterparts, is increasingly a valuable asset. The changing composition of the labor force has also been a catalyst for small enterprises. The increase in the labor-force participation of women and the entry of the baby boom generation into the labor market have increased the supply of exactly the kinds of labor which are most conducive to small firms. The percentage of American mothers with newly born children active in the labor force has increased from 37.5 percent in 1980 to 49.5 percent in 1986. Similarly, the percentage of first-time mothers who are active in the labor force increased from 45.5 percent in 1980 to 57.0 percent in 1986.[4] Not only is the flexibility of small firms more compatible to the schedules of working mothers, but Evans and Leighton (1989) found that between 1975 and 1985 the female self-employment rate increased by more than one-third, while the male self-employment rate increased by about one-tenth. That is, women are increasingly starting their own firms. In addition, the decrease in U.S. real wage rates during the 1970s and early 1980s may also have provided smaller firms, which are presumably labor-intensive, with a competitive advantage over their larger counterparts, which are more likely to be relatively capital-intensive.

The proliferation of consumer tastes, away from standardized mass-produced goods and towards stylized and personalized products has also been a catalyst for small firms. To the extent that relatively small batches of customized products are replacing long production runs of standardized goods, the inherent cost disadvantage of small-scale production will tend to decrease. Several explanations for the destandardization of consumer tastes have been hypothesized, most invoking the notion that consumer demand is derived from a hierarchy of needs, where there has been a "... shift from an economy geared to the provision of a few basic 'gut' needs to one that covers itself with supplying the endlessly diverse needs of the psyche as well" (Toffler, 1985, p. 37). The ascent up the hierarchy of needs is generally attributed to the increase in the U.S. average standard of living, the increase in education levels, and the development of the communication media, providing consumers with access to greater information about the rest of the world. As consumers become more aware of the variety and richness of consumption possibilities, and as they increasingly attain the discretionary income enabling them to actualize some of their wishes, patterns of demand tend to shift away from mass-produced goods towards specialized goods. Of course to the extent that consumer tastes are destandardized, mass-production enterprises no longer maintain a market advantage. When consumers preferred a standardized product at the lowest possible price, firms with a level of production large enough to exhaust scale economies prevailed. But with the advent of demand proliferation, mass-production firms face the loss of consumers to an array of differentiated custom-produced substitutes from small competitors.

The recent deregulation movement in the U.S. may also have contributed to the viability of small enterprises. For example, the relaxation of entry regulations in certain industries, such as telephone manufacturing and financial services, has increased the opportunities for small business. During the early 1980s, small firms experienced higher growth rates and gained market share while the large firms experienced lower growth rates and lost market share in the deregulated industries as a whole (Phillips, 1985).

The final factor contributing to the recent emergence of small firms is the current cluster of innovations that are coming as much from small firms as from large ones. The most convincing evidence in support of this comes from a data base of innovative activity assembled by the U.S. Small Business Administration, and analyzed in our 1987a, 1987b, 1988 papers, and 1990 book. The data base consists of 8,074 innovations introduced into the U.S. in 1982. Of those innovations, 4,476 were identified as occurring in manufacturing industries.

In 1982, the large firms in manufacturing introduced 2,608 innovations. The small firms contributed slightly fewer, 1,923. However, small-firm employment was only about one-half as great as large-firm employment, so that the mean small-firm innovation rate, or number of innovations per million employees, was 322 (Fig. 1.2). By contrast, the large-firm innovation rate in manufacturing was 225. This suggests that although the larger firms contributed just over one-half of the total number of innovations, small firms proved to be more innovative in the sense that they required fewer employees, on average, to produce innovations. While these findings are somewhat startling, they are consistent with the Schumpeterian notion of "creative destruction" and the statistical findings in our 1989b, 1989c and 1989d papers that innovative activity is a strategy which small firms have been using to enter industries and remain viable in industries in which they otherwise would experience an inherent cost disadvantage. We now turn to our main themes.

IV. Small-Firm Growth

Historically small firms have played an important role in industry evolution. Alfred Marshall (1920, p. 263) described this process of industry evolution by analogy, where one can observe "... the young trees of the forest as they struggle upwards through the benumbing shade of their older rivals." Marshall's view of industry dynamics is not so

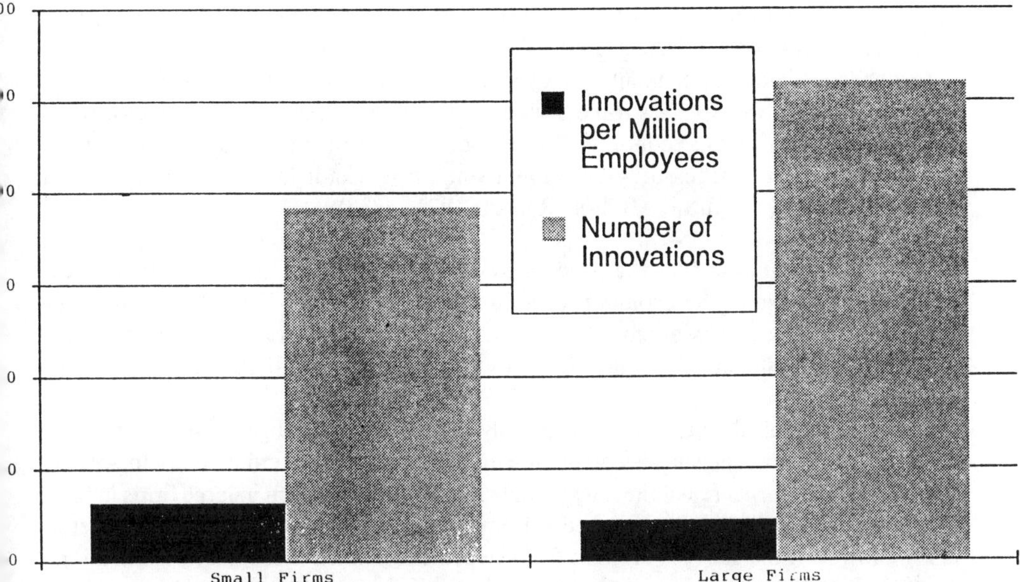

Fig. 1.2. Number of innovations, and innovations per million employees in large and small firms. *Source*: U.S. Small Business Administration Innovation Data Base, 1982.

different from the prevalent view held by most economists in industrial organization today (Carlsson, forthcoming).

Nearly thirty years ago, Mansfield (1962, p. 1023) made a plea for greater emphasis on intra-industry dynamics:

> Because there have been so few econometric studies of the birth, growth and death of firms, we lack even crude answers to the following basic questions regarding the dynamic processes governing an industry's structure. What are the quantitative effects of various factors on the rates of entry and exit? How well can the growth of firms be represented by Gibrat's law of proportionate effect? What have been the effects of successful innovations on a firm's growth rate? What determines the amount of mobility within an industry's size structure?

Although some important studies have provided at least provisional answers to Mansfield's questions, particularly in the area of Gibrat's Law and the variations in firm growth rates, knowledge about the process by which industry structures evolve remains limited.

The extent of intra-industry firm movement is important for several reasons. For example, Simon and Bonini (1958, p. 616) argued that, "As a matter of fact, a measure of mobility... would appear to provide a better index of what we mean by 'equality of opportunity' than do the usual measures of concentration."

The 1971 Bolton Committee in the United Kingdom argued that new firms in an industry would promote new products and ultimately shape the evolutionary path of the industry, as well as constrain any market power exercised by the entrenched firms:

> We believe that the health of the economy requires the birth of new enterprises in substantial number and the growth of some to a position from which they are able to challenge and supplement the existing leaders of industry... This "seedbed" function, therefore, appears to be a vital contribution of the small firm sector to the long-run health of the economy. We cannot assume that the ordinary working of market forces will necessarily preserve a small firm sector large enough to perform this function in the future (Bolton Report, 1971, p. 85).

Despite the recognition that the process by which firms enter, grow, recede, and exit plays a crucial role in the evolution of industrial markets, there have been only a few empirical studies actually attempting to measure it. The chapters by Lazerson, Storey, Contini and Revelli, and Schwalbach in this volume examine different aspects of small firm growth.

Lazerson's analysis suggests that in Italy, where the challenge of small firms has been most vigorous, the success of small enterprises rests on alternative organizational strategies. These firms reject the narrow division of labor common in large firms in favor of an organizational structure based on employees performing a variety of different tasks. However, the success of these firms depends on much more than organizational "superiority". Rather, the evidence seems to indicate that small-firm expansion depends upon a particular social and political order. The continued existence of the extended family, provides a foundation for economic relations based on cooperation and trust (Piore and Sabel, 1984).

These firms form partnerships and invest in other small firms in order to grow by forming networks, i.e. non-hierarchical relationships. However, the firms remain strictly independent enterprises. Networking represents an attempt to preserve the special flexible characteristics of small firms through loosely-coupled units thereby being able to exploit some of the advantages offered by more diversified groups. One key advantage of networks over hierarchical organizational forms is that networks can be more casily disbanded when there are changes in market conditions. The increased volatility of markets during the past two decades has given networks a unique advantage over more formal organizational structures. Tiny firms can do quite big things through networks. These organizational developments differ in many respects from the theories of Williamson (1975), who has argued that firms expand because of dysfunctionals in market relationships and the superiority of bureaucratic forms of management. Small-firm expansion in the Italian survey results in a growth of both markets and hierarchies within the same group of firms, something not predicted by Williamson's dichotomous theory.

As FitzRoy points out in his comment on Lazerson's paper, "Williamson has frequently argued that small-numbers bargaining and asset-specificity create a situation so vulnerable to opportunism that central or vertical hierarchical control should prevail and reduce transaction costs. However, he neglects the importance of high trust personal relationships in attenuating opportunism and also reducing the monitoring and information costs of centralized hierarchy." The lessons from the Emilia model, while specific to Italy, can be quite important for other industrialized countries (Acs and FitzRoy, 1989).

Storey continues to examine the issue of small-firm growth. His argument rests on the observation that smaller firms are not scaled down versions of larger firms, but are unique and distinct from their larger counterparts. This in turn affects how the smaller firm views its performance. Small firms must take into account not only traditional characteristics of growth, but also must deal with issues of *firm failure* and *ownership changes*. The first part of the paper gives an excellent survey of the literature on small-firm growth including both the older studies and the more recent evidence. The starting point of his paper is that small firms are not independent units as predicted by traditional theory. Small firms that grow rapidly often do so in a manner analogous to large firms by acquiring other small firms. However, the motivation for this network of ownership pattern differs between large-and-small firms. While the large firm is likely to acquire existing firms in order to strengthen its market position, the small firm is more likely to start a new firm than acquire an existing one. These observations are inconsistent with the findings of Lazerson where small Italian firms penetrate new markets by spawning new firms without risking their existing activities through networking.

In this Chapter Contini and Revelli use a large sample of Italian firms to examine the relationship between firm growth and firm size, Gibrat's Law. There are several versions of Gibrat's Law which states that the "probability of a given proportionate change in size during a specified period is the same for all firms in a given industry – regardless of their size at the beginning of the period" (Mansfield, 1962, pp. 1030–1031). In fact, there are at least three renditions of Gibrat's Law. The first version postulates that the Law holds for firms which exited the industry as well as for those remaining in existence. The second interpretation is that the Law holds for firms that survive over the period (Hart and Prais, 1956). Thus, according to this interpretation firms that have exited from the industry should not be included in a sample used to statistically test whether Gibrat's Law holds. The third main version is that the Law applies only to firms which are large enough to exceed the minimum efficient scale level of output (Simon an Bonini, 1958).

Recent studies (Hall, 1987; Evans, 1987a and 1987b) have cast considerable doubt on the validity of Gibrat's Law, or the assumption of independence between firm size and the rate of growth. However, an important qualification emphasized by both Hall and Evans is that only surviving firms could be included in their samples used to infer whether or not Gibrat's Law holds. This qualification is apparently not trivial, because the authors each found that smaller firms not only have significantly higher growth rates, but they also have a substantially greater propensity to exit in industry than do their larger counterparts.[5] This left unanswered the question, "If exiting firms are included in the sample along with survivors, will the higher exit rate of small firms tend to offset their greater growth rates? i.e., Will Gibrat's Law hold after all?"

Contini and Revelli compare important Italian results (Revelli and Battagliotti, 1988) with the recent work of Evans, Hall, and Leonard (1986). Their results are generally consistent with the findings from U.S. data. That is, firm size is negatively correlated with firm growth. They also raise important questions about the issues of sample selection bias. Specifically, they are interested in the question: If new firms survive an *initial* period during which they grow rapidly, will this lead to sustained growth? In this case, for those firms that survive, size and growth may not necessarily be negatively related. They found that for small firms lagged growth and size were significant and negative, while for larger firms the sign was positive. This suggests that growth may be persistent among other than the tiniest firms.[6]

Schwalbach examines the traditional hypothesis in Industrial Organization that the observed size distribution of firms is not purely a result of mere chance or luck. Technology and business behavior are seen as additional important determinants of the size distribution. He finds a significant impact of industry specific factors on the *presence* of small plants as well as on the *size distribution* of plants. Specifically, in the Federal Republic of Germany (FRG), small firms are inhibited in industries that have a high capital requirement, high advertising to sales ratios, and are characterized by a high technological environment. These results are consistent with the results of both White (1982) and Acs and Audretsch (1989b) for the U.S. The dynamic analysis reveals that departures from long-run equilibrium are only of a very short duration. While the small-firm employment share remained the same between 1981 and 1986, the share of sales accounted for by small firms increased only negligibly over this period. This leads to a striking conclusion: While there has been a dramatic shift in the share of manufacturing sales and employment accounted for by small firms in the U.S., no such trend is apparent in the FRG.[7] In fact, the FRG and Sweden are the only two deviants in that their average manufacturing firm size increased between 1973 and 1983, whereas it decreased in most other countries, including the U.S., Japan, U.K., Italy, Finland and Denmark (Carlsson, 1989, p. 24). One possible explanation for this disparity between the FRG and the U.S. is that the inherent size disadvantage of small firms relative to their larger counterparts had diminished more in the U.S. than in the FRG.[8] In his comment Revelli discusses alternative specifications of the model to test for long-run equilibrium.

V. Issues in Entrepreneurship

The second main theme in Small Business Economics focuses on entrepreneurship. As the world is caught in a torrent of change there has been a resurgence of interest in entrepreneurship both among economists and the general public (Hébert and Link, 1989). These dynamic stories have been refreshing since most stories told by economists in the post-war period have been of the static variety where entrepreneurs are replaced by production functions. Our two main stories are told by Schumpeter and Knight. In the *Theory of Economic Development*, Schumpeter (1934) calls attention to the role of entrepreneur, who plays a central role in his analysis of capitalist evolution. It is the entrepreneur's *social* function that is central to the book. The entrepreneur, as a member of a social class, is what gives rise to continued self-generated growth. While it is the "essentially unadventurous bourgeois class that must provide the leadership role, it does so by absorbing within its ranks the free spirits of innovating entrepreneurs who provide the vital energy that propels the system. The underlying 'preanalytic' cognitive vision is thus one of a routinized social hierarchy creatively disrupted by the gifted few," (Heilbroner, 1984, p. 690) who are not associated with the established firm.

In *Capitalism, Socialism and Democracy*, Schumpeter draws attention to the role of the large (monopolist) firm as an effective engine of economic progress: "The monopolist firm will generate a larger supply of innovations because there are advantages which, though not strictly unattainable on the competitive level of enterprise, are as a matter of fact secured only on the monopoly level" (1950, p. 101). In this case innovation is typically not the result of outsiders but is *endogenous* to the model. Galbraith supported this latter Schumpeterian view that "There is no more pleasant fiction than that technical change is the product of the matchless ingenuity of the small man forced by competition to employ his wits to better his neighbor. Unhappily, it is fiction" (1956, p. 86).

However, it is also the large corporation that draws attention to Schumpeter's gloomy prospects for economic progress. The ideologically plausible capitalism, as Schumpeter himself wrote, contains no purely economic reason why capitalism should not have another successful run. The socialist future of Schumpeter's drama, therefore, rests wholly on extraordinary factors. The large corporation, by taking over the entrepreneurial function, not only makes the entrepreneur obsolete, but undermines the *sociological* and *ideological* functions of capitalist society as Schumpeter himself notes (1950, p. 134):

> Since capitalist enterprise, by its very achievements, tends to automatize progress, we conclude that it tends to make itself superfluous – to break to pieces under the pressure of its own success. The perfectly bureaucratized giant industrial unit not only ousts the small or medium-sized firms and "expropriates" its owners, but in the end it also ousts the entrepreneur and expropriates the bourgeoisie as a class which in the process stands to lose not only its income but also what is infinitely more important, its function. The true pacemakers of socialism were not the intellectuals or agitators who preached it but the Vanderbilts, Carnegies and Rockefellers.

The extent to which the large corporation replaces the small- and medium-sized enterprise will negatively influence growth as the resulting economic concentration starts to have a feedback effect on entrepreneurial values, innovation, and technological change declines in the large corporation, bringing slower economic growth.[9] Technology as "the means by which new markets are created, the source of that 'perennial gale of creative destruction', that fills the sails of the capitalist armada" (Heilbroner, 1984, p. 686) may die out. To this story we return below.

While Schumpeter makes a functional distinction between the entrepreneur and the capitalist (the financial function) for Knight (1921), the entrepreneurial and capitalist function are inextricably intertwined. Entrepreneurs must finance themselves and bear the risk of their failure. Thus, for Knight, the superior foresight of the entrepreneur, and his willingness to bear risk must go hand in hand. Who becomes an entrepreneur is determined not by personality (McClelland, 1961) but by (1) entrepreneurial ability, and (2) the extent to which individuals form accurate estimates of their entrepreneurial abilities.[10] Recently Lucas (1978), Kihlstrom and Laffont (1979), and Jovanovic (1982) have built formal models of Knight's view. Jovanovic considers a model where individuals are unsure of their abilities when they enter business, but uncover their true efficiencies over time with a Bayesian learning process.[11]

The first of three chapters on entrepreneurship in this volume is an empirical examination of self-employment in the U.S. by Evans and Leighton. Whether the self-employed are entrepreneurs depends on one's definition. The self-employed are Knightian entrepreneurs because they have control over their workplace and bear risk as residual income claimants. They are not necessarily Schumpeterian entrepreneurs because many operate routine businesses. But in any case the self-employed operate, by number, most businesses – all sole proprietorships and many small corporations.

They report several key findings: (1) the probability of switching into self-employment is roughly independent of age and total labor market experience;[12] (2) the failure rate of self-employment decreases with the duration in self-employment falling from about 10 percent in the first year to about 0 percent in the eleventh year;[13] (3) the fraction of the labor force that is self-employed increases with age until the early 40s and then remains constant until the late 50s, when many workers became self-employed after retirement; and (4) the self-employed have a high internal locus of control supporting a major psychological theory. They also find some evidence that unemployed workers and low-paid wage workers become entrepreneurs. This is consistent with the findings of Storey and Jones (1987) for the United Kingdom.

In this chapter, Kirchhoff is also concerned with economic dynamics. However unlike Evans and Leighton, he builds on a Schumpeterian and not a Knightian dynamic, being concerned with rapidly growing small firms in a technologically fertile environment, rather than with self employment. He argues that *entry* is a necessary condition for economic development if long run market concentration and declining innovation rates are to be avoided.

To test Schumpeter's creative destruction hypothesis Kirchhoff argues that increasing wealth concentration should not be evident over time among the largest industrial corporations. He tests the proposition that, "Total Assets of the largest 500 industrial firms did not increase as a percentage of total industrial assets over the 1970-80 time period." The data utilized is the COMPUSTAT files from 1970 through 1980, which also contain 10 years of historical data. The file contains information on all publicly traded firms in the U.S. He found that the 500 largest firms in 1980 (determined by assets) held 16.55 percent of all corporate assets, a slight decline from 16.82 percent in 1970. Since there has been a shift in business activity from manufacturing to services, it is possible that these results were influenced by the disproportionate growth of assets in services. However, the percentage of assets of the largest 500 as a percentage of total assets of all industrial corporations shows no concentration.[14]

It is possible to disaggregate the COMPUSTAT files and allocate asset growth to either internal growth or mergers. Over the 20 year period 82 firms entered the sample. Consistently the 418 large firms in the sample had growth rates below the average. While the 82 new firms had growth rates above the average, once they became "large" their growth rates tapered off. This analysis suggests that a negative correlation between firm size and growth of assets exists.

Dunkelberg and Cooper, also in the Knightian tradition, analyze data collected from 2,994 new firms over a four-year period beginning in 1985. The data were generated from the membership files of the National Federation of Independent Business (NFIB). The membership is quite representative of the population of small firms in the U.S. They set up a production function model where they compare the capital inputs for complimentarity and substitutability for given inputs. Their results indicate that the higher the quality of human capital invested (measured by years of education) the fewer hours entrepreneurs worked per week. Large amounts of financial capital were associated with additional rather than fewer hours worked by the owner. Thus, it does not appear that in practice larger financial capital investments are a substitute for human capital.[15] We now turn to the question of technology.

VI. Technology, Strategy and Flexibility

The third main theme in Small Business Economics is the role of technology and innovation in economic change. It should be apparent from the discussion in section III above that technological change is one of the main forces contributing to the shift in the size distribution of firms, and the increasing relative importance of small firms.

The post-war model of economic development was dominated by the large corporation using mass-production technologies in an environment of stable prices. At the turn of the century the large corporation, through vertical and horizontal integration, had been able to fix input and output prices; in the 1930s collective bargaining ensured that wages were fixed, balancing production and consumption; a decade later public policy stabilized the level of aggregate demand, the price level, interest rates, and the exchange rate. Stable markets were necessary to accommodate mass-production technologies characteristic of big business. The specialized machinery needed by this technology was expensive and had to be amortized over a long period of time. This "fixed-price" environment made the existence of mass-production possible in an otherwise unstable world. According to Piore and Sabel (1984), the economic crisis of the 1970s resulted from the inability of firms and policy makers to maintain the conditions necessary to preserve mass-production, stability of markets. Their claim is that the present deterioration in economic performance results from the limits of the model of industrial development that is found in mass-production: the use of special-purpose machines and of semi-skilled workers to produce standardized products. The endogenous instability of the mass-production model based on so many production and social rigidities over the past century has given rise to what the authors call an "industrial divide". An "industrial divide" is a moment in history when the path of technological development itself is at issue. The central claim of the authors, therefore, is that we are living through the second "industrial divide". For example, Piore and Sabel observed that a distinction between the 1930s and the 1970s was that, in the latter, there was great confusion over "how to organize technologies, markets, and hierarchies...". In fact, if the Great Depression represented a *macroeconomic crisis*, the economic problems in the 1970s and 1980s were essentially *microeconomic* in that the focus was on the choice of technologies, organization of firms and markets (FitzRoy and Acs, 1989).

Mills and Schumann (1985) develop a model where the existence of available technologies and entrepreneurial strategies affords a tradeoff between static efficiency and flexibility. Their theory associates greater flexibility with smaller firm size, since smaller firms tend to achieve greater flexibility through increasing reliance on variable factors of production. This implies that flexible technologies have lower capital requirements than do inflexible technologies. Since flexibility apparently varies inversely with firm size, Mills and Schumann's thesis suggests that flexible production is a strategy which small firms can employ to remain viable in a relatively capital-intensive industry. In fact, Caves and Pugel (1980) found that capital-output ratios are greater for large firms than for small firms within a given industry. Thus, small firms in capital-intensive industries presumably survive by adapting a strategy of flexible production and absorbing a relatively large share of market output fluctuations.

In our 1988 paper (Acs, Audretsch and Carlsson) we provide one of the first empirical tests of the Piore and Sabel thesis that flexible production will tend to promote the relative viability of small firms. We conclude that at least certain flexible technologies have promoted the viability of small firms. An implication of our 1988 paper was that if small firms are growing relative to large firms and accounting for an increased share of sales in the engineering industries, the mean *plant size* in these industries would be expected to be decreasing over a similar period.

The purpose of our contribution in this volume is to examine data from the U.S. Bureau of the Census to test whether the shift in mean *plant size* is also related to the application of flexible technologies. A casual observation on changes in mean plant size, mean firm (enterprise) size, number of establishments, number of firms, and employment in the 106 four-digit Standard Industrial Classification (SIC) engineering industries, between 1972 and 1982, strongly supports the deconcentration thesis, and suggests a structural change in the engineering industries has taken place. We find that the mean plant size has tended to decrease the most in those engineering industries where there has been the greatest application of programmable robots and numerically controlled machines. Inflexible technologies have tended to promote larger plant size.

Dodgson's chapter continues more than a decade of research at the Science Policy Research Unit (SPRU) at the University of Sussex which has shown that small firms are significant innovators. This and similar work elsewhere (Acs and Audretsch, 1987b, 1988, 1989e) has successfully challenged the old notion that it takes a big R&D budget to be a successful innovator. In his chapter Dodgson takes this research a step forward by suggesting that technology strategy is important for small firms, as well as for large, in the innovation process.

His paper is important in several ways. First, like the paper by Lazerson it is a case study of small firms, with a particular orientation towards organizational growth. However, it extends the issue by (1) being interested in isues of technology and (2) addressing the important issue of strategic management of technology in small firms. Advanced technologies are enormously complex. Complexity results from the convergence of technologies between, for example, electronics and mechanics to create 'mechatronics'. Few firms possess internally the range of skills required to merge previously discrete technologies. Given the high cost of R&D investment, and the potentially long time scale before returns are forthcoming from such investments, technology needs to be considered strategically. Firms often have to collaborate in their technological activities. Dodgson offers these hypotheses for a technology strategy: (1) small firms must dedicate considerable resources to the R&D effort, and (2) there must be a high level of integration between a firm's internal functions and between its activities and the activities of other firms in complementary areas. As Hull points out in his comment, the key to innovativeness is not so much the *creation* of knowledge as the *exploitation* of knowledge.

In this chapter Carlsson integrates some of the issues raised previously by further analyzing the metalworking industry. His comparative analysis of the role of small firms in the machine tool industry shows how the Japanese followed strategies that allowed them to increase their share of the market at the expense of U.S. firms. Among the strategies pursued by Japanes firms was collaboration with other firms in their technological activities. While U.S. and European machine tool manufacturers were building complex and sophisticated NC machines, the Japanese, realizing the limits of this market, began to make more general-purpose machines. The potential number of customers now increased dramatically for the first time allowing machine tool firms to take advantage of scale economies in production. The Japanese were simply the first to reap the benefits. Up to the mid-1970s, the industry consisted almost entirely of small firms. Since the Japanese machine tool makers are basically assemblers, whereas Western firms tend to be more vertically integrated, the size differences in terms of employment between Japanese and Western firms underestimate the true differences.

There were several factors besides exploitation of scale economies which put the Japanese ahead. The introduction and integration of electronics into an industry previously dominated by mechanical technologies required new technological skills that small firms did not have. The Japanese had special links to larger industry groups. Of the ten largest machine tool firms in Japan, at least four belonged to such a group. One suspects that belonging to such a group helped develop new technologies. While there were few such examples of technological "cooperation" in Europe, there were none in the U.S. Many firms have been taken over by large firms (conglomerates), but these acquisitions appear to be motivated more by financial gain rather than vertical integration. In many instances these takeovers have resulted in U.S. machine tool makers having their overheads cut, and engineering staffs reduced, further weakening their competitiveness vis-à-vis the Japanese.

Also, whereas the Japanese firms have had strong links between machine tool makers, the producers of numerical controllers, western machine tool firms have often been fiercely independent in terms of both technical development and ownership. By developing their own controllers they have remained outside industry groups. The results have appeared to be that the Japanese strategy of closer integration between suppliers of technology and machine builders has resulted in a substantial lead over their U.S. and European counterparts.[16]

VII. Small Firms, New Entry and Employment

The fourth theme in Small Business Economics is the role of economic policy in promoting or hindring new firm formation. While this conference has not dealt with the issue in a formal fashion, it was nonetheless an issue of much debate. The vast literature on labor market change and small firms has been recently surveyed by Storey and Johnson (1987) and FitzRoy (1989) and does not need repeating here. However, as we saw in section II, one of the most remarkable findings in the growing literature on small firms is that their share of employment in U.S. *manufacturing* has increased substantially in recent years, while shares have remained constant in the F.R.G. (Acs and Audretsch, 1989a). We suggest that rapid employment growth in the U.S. and decline or stagnation in the main European economies (with the exception of Italy) may be related to the more dynamic small firm sector in the U.S., with its generally lower barriers to new entry (Acs and Audretsch, 1989d and 1989c) and high levels of turbulence (Acs and Audretsch, 1989f).[17]

The main sources of these differences in the employment growth can be traced to misguided government policies in Europe supporting large firms, as well as a much larger venture capital market in the U.S., and from the willingness of scientists and experienced managers to leave secure jobs and share the entrepreneurial risks in new enterprises.[18]

In the U.S. small high-tech firms are responsible for much of the innovation which has compensated for the decline of traditional industries. In general unions are weak in the firms that innovate (Acs and Audretsch, 1988), while profit sharing and work sharing are most prevalent there (Smith, 1988). Of course, small high-tech firms account for perhaps no more than five percent of the new jobs. Most of the jobs are in lower paid services and manufacturing, and this has led to several critiques of job creation in the small-firm sector as a solution to unemployment problems.

It is perceived that workers with the same skills and other personal characteristics may sometimes be paid more in large firms than in small firms.[19] The more bureaucratic and regimented working conditions of a large organization at the same time lead to greater worker dissatisfaction and workers in large firms are much more prone to strike (Prais, 1981). Higher pay in large firms may include a compensating differential for difficult working conditions. The long and the short of it is that a low-paid job may be preferred to no job at all, especially by those not receiving generous unemployment benefits. From the point of experience, even a low-paid job will provide intangible benefits in the form of work experience and work references. In fact, the average tenure at a low paid job is less than six months. It is also quite conceivable that a job that is unacceptable for some workers is preferable to lengthy unemployment for others. There is convincing evidence that long bouts of unemployment erode human capital and motivation, and over time lead to exclusion from the labor market. There is little evidence that being unemployed facilitates the search for employment, while the lack of contact in the workplace may handicap search by the unemployed (FitzRoy, 1989b).

Job creation and small and new firm entry in Europe has been severely discouraged by decades of government policy in support of large corporations and quasi-monopolistic suppliers of state industries (Geroski and Jacquemin, 1985). New firm entry would be encouraged by labor market flexibility and deregulation as well as access to the R&D infrastructure. Existing state subsidies and other support for large corporations should be reduced. Indeed, if they are so efficient why the subsidies in the first place? Enlargement of the small and medium firm sector, in turn, would increase competition, enhance the overall rate of return on capital, and most important expand employment, as we have seen in the U.S. Even in "centrally planned economies" like the G.D.R., Poland and Hungary, where decades of policies have favored large firms over small ones, strengthening and expanding the small firm sector is considered a prerequisite to the revitalization of the economy. In the final chapter Román is quite clear why the small firm sector must be expanded in Hungary. It is because many large firms are relatively inefficient!

As Blanchard and Summers (1988, p. 182) explain, "European experience of the 1980s poses a profound challenge to standard Keynesian and classical theories of economic fluctuations." Focusing employment policy exclusively on aggregate demand, or on wages and the labor market, will thus miss important channels through which employment, competition and economic welfare can all be influenced simultaneously without additional public expenditure (FitzRoy, 1989a).

VIII. The European Challenge

The performance of the U.S. economy at maintaining full employment along with providing international leadership in high-technology markets during the latter part of the 1980s, has not gone unnoticed in Europe. In this introductory chapter we have shown that small firms have played a crucial role in creating jobs, as well as contributing to innovative activity. In particular, we suggest, and provide at least some evidence in support of the hypothesis that a *restructuring* of U.S. markets has taken place (Acs, 1984), causing a shift in the size distribution of firms towards a greater presence of small firms. Not only have small firms been the major engine for job generation, but as a result, they are playing a more important role across the economy. While Europeans have become increasingly aware of the American success, there is little questioning of the "conventional wisdom" that the source of this success is from greater efficiency enjoyed by the giant corporation. As 1992 nears the "European Challenge" is perhaps best summed up by FitzRoy (1989b, p. 28) who suggests that Europeans should "...abandon their cherished but unrealistic faith in economies of scale, and institute a thoroughgoing reversal of current policy towards large firms, preferably coupled with support for venture capital and new start-up and small firms."[20]

Despite the important contributions from small firms in industrial economies, a conventional wisdom oblivious to these contributions persists in the realm of public policy. This conventional wisdom, which thrives on both sides of the Atlantic, advocates public policies which are effectively *biased* towards subsidizing larger enterprises. An irony may be that, just at a time when technological change depends upon a vital small-firm sector, public policy seems to be moving in a direction from an implicit towards an explicit nurturing of larger enterprising at the expense of smaller firms (Adams and Brock, 1988).

For example, in 1986 the U.S. Secretary of Commerce, Malcolm Baldridge, asserted, "We are simply living in a different world today. Because of larger markets, the cost of research and development, new product innovation, marketing, and so forth... it takes larger companies to compete successfully" (Baldridge, 1986). Baldridge based his argument on the observation that the American share of the largest corporations in the world had fallen considerably between 1960 and 1984. He warned that programs promoting the largescale enterprise must "... not be stopped by those who are pre-occupied with outdated notions about firms size".[21] While it is definitely true that increasing costs of R&D are driving merger activity in some industries, most notably the pharmaceutical industry, another and perhaps more general response is to enter into cooperative R&D agreements, joint ventures, and networking arrangements, thus spreading the risks and drawing upon the competence of other firms as a complement to one's own resources.

An example of this conventional wisdom surfaced during the Reagan Administration's proposed changes in the antitrust laws, particularly in the areas of merger policy, collusion, and joint ventures and cooperative R&D arrangements. The Reagan Administration advocated emasculating the antitrust statutes and promoting horizontal mergers as a means of enhancing the international competitiveness of U.S. firms. It was argued that, "... if our industries are going to survive there have to be additional consolidations to achieve needed economies of scale". Despite the general euphoria that seemed to surround U.S. takeovers in the 1980s, Scherer (1988), in fact, questions both the theoretical and empirical basis that takeovers actually increase corporate efficiency.

This conventional wisdom has at least as great a following among policy makers in Europe. More than two decades ago J.J. Servan-Schreiber warned Europeans to beware "The American Challenge", in the form of "dynamism, organization, innovation, and boldness that characterize the giant American corporations" (p. 153). Because giant corporations are needed to amass the requisite resources for innovation, Servan-Schreiber advocated "... creation of large industrial units which are able both in size and management to compete with the American giants", (p. 159) through the selection by government of "... fifty to one hundred firms which, once they are large enough, would be the most likely to become world leaders of modern technology in their fields" (p. 160). Ironically, with the European integration that is expected in 1992, Servan-Schreiber's policy prescriptions are now more than ever likely to be followed. The long-standing policy tradition in Europe of cartellization, encouraging mergers, and subsidizing large-scale enterprises is being reinforced rather than questioned, as 1992 nears (Cecchini, 1988).[22]

The papers in this book do cast considerable doubt onto the conventional wisdom about the source of innovative activity, technical change, and employment that is embedded in much of public policy. It is clear that small firms apparently have played a key role in the process of technological change as well as in the dynamic process by which industries evolve. Servan-Schreiber may have been correct to prophesize an American challenge, but this challenge is more likely to emanate from the high-technology innovative small firms than from the giant corporations which are on their way to becoming the dinosaurs of yesterday.

Notes

* We wish to thank Bo Carlsson, David S. Evans, Joachim Schwalbach, and David J. Storey for helpful suggestions. All errors and omissions remain our responsibility.

1. For a survey of the literature see Brock and Evans (1989).
2. For an international survey of the evidence on the emergence of small firms see Sengenberger et al. (forthcoming).
3. "The Rise and Rise of America's Small Firms," *The Economist,* January 21, 1989, pp. 33–74.
4. These figures are from the Bureau of the Census, United States Department of Commerce.
5. For further evidence on the U.S. see Dunne, Roberts and Samuelson (1987).
6. For similar results in the U.K. see Storey et al. (1987).
7. Similar results were also found by Hull (1986) for the FRG. For very small firms, less than 20 employees, the results are less conclusive.
8. See Acs and Audretsch (1989a) for further discussion and explanations.
9. Some evidence for this is found in Acs and Audretsch (1988).
10. Probably the most significant economic analysis of the entrepreneur in this decade is by Casson (1982).
11. Pakes and Ericson (1987) present an alternative to Jovanovic's model, which they dub the passive learning model. In their alternative model firms can actively accelerate the learning process by investing in R&D, thereby endogenously raising the level of innovation.
12. This finding appears to contradict much of the U.K. based research on self-employment (Storey and Johnson, 1987). Also see Blau (1987).
13. For those interested in firm failure, see Phillips and Kirchhoff (1989).
14. It was pointed out by David J. Storey that the percentage of total assets held by the top 500 companies does appear not to depend on whether their shares of total employment or output are going up or down.

In fact this is precisely the case. While the employment of the 500 largest U.S. firms has decreased, their share of both sales and assets have not declined.

15. It was Schultz (1975) who redefined entrepreneurship as the ability to deal with disequilibria, and found human capital to be a strong explanatory variable. We should also note that there are important selection problems here that will have to be addressed in further research.
16. See Aoki (1989), Yokokara (1988) and FitzRoy and Acs (1989) for detailed discussion of the small firm sector in Japan.
17. It should be pointed out that small firms are relatively more important in Europe and Japan than in the U.S. (Román, this volume). However, the rate of change in the relative presence of small firms has been greater in the U.S than in Europe.
18. Recently, the venture capital market has expanded rapidly in the U.K., while it is still of modest importance in the Federal Republic of Germany, for example.
19. In the F.R.G., even if there is an earnings gap between large and small firms, compared with other countries such as the U.S. or Japan, this gap is relatively narrow. Average earnings in small firms in the Federal Republic are 90 percent of those in firms with more than 500 employees. The figures for Japan and the U.S. are only 77 percent and 57 percent respectively. A fundamental cause of this relatively small gap, in international terms, lies in the German system of central, sector-wide collective bargaining (OECD, 1985).
20. It could be argued that the U.K. has had a decade of policies that reflect this view. Unfortunately, there is no way to demonstrate if these policies have been responsible for the economic *revival* of Britain in the 1980s, or if they have hindered the recovery. We believe, that despite the unevenness of the recovery the United Kingdom has experienced a renaissance in this decade. In the best case these policies have been a positive influence, and in the worst case have been neutral.
21. Statement of the Honorable Malcolm Baldridge, Secretary, Department of Commerce, *Merger Law Reform: Hearings on S.2022 and S.2160 Before the Senate Committee on the Judiciary*, 99th Congress, 2nd Session 18, 22, 1986.
22. However, if scale economies are becoming less important, then we need to both broaden and deepen our understanding of market structure i.e., the size distribution of firms. According to Carlsson (1989, p. 36) "The results of the present research suggest that industrial organization economists need to concern themselves more than they currently do with understanding the mechanisms which generate the absolute sizes of firms and plants in various industries".

References

Acs, Zoltan J., 1984, *The Changing Structure of the U.S. Economy: Lessons from the Steel Industry,* New York, NY: Praeger.

Acs, Zoltan J. and David B. Audretsch, 1987a, "Innovation in Large and Small Firms", *Economics Letters* 23, 109–112.

Acs, Zoltan J. and David B. Audretsch, 1987b, "Innovation, Market Structure and Firm Size", *Review of Economics and Statistics* 69, November, 567–575.

Acs, Zoltan J. and David B. Audretsch, 1988, "Innovation in Large and Small Firms: An Empirical Analysis", *American Economic Review* 78 (September), 678–690.

Acs, Zoltan, J. and David B. Audretsch, 1989a, "Job Creation and Firm Size in the U.S. and West Germany", *International Small Business Journal* 1(4), 9–22.

Acs, Zoltan J. and David B. Audretsch, 1989b, "Entrepreneurial Strategy and the Presence of Small Firms", *Small Business Economics* 1(3), 193–214.

Acs, Zoltan J. and David B. Audretsch, 1989c, "Births and Firm Size", *Southern Economic Journal* 55, October, 467–475.

Acs, Zoltan J. and David B. Audretsch, 1989d, "Small-Firm Entry in U.S. Manufacturing", *Economica* 56 (May), 255–266.

Acs, Zoltan J. and David B. Audretsch, 1989e, "R&D, Firm Size, and Innovative Activity", Discussion Paper No. (FS IV-89-6) Wissenschaftszentrum Berlin, April.

Acs, Zoltan J. and David B. Audretsch, 1989f, "Technological Regimes, Learning, and Industry Turbulence", Discussion Paper No. (FS IV-89-12) Wissenschaftszentrum Berlin, May.
Acs, Zoltan J. and David B. Audretsch, 1989g, "Patents as a Measure of Innovative Activity", *Kyklos* 42(2), 171–180.
Acs, Zoltan J. and David B. Audretsch, 1990, *Innovation and Small Firms*, Cambridge, Ma. The MIT Press.
Acs, Zoltan J. and David B. Audretsch, and Bo Carlsson, 1988, "Flexible Technology and Firm Size", RPIE Working Paper, 1988 : X, Case Western Reserve University, March.
Acs, Zoltan J. and Felix R. FitzRoy, 1989, "Inside the Firm and Organizational Capital: A Review Article", *International Journal of Industrial Organization* 7(2), 309–314.
Adams, Walter and James W. Brock, 1988, "The Bigness Mystique and the Merger Policy Debate: An International Perspective," *Northwestern Journal of International Law & Business* 9 (Spring), 1–45.
Aoki, M., 1988, *Information, Incentives and Bargaining in the Japanese Economy* (Cambridge University Press, Cambridge).
Armington, Catherine and Marjorie Odle, 1982, "Small Business – How Many Jobs?", *The Brookings Review* 1 (Winter), 14–17.
Audretsch, David B., 1989, The Market and the State: *Government Policy Towards Business in Europe, Japan, and the U.S.A.*, New York: New York University, Press.
Birch, David L., 1981, "Who Creates Jobs?", *The Public Interest* 65 (Fall), 3–14.
Blanchard, O.J. and L.H. Summers, 1988, "Beyond the Natural Rate Hypothesis", *American Economic Review* 78 (May), 182–187.
Blau, David, 1987, "A Time Series Analysis of Self-Employment," *Journal of Political Economy* 95 (June, 445–467).
Brock, William A. and David S. Evans, 1986, *The Economics of Small Business*, New York, NY: Holmes & Meier.
Brock, William A. and David S. Evans, 1989, "Small Business Economics", *Small Business Economics* 1(1), 1989, 7–20.
Brown, H. Shelton and Bruce D. Phillips, 1989, "Comparisons Between Small Business Data Base (USEEM) and Bureau of Labor Statistics (BLS) Employment Data: 1978–1986," *Small Business Economics,* 1(4).
Carlsson, Bo, 1984, "The Development and Use of Machine Tools in Historical Perspective", *Journal of Economic Behavior and Organization* 5, 91–114.
Carlsson, Bo, 1989, "The Evolution of Manufacturing Technology and its Impact on Industrial Structure: An International Study," *Small Business Economics*, 1(1), 21–38.
Carlsson, Bo, "Industry Dynamics: An Overview", in Bo Carlsson, ed., *Industry Dynamics*, Boston, Kluwer Academic Publishers, forthcoming.
Casson, Mark, 1982, *The Entrepreneur: An Economic Theory,* Totowa, N.J.: Barnes & Noble.
Caves, Richard E., and Thomas A. Pugel, *1980, Intraindustry Differences in Conduct and Performance: Viable Strategies in U.S. Manufacturing Industries.* New York: New York University Press.
Cecchini, Paolo, 1988, *The European Challenge: 1992,* Alderschot: Wildwood House.
Dunne, T., M. Roberts, and L. Samuelson, 1987, "The Impact of Plant Failure on Employment Growth in the U.S. Manufacturing Sector," unpublished paper, Pennsylvania State University.
Evans, David S., 1987a, "The Relationship Between Firm Growth, Size, and Age: Estimates for 100 Manufacturing Industries", *Journal of Industrial Economics* 35 (June), 567–581.
Evans, David S., 1987b, "Tests of Alternative Theories of Firm Growth", *Journal of Political Economy* 95, 657–674.
Evans, David S. and Boyan Jovanovic, 1989, "Estimates of a Model of Entrepreneurial Choice under Liquidity Constraints", *Journal of Political Economy* 97.
Evans, David S. and Linda S. Leighton, 1989, "The Determinants of Changes in U.S. Self-Employment, 1968-1987", *Small Business Economics* 1(2), 111-120.
FitzRoy, Felix, R., 1989a, "Firm Size, Efficiency and Employment: A Review Article", *Small Business Economics* 1(1), 75–80.
FitzRoy, Felix R., 1989b, "Wage Structures, Employment Problems and Economic Policy", Working Paper prepared for The Commission of the European Communities (March), forthcoming, *Small Business Economics.*

FitzRoy, Felix R. and Zoltan J.; Acs, 1989, "The New Institutional Economics of the Firm and Lessons from Japan", Discussion paper (FS IV 89–16), Wissenschaftszentrum Berlin (January).

Florida, R.L. and M. Kenney, 1988, "Venture Capital, High Technology and Regional Development", *Regional Studies* 22 (February), 33–48.

Galbraith, John K., 1956, *American Capitalism: The Concept of Countervailing Power*, revised edition, Boston, MA: Houghton Mifflin.

Geroski, Paul A. and Alexis Jacquemin, 1985, "Industrial Change, Barriers to Mobility and European Industrial Policy", *Economic Policy* 1 (November), 172–217.

Hall, Bronwyn H., 1987, "The Relationship Between Firm Size and Firm Growth in the U.S. Manufacturing Sector", *Journal of Industrial Economics* 35 (June), 583–605.

Hart, P.E. and S.J. Prais, 1956, "The Analysis of Business Concentration: A Statistical Approach", *Journal of the Royal Statistical Society* 119 (part 2), 150–191.

Hébert, Robert F. and Albert N. Link, 1989, "In Search of the Meaning of Entrepreneurship", *Small Business Economics* 1(1), 39–50.

Heilbronner, Robert L., 1984, "Economics and Political Economy: Marx, Keynes and Schumpeter", *Journal of Economic Issues* 18 (September), 681–695.

Horovitz, Paul M. and Richardson Pettit (eds.), 1984, *Small Business Finance*, Greenwich, CT: JAI Press.

Hull, Christopher, J., 1986, "Job Generation in the Federal Republic of Germany – A Review, 'Wissenschaftszentrum Berlin, (II/LMP 86-12).

Jovanovic, Boyan, 1982, "Selection and Evolution of Industry", *Econometrica* 50 (May), 649–670.

Kihlstrom, R. and J. Laffont, 1979, A General Equilibrium Entrepreneurial Theory of Firm Formation Based on Risk Aversion, *Journal of Political Economy* 87, 719–748.

Knight, Frank, 192, *Risk, Uncertainty and Profit*, New York, NY: Houghton Mifflin.

Leonard, Jonathan S., 1986, "On the Size Distribution of Employment and Establishments", NBER, Working Paper No. 1951.

Lucas, Robert E., Jr., 1978, "On the Size Distribution of Business Firms", *Bell Journal of Economics* 9 (Autumn), 508–523.

Mansfield, Edwin, 1962, "Entry, Gibrat's Law, Innovation, and the Growth of Firms", *American Economic Review* 52 (December), 1023–1051.

Marshall, Alfred, 1920, *Principles of Economics*, 8th edition, London: Macmillan.

McClelland, David C., 1969, *The Achieving Society*, New York: The Free Press.

Mensch, Gerhard, 1979, *Stalemate in Technology*, Boston, MA: Ballinger.

Mills, David E., and Laurence Schulmamm, 1985, "Industry Structure with Fluctuating Demand," *American Economic Review*, 75 (September 758–767).

Nelson, Richard R. and Sidney G. Winter, 1982, *An Evolutionary Theory of Economic Change*, Cambridge, MA: Harvard University Press.

OECD, 1985, "Employment in Small and Large Firms: Where have the Jobs Come From?", in OECD Employment Outlook 1985, Paris.

Pakes, Ariel and Richard Ericson, 1989, "Empirical Implications of Alternative Models of Firm Dynamics", Working Paper No. 2893, National Bureau of Economic Research.

Piore, Michael, J. and Charles F. Sabel, 1983, "Italian Small Business Development: Lessons for U.S. Industrial Policy",in John Zysman and Laura Tyson (eds.), *American Industry in International Competition*, Ithaca, NY: Cornell University Press.

Piore, Michael, J. and Charles F. Sabel, 1984, *The Second Industrial Divide: Possibilities for Prosperity*, New York, NY: Basic Books.

Phillips, Bruce D., 1985, "The Effects of Industry Deregulation on the Small Business Sector", *Business Economics* 20, 28–37.

Phillips, Bruce D. and Bruce A. Kirchhoff, 1989, "Formation, Growth and Survival: Small Firm Dynamics in the U.S. Economy", *Small Business Economics* 1(1), 65–74.

Prais, S., 1981, *Productivity and Industrial Structure*, Cambridge, MA: Cambridge University Press.

Revelli, R. and T. Battagliotti, 1988, "Modelli di Crescita Delle Imprese: il Caso Italiano", mimeo, R&P, Torino.

Scherer, F.M., 1980, *Industrial Market Structure and Economic Performance*, 2nd edition, Chicago, IL: Rand McNally College Publishing Co.

Scherer, F.M., 1988, "Corporate Takeovers: The Efficiency Arguments", *Economic Perspectives* 2 (Winter), 69–82.

Schultz, Theodore W., 1975, "The Value of the Ability to Deal with Disequilibria", *Journal of Economic Literature* 13, 827–847.

Schumpeter, Joseph A., 1934, *The Theory of Economic Development,* Cambridge, MA: Harvard University Press.

Schumpeter, Joseph A., 1950, *Capitalism, Socialism and Democracy*, 3rd edition, New York, NY: Harper and Row.

Sengenberger, Werner, Gary Loveman, and Michael Piore, eds. 1989, *The Reemergence of Smaller Units of Employment – Developments of the Small and Medium-Sized Enterprise Sector in Industrialized Countries,* mimeograph, Cambridge, MA.

Servan-Schreiber, J.-J., 1968, *The American Challenge,* London: Hamisch Hamilton.

Simon, Herbert A. and Charles P. Bonini, 1958, "The Size Distribution of Business Firms", *American Economic Review* 48 (September), 607–617.

Smith, S.C., 1988, "On the Incidence of Profit and Equity Sharing", *Journal of Behavior and Economic Organization* 9, 45–58.

Soete, Luc L.G., 1979, "Firm Size and Inventive Activity: The Evidence Reconsidered", *European Economic Review* 12, 319-340.

Storey, David J., Kevin Keasey, Robert Watson an Pooran Wynarczyk, 1987, *The Performance of Small Firms*, Croom Helm: London.

Storey, David J. and A.M. Jones, 1987, "New Firm Formation – A Labour Market Approach to Industrial Entry," *Scottish Journal of Political Economy* 34 (February), 37–51.

Storey, David J. and Steven Johnson, 1987, *Job Generation and Labour Market Changes*, London: Macmillan.

Toffler, Arvin, 1985, *The Adaptive Corporation*, New York, NY: Bantam Books.

White, lawrence J., 1982, "The Determinants of the Relative Importance of Small Business", *Review of Economics and Statistics* 64 (February), 42–49.

Williamson, Oliver E., 1975, *Markets and Hierarchies,* New York, NY: Macmillan Publishing Co.

Yokokara, Takashi, 1988, "Small and Medium Enterprise", in Ryutaro Komiya, M. Oluno, and K. Sazumura, eds., *Industrial Policy of Japan*, New York: Academic Press, 513–539.

A. SMALL-FIRM GROWTH

2. Transactional Calculus and Small Business Strategy*

MARK H. LAZERSON

I. Introduction

The prolonged economic stagnation and widespread unemployment of the recent decade have stimulated an unexpected reappraisal of the place of the small manufacturing sector in advanced industrial societies; until recently, this sector was considered an impediment to modernization and development (Berger 1980a; 1981). Indeed, in the United States where the number of small firm establishments have recently swelled (Granovetter 1984), there are growing doubts about the capacity of large mass production organizations to satisfy the needs of an advanced society (Piore and Sabel 1984).

Nowhere among the advanced capitalist countries has the challenge of small firms been more vigorous than in Italy, the fifth largest capitalist industrial power. There, manufacturing firms having a work force of fewer than fifty persons engage 46 percent of the work force, and the average manufacturing firm engages only 7.9[1] persons or 7.4 persons per plant. These data include owners and family help. This compares to an average of 59.9 employees in American manufacturing firms.[2] Average firms size in Italy is 21 percent lower today than in 1971, despite a 40 percent increase in the number of industrial firms during the same period.[3] Though small firms have been accorded an important role in the initial period of industrialization (Mendels 1972), the increased density of small firms in the last ten years is closely correlated with both rising wealth and technological progress. In fact, it is only in Italy's poorest and most underdeveloped regions that small firms been declining in number (Weiss 1984, p. 221).

My focus on the boom among Italian small firms is not intended to deny the importance of broader macroeconomic influences (Minsky 1985) in explaining economic growth, nor the reality that a vibrant industrial sector depends on both small firms and large firms (Oakey 1984). But there is also growing evidence that the success of small enterprises rests on alternative organizational strategies. Research centered in Emilia Romagna, a mixed agricultural-industrial region of north central Italy with four million inhabitants (see note 1, p. 50), has detailed how small firms have often achieved better economies of scale than large ones through the creation of specialized industrial districts where an agglomeration of producers in one industry work in close physical proximity (Brusco 1982; Sabel 1982; Solinas 1982; Piore and Sabel 1984). In this so-called Emilian model, the narrow division of labor common to large firms is rejected in favor of an organizational structure based on employees who perform a variety of different tasks (Rieser and Franchi 1986; Agenzia Industrial Italiana 1984).

However, it would be a mistake to conclude that the economic vitality of these small firms rests solely on the technical superiority of their individual strategies within the marketplace. Rather, the evidence seems to indicate that small firm expansion depends

Z.J. Acs and D.B. Audretsch (eds.), The Economics of Small Firms: A European Challenge. 25–41.

upon a particular social and political order. The continued existence of the extended family, in modified form (Pitkin 1985), provides a foundation for economic relations based on cooperation and trust. The importance of such non-market relationships for economic success also explains the heavy reliance ex-worker owners place on turning to friends and former colleagues in their search for employees. These social factors are reinforced by national and local policies grounded in tax, company, and labor relations legislation that assist small firms. But, in addition to state intervention, there is a rich network of private economic associations and political organizations that have constructed an environment in which markets prosper by promoting cooperative behavior and by providing small firms with the infrastructural needs that they could not afford alone. To capture the complexity of these phenomena, there is a need for additional research on how sociological variables contribute to the existence of markets.

The Research

The centrality of the social environment to any analysis of markets emerges from my research on the creation of firm networks, a strategy used by small Emilian firms to expand although maintaining the legal and organizational structure of a small company. In this article, I focus upon fifteen small mechanical-engineering companies in Modena, a prosperous province of 600,000 people within the region of Emilia-Romagna (see note 1, p. 69). The data are based upon plant visits, open-ended interviews with employers, and business association and trade union representatives. The fifteen firms were drawn from a 1985 quantitative survey of 219 Modena firms (Rieser and Franchi, 1986), representing the universe of mechanical engineering firms with eight or more persons[4] associated with the Modena branch of the National Confederation of Artisans (CNA), a small-business association that sponsored the research. Three other companies in the survey reported establishing network firms but refused to cooperate with my investigation. Another company expanded through a merger. In Modena in 1985, the CNA represented 53 percent of all mechanical-engineering artisanal firms.

Network Firms

The 15 companies formed partnerships or invested capital in other small firms in order to expand horizontally or vertically. The additional firm may have been newly formed for this purpose or have already been in existence. In some cases, the additional firm was really a satellite-firm in that it was dependent upon the first for its existence. In other cases, there was no such relationship of dependence and indeed the second firm might eventually outgrow the spawning firm. The firms also remain strictly independent legal entities with separate accounting procedures, work forces and workshops. Network-firms represent an attempt to preserve the special characteristics of small firms through loosely-coupled units yet exploit some of the advantages offered by more diversified economic groups. These organizational developments differ in many respects with the theories of Oliver Williamson, who has argued that firms expand because of dysfunctions in market relations and the superiority of bureaucratic forms of management (1975). Small-firm expansion in my Modena survey actually resulted in a growth of both markets and hierarchies within the same group of firms, something not predicted by

Williamson's dichotomous theory. Furthermore, my Modena data indicated that the role of law and labor relations is a major variable in shaping the small firm's decision to expand. Issues of hierarchies and markets completely ignore the critical role of the state in economic structure, nor do they help analyze how social and political institutions serve to eliminate some of the more negative aspects of markets, avoiding the need for bureaucratic forms of control.

To better situate the discussion of network-firms, my paper begins with a brief exegesis of the phenomenon of decentralized production and the relative decline of the large factory. I argue that, although this development is not easily reconcilable with the justification for large firms provided by Chandler (1977), it can be subsumed within Williamson's argument. After an abbreviated synopsis of Williamson's principal claims and the position of his adversaries, I proceed with a description of the particular organizational and legal structure in which small Italian firms operate. I then analyze the field research on network-firms and small-firm strategy and compare my empirical findings with the theory presented by Williamson.

II. The Decentralization of Production

Many of the technical justifications for large factories have been undermined. Though it is true that small firms may be less efficient than mass production facilities, such processes do not dominant manufacturing. Evidence suggests that even in industrialized economies manufacturing employment is concentrated in small batch and project production (Sayer 1986, pp. 57, 70). For example, in the United States and the United Kingdom 75 percent of manufacturing production (by value) is made by means of batches (Littler 1985, p. 19). Rarely has manufacturing resembled the widget-tightening contortions of Charlie Chaplin's *Modern Times*. Centralized manufacturing sites may have once been a function of the steam engine and water wheel that required production to be physically linked to the power source, as in the English textile factories studied by Marx. But these reasons have been rendered superfluous by the advent of electricity and small electric motors that permit production to be widely dispersed (Brusco 1975). Telecommunications, improved transportation facilities, and lightweight microelectronics have further enhanced possibilities for decentralized production.

There remain, however, the social explanations for large factories that marxists have attributed to the capitalists' need to overcome worker resistance (Marglin 1974). But the twentieth century rise of trade-union power in large industries has undercut many of the advantages that once employers gained from that form of organization. Today industrial relations experts argue that small factories are less strike-prone than large ones (Prais 1982). The advantages of smaller, decentralized firms have not been overlooked by large industrial organizations seeking to enhance their control over the external environment, and the widespread dispersion of production by large corporations around the world has forced governments, suppliers, and especially labor unions to retrench (Scott and Storper 1985).

III. Explanations for the Growth of Large Firms

There is nothing contradictory about the superior efficiency of small, decentralized production units and the tendency of large firms to take over smaller firms, if one assumes that production is not transferred to larger units. But Chandler's explanation of the concentration of industry in the hands of a few large corporations is based largely on the centralization of production to improve coordination and throughput speed, even though the small-firm organizational model has proved is not always necessary or important (1977). On the other hand, Oliver Williamson's theory of firm expansion, which highlights transaction costs and not economies of scale or technological aspects of production, should be as applicable to the growth dynamics of both small and large firms (1975).

Williamson explains the combined presence of large, complex firms and small firms in the economy as a reflection of the relative efficiencies of hierarchies and markets in reducing transaction costs, which are involved in economic exchanges with buyers, sellers, suppliers, and distributors. In cases of nonrepetitive transactions, markets will usually prevail. Here, markets are efficient because the buyer is not dependent upon the seller as in long-term contracts, where the latter is prone to squeeze the former, or in Williamson's terms, behave opportunistically. Markets also are more efficient in cases of standardized and non-complex products. The market for these products is quite large and price comparisons are easy to make because quality can be instantly compared. The market will also function quite well if the barriers to entry are low and the production technology well known.

But Williamson says that, in long term economic relationships based on the buyer's specific needs and the seller's special knowledge of them, the transaction costs are high because the size of the market is limited. The buyer has to invest expensive resources to protect himself from the seller's opportunism, whether it be in legal fees, quality controls, or administrative costs to assure contractual performance. He also pays inflated prices. Thus, in the case where the buyer is tied to a few sellers (reduced to small-numbers bargaining) and where the items are not fungible because of asset specificity, it is more efficient for the buyer to swallow the seller's company. It eliminates both Williamson's joint problem of bounded rationality, caused by the buyer's lack of adequate information about the seller's operations, and of opportunism, which derives from the seller's ability to conceal information from the buyer. In the newly expanded firm, bureaucratic rule backed by hierarchical power will limit opportunism, and organizational integration will restore transparency to economic transactions.

Williamson's analysis has been subjected to extensive criticism on a variety of grounds. Transactional economic analysis fails to recognize that within one organization opportunistic behavior may actually be more difficult to monitor and more costly than in separate organizations (Perrow 1981). There is also a strong counter-argument that loose coupling among independent economic organizations avoids the rigidities and expensive overhead associated with tightly coupled multi-functional firms (Perrow 1986). Williams has also been taken to task for his neo-classical economic assumption that competitive market forces and organizational hierarchies discourage human beings from acting egoistically in economic transactions. Much economic activity is underpinned by long-established and stable networks of personal and affective relationships

(Granovetter 1985). Part of the strength of the Japanese models may also be located in those relations of reciprocity and trust that are interwoven with market transactions (Dore 1983). Williamson himself has recently recognized the importance of cultural and institutional forces (1985). Finally, economic efficiency may be a motive for firm expansion but there are numerous historical cases of how it has suffered when business hierarchies have been formed to monopolize markets (Du Boff and Herman 1980).

IV. The Emilian Model

The Emilian model of small, highly specialized industrial firms does not seem to conform to Williamson's explanation of business behavior, even though many of these firms are enmeshed in types of economic transactions that would make them ripe for hierarchical integration. Small-numbers bargaining is rife. The CNA survey of 219 firms revealed that 48.5 percent of Modena firms that supply other firms have 10 or fewer regular customers (Rieser and Franchi 1986, p. 25). The very specialized, non-standardized production which allows Emilian producers a niche in the market clearly is asset specific and often involves only a few producers, two elements that should aggravate the twin-headed problem of bounded rationality and opportunism. Though it is true that some of the technologies employed are fairly simple, many of them described by Sable (1982) are quite sophisticated. Market entry costs for a small firm are lower than for a large firm, but acquiring a skilled work force and the necessary capital still takes many years, slowing entry into the marketplace.

It also seems that the dense web of market relations, often marked by long-established reciprocal relations and interfamily connections, is one of the strengths of the Emilian model (Bagnasco 1985, p. 26). Clustered in municipally-sponsored industrial parks or districts, small firms cooperate with one another to perform a multiplicity of tasks that in the past a large factory may have completed under one roof (Solinas 1982; Becattini 1979). This spatial division of production (Marshall 1970) allows small firms to enjoy economies of scale "at the level of one or a very few machines, not whole factories" (Sabel 1982, p. 226). Efficiency is achieved by rapid responses to market needs, based on a flexible organizational structure and substantial subcontracting to other small firms to allow specialization and maximum use of existing plant and equipment (Brusco and Sabel 1981; Rieser and Franchi 1986). These strategies increase rather than decrease inter-firm dependency. The market exchanges also accelerate the rapid exchange of information and stimulate innovation (Messori 1986, p. 418). Even if one accepts doubtful Williamson's claim that information flows are reduced with market transactions, productive structures based on loosely-coupled units can be rapidly substituted in case of difficulties, thus enhancing the capacity of buyers to respond rapidly to negative information. The effectiveness of these arrangements seems to have reduced the need for firms to expand in order to protect themselves from the caprices of the external environment.

The Social and Political Context

The organization of small firms in Modena is strongly marked by the province's particular political and social characteristics. Indeed, Modena was selected because of its advanced small firm sector, not because of its representativeness. Its exceptionalism is apparent when compared to other areas, e.g., Naples, where exploitation of labor and tax violations are widespread in small firms (Capecchi and Pugliese 1978; Botta, Fonte, Improta, Pugliese and Ruggiero 1976), and the Veneto region, also prosperous but under Christian Democratic control and relatively union free (Bagnasco and Trigilia 1984). In Modena almost 20 percent of employees in small firms are union members,[5] a proportion between two and four times higher than the Italian average. This relative union strength derives from the dominance of the Communist Party, which, with a near electoral majority compared to less than 30 percent elsewhere in Italy, has governed both the province and region alone or in coalition with other parties since the end of World War II.

Approximately 60 percent of small firms in Modena are members of the National Confederation of Artisans (CNA), a national organization founded in the immediate post-war period that represents 300,000 artisanal firms. The CNA has close organizational ties with the Italian Communist Party and to a lesser extent with the Socialist Party, and its membership is disproportionately concentrated in Emilia Romagna and Toscany, where the Communist Party has been historically dominant.

The CNA, which also performs accounting and bookkeeping services for many of its member firms, self-polices the local and national wage scales negotiated with trade unions. The CNA sees violation of these rules, along with fiscal evasion and non-payment of employment taxes, as a form of unfair competition among its member firms. The local Communist Party's interclassist social formation, comprised of both workers and artisans, also allows it to act as a social mediator. In the province of Modena, strong zoning controls and industrial parks assure affordable workshops and restrain real-estate speculation in commercial property. A specialized agency of Emilia-Romagna, financed by the region and fees from businesses, promotes the exchange of information and resources among small enterprises. It also assists in the development of networks for the commercialization of products produced by small firms.

V. The Artisanal Firm

Artisanal status in Italy is a legal classification based primarily on the size of the company's work force, not the form of its productive activity.[6] Artisanal firms are permitted to hire anywhere from 8 to 40 employees; the lower limit applies to transportation firms and the upper to handicraft firms. Most small manufacturing firms are restricted to 22 employees, or 18 if they do not employ apprentices. The limit includes any family members, with exclusions allowed only for one partner and any handicapped persons. Employment levels, however, may be exceeded by 20 percent for a period of up to three months per year. The CNA survey reports that between 1981 and 1985 there was a slight increase in the average firm work force from 10.9 to 12.19 (Rieser and Franchi 1986) This is considerably larger than the average mechanical engineering firm in Modena which has only 2.46 persons including owners and family help.

Of the firms in the larger survey, 80 of the 219 firms surveyed were not strictly artisanal enterprises. Nevertheless these firms were all small–only 18 had a work force larger than 20 persons, of which seven had more than thirty. Among the network firms ten were artisanal firms. The data for the 15 firms surveyed is contained in Table 2.1.

Table 2.1.

COMPANY DESCRIPTION

Firm	Year est.	Work force	Company form	Principal product
BGHI	1967	28	L.P.	Machinery for broom making
GMB	1977	13	Artisan	Hydraulic compressors
AUTL	1972	11	Artisan	Robot and control panels
OO	1968	12	Artisan	Automatic gates
FSS	1971	11	L.P.	Plastic products
DMM	1963	9	Artisan	Industrial furnishings
TMM	1970	12	Artisan	Automated equipment
BT	1961	62	Share co	Ceramic ovens
GEC	1978	12	L. Part.	Lamps
CIS	1979	15	L. Part.	Machinery for ceramic industry
CIS1	1974	15	Artisan	Electronic systems
ORM	1954	13	Artisan	Rebuilt engines
FROS	1970	14	Artisan	Metal finishing
RENF	1971	13	Artisan	Metal hardening
CEC	1978	12	Artisan	Plastic dies

Key: L.P. = Limited Partnership; Share Co. = Incorporated firm.

Because of the legislative, ideological and historical underpinnings of the artisanal firm, conceived of as standing between capital and labor (Cavazzuti 1978; Weiss 1984), the law mandates that the artisan "must commit a substantial portion of his own labor to the productive process."[7] Completely mechanized firms are denied artisanal status, whereas firms that rely on assembly-line production are restricted to 12 employees. Partnerships and cooperatives are permitted artisanal status, but only if a majority of the owners are directly engaged in production. Limited partnerships and shareholder companies are excluded from artisanal status.

Though artisan-entrepreneurs are allowed to be registered owners of only one firm, the law permits them to invest in or form partnership interests with other artisanal firms. Through this method, small producers can integrate their resources with other artisans to expand their range of services and production without losing the flexibility, informality, and low overhead of small firms.

State Incentives

The legal definition of smallness is also of considerable importance because it is associated with special dispensations from labor laws as well as other benefits. In Italy, firms with fewer than 16 employees may dismiss employees with relative impunity, unlike larger firms that are subject to the Workers' Charter, which mandates substantial fines and the reinstatement of employees dismissed without justification[8] (Lazerson 1985). Regardless of this labor law, the national contract that regulates labor relations in artisanal firms also allows small firms more latitude in dismissing employees for economic reasons than industrial firms. Union organizing activities are also relatively unprotected in firms with fewer than 16 employees.

Artisanal status confers substantial loan and tax advantages and reduced administrative expenses. Artisanal firms are entitled to obtain state subsidized loans for machinery and workshops of up to 120 million lire ($92,300) at five percentage points below the prevailing interest rates. In Emilia Romagna, regional loans are also available for up to 60 million lire at about three points below prevailing rates. Though these loans are inadequate for established artisan manufacturing firms that need to modernize, they provide seed capital for one or two skilled workers who wish to become self-employed, which is how most artisanal firms originate. These subsidized state loans equalled 64 percent of artisanal investment requirements between 1953 to 1976 and accounted for 75 percent of new artisanal firms established between 1961 and 1971 (Weiss 1984, pp. 226–227). Other additional incentives are provided by exemptions from some property taxes, exemption from maintaining inventory records and protection against bankruptcy proceedings. The artisan's share of social-insurance contributions for their workers is 40 percent of the employee's gross wages, four points lower than for industrial firms. Artisans' contributions to their own pensions are also heavily subsidized by the state. Nevertheless, the evidence seems to indicate that artisans receives less support from the state than large industries and state-run firms, and that more state subsidies have generally flowed to the depressed south than to the small firm industries of North Central Italy (Forte, Bevolo, Clerico, and Rosso 1978; Ranci 1983).

An entrepreneur's decision to expand through a network-firm is ultimately determined by market factors. But market criteria are continually structured by state regulations that pattern the forms under which capital is aggregated and reproduced: company and bankruptcy laws, taxation and fiscal policies, and labor laws. In artisan firms all of the personal property of the owners is at risk in case of a law suit. Though the numerous advantages of artisanal status, along with liability insurance, usually outweigh this risk, manufacturing firms with substantial sales and commercial activities may decide to set up a limited corporation for those businesses exposed to greater risks and preserve the already existing artisan structure for the productive realm. Incorporating the sales division as a limited company is often also necessary because artisan status does not cover commercial activities that are more than incidental to the firm's principal business.

Labor relations is central to understanding the growth strategies of small firms but not for the reasons usually offered. Both in Italy and abroad, especially in the United Kingdom, it is argued that small firms' principal attraction to business is as a haven from unions (Bin 1983; Rainnie 1985, pp. 148–150). In Italy developments in industrial relations of the late 1960s and 1970s left small firms in a privileged position where they were both exempted from the Workers' Charter of 1970 and relatively untouched by an unprecedented wave of trade union militancy. In perspective, however, labor relations, particularly exemption from protective labor law legislation, appear to be only one factor among many for the fluorescence of the Emilian model (Murray 1983). In Modena, wages are higher than the national average (Brusco 1982), and, since 1979, employees in artisan workshops have been guaranteed the same wage increases as those in large industrial firms.[9] My interviews with union representatives indicated that small firms, especially in the largely male mechanical-engineering sector, often pay higher wages than large companies. However, lower wages prevail in the clothing and textile sectors of Modena that employ mostly female workers (Solinas 1982). Evasion of social insurance by small employers is also uncommon in the province of Modena, unlike in Southern Italy.[10]

Of perhaps greater relevance is the priority that small employers place on not hiring more than 15 employees, above which level the provisions of the Workers' Charter take effect. Of the firms studied, four had already surpassed that threshold. Between 1981 and 1985, one firm lost its exempt status when its work force and two other firms were exempted after a decrease in size. In both cases, the drop in employment seemed unrelated to the law. One of the employers expected that improved economic conditions would soon permit an expansion of the work force future and the other employer intended to hire an additional employee that would expand the work force beyond 15. On the other hand, several employers were very conscious of the 15-employee limit and refused to exceed it. The fact that fewer than 15 percent of the 219 firms surveyed had more than 15 employees offers circumstantial evidence that the Workers' Charter weighs as an important consideration in the decision to expand. On the other hand, the effective threshold of the law is really higher, since employers with fewer than 50 to 100 employees have considerable flexibility in dismissing employees and often are only obliged to pay monetary damages rather than reinstate the employee (Treu 1975, 1976; Centro Nazionale di Prevenzione e Difesa Sociale 1984). Trade unions also are more flexible in negotiating dismissals with smaller firms even when regulated by the Workers' Charter. Equally important is the presence of a trade union in the firm that can constrain the employer's decision to dismiss (Lazerson 1985). Trade unions represented employees in 11 of the 18 firms. Even in firms unrepresented by unions, there seemed to be some evidence that trade unions' institutional power in Modena afforded employees limited protection. One employer of a non-union firm told me that he renegotiated the dismissal of two employees after the union had intervened.

Though employers clearly preferred a free hand to hire and fire, work force turnover was under five percent annually and dismissals infrequent in both union and non-union firms. Of the 14 firms, two firms had dismissed employees for economic reasons and two others for personal reasons. Of course, in a number of the firms there were also periods of informal lay-offs and reductions in work hours. But employment stability was a major concern of the employers, a reflection of the relative skill of the work force. Since most employees were trained on the job, employers loathed losing employees for economic reasons. These costs also made them wary about expanding their work force, preferring to meet increased demand by subcontracting to other firms. This policy served to discourage employees from seeking work in larger firms because it increased their job security in case of economic difficulties. The employers' widespread view that employment should be seen as permanent was best captured by one employer who said that a firm should not be a "seaport where people come and go."

VI. The Importance of Direct Supervision

The general pattern that emerged from the research indicated that avoiding unions, paying low wages, or firing employees were not policies of small Modena employers. Rather, their key concerns were to assure the continuance of personal ties between themselves and their employees without the mediation of managers. In only two of the fourteen firms did employees supervise other employees. Employers feared that the close relations with their employees, which were described as "familial" and "collaborative", would be undermined in a larger firm. Even one relatively large non-artisanal firm in the survey favored decentralized manufacturing sites in close proximity to one another to preserve small work groups. The emphasis on close ties between employer and employees was even present in firms where all employees were union members and strikes had occurred. Strikes were usually called to renew regional or national contracts rather than to protest local conditions. Indeed, one of the few strikes that was aimed at the local employer resulted from the union's and CNA's opposition to a factory-level contract that exceeded the recommended wage increase for the province. In any case, strikes would almost always be followed by employees working overtime to make up lost production, a practice opposed by unions in large firms.

Unionization in these small firms seemed more an affirmation of solidarity with the working-class outside the plant rather than a claim to institutionalize an adverse relationship with the employer inside the plant. Only four of the thirteen firms with unionized work forces negotiated contracts at the firm-level in addition to the national and regional labor accords that apply to all employees, whether union members or not. And of these four, only one was negotiated with the participation of the union. Employers opposed firm-level contracts because of a desire to maintain a direct relationship with their employees and avoid rigid work rules. Flexible work schedules, frequent job rotation, overtime work (often in excess of that contractually permitted), a six-day work week, individual bonuses for workers, and pay scales sometimes above the union standard were aspects of small firm labor relations that conflicted with national union policies. But since these practices normally resulted in higher wages, union members in small firms rarely objected. The handful of employees who attempted in the 1970s to challenge these practices and apply the rigid contract provisions of large firms were rapidly eased out of the firms I surveyed.

This absence of sharp social conflict between employees and their artisan-employers reflects the social origins of the artisans themselves and the vision of the artisanal-entrepreneur as a logical culmination of a skilled worker's career. The overwhelming majority of the artisans surveyed (Rieser and Franchi 1986, p. 17) had been previously employed as skilled workers in larger firms, though some had came from artisanal enterprises. Indeed, union-shop stewards surveyed in large firms in the province of Modena defined artisan-owners as members of the working-class (Franchi and Rieser 1983). A similar identity of interests with small-firm owners combined with a hostility toward large industrialists was also expressed in surveys of workers in the neighboring Communist region of Tuscany (Bagnasco 1985, p. 34). Evidence of this social affinity between artisans and their employees was reported in the CNA survey, which revealed that 47.3 percent of new partners hired between 1981 and 1986 came from within the firm.

The Importance of Personal Ties

The informal arrangements between owners and employees was also solidified by small firms' preference for hiring people recommended by other firms and friends. Employers in the CNA survey hired 42.9 percent of their employees in this way as against only 16.3 percent hired through the state employment office, from which larger firms are required to draw many of their employees. Perhaps because of this reliance upon a closed network of trusted people, employers did not rely upon the oppressive forms of simple control that have been described by Edwards (1979). The dominant impression I gained was that conventional instances of low trust attitudes toward labor were absent (Fox 1974). Only a minority of firms used time clocks, and some that did required everyone, including the partners, to use them. Employers were often permitted some flexibility in working hours. Nor were piece rates or any work incentive pay systems used, reflecting both the essentially non-repetitive nature of the work process and the employer's preference for self-motivated employees. In any case the relative absence of white-collar employees and well-defined lines of authority in small firms would have made direct control strategies ineffective (Friedman 1986).

Although network-firms served to preserve the intimate work relations between owner and employee, they often required the selection of new partners to manage them, the necessity of "having someone there" as two partners of a firm expressed it. According to the CNA survey, new partners were added principally to help manage and operate the firm. The partner's contribution to firm capital and his specialized skills were no more than secondary considerations. Hired managers were normally rejected because of the importance placed on ownership. However, the selections of new partners was always problematic because of the question of trust. The fear of not finding reliable and agreeable partners often was reflected by artisan-owners' selection of relatives or work colleagues as partners. In most cases artisan-owners preferred not to expand rather than risk adding a partner to share the new work obligations.

VII. Market Reasons for Expansion

Though the problem of labor relations and company law were common to all types of small firms contemplating expansion, the precise reasons for establishing network-firms depended on the market position of the company. In general, artisans and small firms fell into two categories: those that marketed finished products and those that were subcontractors for other firms, usually performing usually only one phase of the production process. Of the 219 firms surveyed, 54.3 percent performed primarily subcontract work and the remainder produced mostly their own products. However, of the companies that established network-firms, only 3 out of 18 or 16 percent were primarily subcontractors. In general, small firms with their own product-lines were larger, employed more white-collar employees because of marketing and design needs, and were more likely to use subcontractors themselves. Indeed, this widespread use of subcontractors demonstrates that even within the small-firm sector a core and dependent periphery is visible.

For subcontracting firms, cost reduction was the principal objective, and if they established network-firms, it was to satisfy that goal rather than to enhance their control over the market. A good example was provided by three independent subcontracting firms that performed different finishing operations on steel-roller bearings for a large constructor of heavy machinery. In the past, the roller bearings would make three round-trips in and out of the large factory and to and from the three smaller firms. But the severe recession of 1981-1982 that intensified competition forced the three firms to establish a jointly-owned storage firm to reduce transportation and inventory costs. The three round-trips were reduced to one, and the placement of a storage facility near to two of the small firms allowed much of the transport to be handled by cheap hand-operated dollies. This particular form of vertical integration also sharply increased inter-firm dependency.

In some cases, reliance upon network-firms was required because small firms did not have any well-established relationships, either because business transactions took place in unfamiliar regions or involved third parties that supplied financing. Thus, a manufacturer of broommaking machines was forced to establish a small firm in Spain to assist in the servicing and marketing of its products there. The inability to directly control its foreign distributor nearly ruined one lamp manufacturer after its French sales representative of imitation brass lamps abruptly went bankrupt, leaving the company without an outlet in France, which had absorbed much of its production. A manufacturer's link-up with financial services is sometimes required because the buyers are unknown to the financing agent, even if the latter has a privileged relationship with the seller. Integration of financing services also serves to facilitate sales, especially when the buyer is located abroad. This was exemplified by a very prosperous and well-established ceramic-oven manufacturer that established a separate financing firm to assist its customers with loan and leasing arrangements.

The expansion strategies of small firms with their own product-lines were conditioned by the widespread division of labor that marks subcontract work. Thus, in none of the companies I visited were network-firms initiated to expand existing production. In the face of the potential costs of increased labor and capital inputs, firm owners usually preferred to subcontract any excess production rather than expand. Often these tasks could be outsourced to other small or large firms in the local area that might even be more price competitive. Indeed, a firm's decision to create new network-firms was often premised on the elimination or reduction of some of its existing production facilities in order to replace low-value items with higher-value ones.

Critical in an enterprise's calculations was that the network-firm structure lead to greater control over the three key phases of the production process: design, final assembly, and marketing. These three functions not only helped insulate firms from competitors but also guaranteed them substantial autonomy in the market place, an autonomy that rested considerably on greater freedom to use subcontractors. The possibility that this increased outsourcing of production might impose higher transaction costs appeared to be a minor consideration unless it compromised the strategic core of the firm's market position, e.g., if outsourcing risked revealing product and design secrets to competitors with whom it might share the same subcontractor. But such sensitive production phases could be kept in-house or entrusted to subcontractors with whom a long relationship of trust had been established. Other problems of subcontracting involved quality control, particularly when final customers demanded more exacting warranties and the additional accounting and bookkeeping expenses. However, most firm owners believed that the higher transaction costs resulting from accounting expenses for network and subcontracting firms were preferable to the less desirable alternative of not knowing the cost of each phase of production, a problem that often arose with internal systems of control.

Network-firms were useful vehicles to launch new products and facilitate access to new markets and technologies. One example of how network-firms were used to restrict opportunism in strategic areas, yet not compromise the small firm's flexible structure, was provided by a machine shop with 12 employees. In the past, it had specialized in ceramic boring tools but now produced automated box handling and robotic equipment because of a severe crisis in the ceramic-tile industry. Though staffed with a skilled work force, the firm was dependent on an engineering firm located in the same building for design concepts. To preserve this relationship, the small firm bought a five percent interest in the engineering firm that gave it first right to produce any new invention. But the opportunity for a complete merger was rejected by the machine shop because of concern that it posed an unacceptable risk should the economic environment worsen. Here, the fear of opportunism and dependence on a single firm led to some integration and reduced dependence on the market, but the need to maintain loose-coupling limited the move toward hierarchies. A similar concern for assuring a flow of new products led a manufacturer of automated equipment used in the ceramic and tile industry to transform a once independent subcontractor into a network-firm. This association with an electronics firm with its own design capacity and contacts outside the ceramics industry promised to enhance the primary firm's market autonomy.

Network-firms also allow enterprises to penetrate new markets without risking their existing activities. Two of the firms studied first started out designing and producing plastic injection molds and dies, only to later enter the more lucrative market of plastic fabrication. Plastics production is highly valued because it permits a direct relationship with consumers and increases a firm's options. However, a die-making firms that takes the step toward the actual production of plastics risks losing its customers who are also plastic-makers. This risk is reduced if the plastics production is contained within a network-firm that appears to be formally independent.

Finally, network-firms at the retail level not only provide secure market outlets for finished goods, but offer the opportunity to illegally escape taxes. If a manufacturer is linked with a consumer retail outlet, it facilitates evasion of the country's tax laws. In transactions of goods between companies, an official receipt is normally demanded by the buyer in order to deduct the cost of the purchased item against gross income for tax purposes. However, a retailer who sells primarily to consumers can easily conceal most of his income because sales are often made without receipts, despite the passage of a new law requiring them. The real costs of products can also be easily concealed in transactions with a network-firm. In this way, one manufacturer avoided declaring about 25 percent of its income.

VIII. Conclusions

It is possible that the present organizational development discussed here is only a reflection of the youth of the firms, and that as they mature network-firms will be merged into a single integrated firm. Ten years ago none of these firms had even established networks. Nevertheless, the firms' motivations for integration and combination only infrequently parallelled those suggested by Williamson. On the contrary, there is evidence that the more continuous and long-term the exchange relations between economic agents, the less likely is the need to formalize them legally. Certainly from the standpoint of manufacturing flexibility, production costs, and insulation from economic difficulties, market relations seemed most attractive. The exceptions occurred when transactions with the external environment touched upon what I have defined as the strategic core or the commanding heights of the market – design, marketing, and assembly functions. But here the rationale for vertical integration and greater intra-firm coordination was not to reduce transaction costs but to obtain a more secure position within the market. Even more incongruous with the dichotomous vision of hierarchies and markets was the fact that, within a single firm, movements toward hierarchy and away from markets in one area were often counter-balanced by a greater dependence on markets in other areas.

The other critical issue that the market and hierarchies distinction does not adequately address is that of the legal and social environment within which firms operate. Before firms choose markets or hierarchies, they are affected by state policies which promote certain forms of business combinations more than others, often for reasons that are socially and politically, rather than economically, motivated (Berger 1980b). The strategies of Italian small firms would appear very different if tomorrow the entire legal structure promoting artisanal firms was withdrawn. The is also true for the special labor laws that make some organizational choices more attractive than others.

Analysis of social formation must also require consideration of those particular national structures that encourage cooperation and solidarity, values that are not equally distributed and nurtured across national boundaries. In my research in Modena, these institutions included the local administration, the Communist Party and the CNA. But in the Veneto region to the north of Emilia Romagna, they also include the Christian Democratic party and its vast capillary network (Bagnasco and Trigilia 1984). These political and social institutions' encouragement of collaborative arrangements and continuous intervention in the market have been necessary to prevent capitalism from destroying the environment in which it flourishes (Polanyi 1957), an event that would perhaps leave us only with hierarchies and no markets.

Notes

* Field research for this paper was supported by an N.S.F.-N.A.T.O. Post-Doctoral Research Fellowship at the Instituto Giuridico of the University of Bologna, where I was a guest of Professors Giuseppe Caputo and Vincenzo Ferrari. I am especially indebted to Sebastiano Brusco and Vittorio Rieser of the University of Modena and Ivan Bignardi and Mauro Ronchetti of the Modena branch of the Confederazione Nazionale dell'Artigianato for their cooperation during my investigations. James Form, Mark Granovetter and Charles Perrow helped me strengthen this paper.

1. Source: *Annuario di statistico Italiano*. 1986. "6th censimento generale dell'industria, del commercio, dei servizi e dell'artigianato, 26 october 1981." pp. 347, 353. Rome: ISTAT. In calculating the percentage of manufacturing firms with a workforce of less than 50, I have excluded agricultural, construction and energy firms. Work force is defined as including employees, owners and family help.
2. County Business Patterns, 1968-1977: Ten Year History. U.S. Bureau of the Census, July, 1981.
3. Source: *Annuario di statistico Italiano*. 1986. "6th censimento generale dell'industria, del commercio, dei servizi e dell'artigianato, 26 october 1981." p.347. Rome: ISTAT.
4. Italian employment data usually refers to the entire workforce, defined as including all owners, family help and employees.
5. This information was obtained through the provincial office of the Modena CGIL.
6. "La legge quadro per l'artigianato." Law of August 8, 1985, number 443.
7. "La legge quadro per l'artigianato." Law of August 8, 1985, number 443, article 2.

8. "Statuto dei Lavoratori, Law No. 300 of May, 1970.
9. *Contratto Collettive Nazionale di Lavoro*,of June 14, 1984 for the mechanical engineering firms of the Province of Modena.
10. Interview with inspector of the Italian Department of Health and Welfare (INPS) for the province of Modena.

References

Agenzia Industrial Italiana, 1984, *Osservatorio sulla subfornitura: III rilevazione – Settembre, 1984* Torino: Agenzia Industriale Italiana.

Bagnasco, Arnaldo, 1985, "La costruzione sociale del mercato: strategie di impresa e esperimenti di scala in Italia," *Stato e Mercato* 13, 9–45.

Bagnasco, Arnaldo, and Carlo Trigilia, 1984, *Societa e politica nelle aree di piccola impresa: Il caso di Bassano*, Venice: Arsenale.

Becattini, Giacomo, 1979, "Dal 'settore' industriale al 'distretto'industriale: alcune considerazione sull'unita di indagine dell'economia industriale," *Rivista di economia e politica industriale* 1, 7–22.

Berger, Suzanne, 1980a, "Discontinuity in the Politics of Industrial Society," in Susan Berger and Michael Piore (eds.), *Dualism and Discontinuity in Industrial Societies*, Cambridge: Cambridge University Press.

Berger, Suzanne, 1980b. "The Traditional Sector in France and Italy," in Susan Berger and Michael Piore (eds.), Cambridge: Cambridge University Press.

Berger, Suzanne, 1981, "The Uses of the Traditional Sector in Italy: Why Declining Classes Survive," in Frank Bechhofer and Brian Elliott,(eds.) *The Petite Bourgeoisie: Comparative Studies of the Uneasy Stratum*, London: Macmillan.

Bin, Mario, 1983, *La piccola impresa industriale: Problemi giuridici e analisi economica*, Bologna: Mulino.

Botta, Paolo, Maria Fonte, Lucia Improta, Enrico Pugliese and Francesca Ruggiero, 1976, "La struttura del settore calzaturiero a Napoli," *Inchiesta* 23, 61–83.

Brusco, Sebastiano, 1975, "Organizzazione del lavoro e decentramento produttivo nel settore metalmeccanico," in FLM of Bergamo (ed.), *Sindacato e piccola impresa: Strategia del capitale e azione sindacale nel decentramento produttivo*, Bari: De Donato.

Brusco, Sebastiano, 1982, "The Emilian Model: Productive Decentralization and Social Integration," *Cambridge Journal of Economics* 6, 167–184.

Brusco, Sebastiano, and Charles Sabel, 1981, "Artisan Production and Economic Growth," in Frank Wilkinson (ed.), *The Dynamics of Labour Market Segmentation*, London: Academic Press.

Capecchi, Vittorio and Enrico Pugliese, 1978, "Bologna Napoli: due citta a confronto," *Inchiesta* 35–36, 3–54.

Cavazzuti, Franco, 1978, "Le Piccole Imprese," in Francesco Galgano (ed.), *Trattato di diritto commerciale e di diritto pubblico dell'economia*, vol. 2, Padova: Cedam, 1978.

Centro Nazionale di Prevenzione e Difesa Sociale, 1984, "L'Applicazione dello statuto dei lavoratori dal 1974 al 1981: Ricerca Campionaria in Otto Province," *Quaderni della giustizia* 36, 68–103 and 38, 94–125

Chandler, Alfred, 1977, *The Visible Hand: The Managerial Revolution in American Business*, Cambridge: Harvard University Press.

Dore, Ronald, 1983, "Goodwill and the Spirit of Market Capitalism," *British Journal of Sociology* 34, 459–82.

Du Boff, Richard and Edward Herman, 1980, "Alfred Chandler's New Business History: A Review," *Politics and Society* 10: 81–110.

Edwards, Richard, 1979, *Contested Terrain: The Transformation of the Work Place in the Twentieth Century*, New York: Basic Books.

Forte, Franco, Bevolo, Maripina, Clerico, Giuseppe, and Rosso, Loretta, 1978, *La redistribuzione assistenziale*, Milan: Etas Libri.

Fox, Alan, 1974, *Beyond Contract; Work Power and Trust Relations* London: Faber.

Franchi, Maura, and Rieser, Vittorio 1983, *Esperienza e cultura dei delegati: un indagine nella realta metalmeccanica modenese*, Reggio Emilia: Bonhoeffer Edizioni.

Friedman, Andrew, 1986, "Developing the Managerial Strategies Approach to the Labour Process," *Capital & Class* 30, 97–124.

Granovetter, Mark, 1984, "Small Is Bountiful: Labor Markets and Establishment Size," *American Sociological Review* 49, 323–334.

Granovetter, Mark, 1985, "Economic Action and Social Structure: The Problem of Embeddedness," *American Journal of Sociology* 91, 481–510.

Lazerson, Mark, 1985, *Labor Conflict Within the Shadow of the Law: The Italian Workers' Charter of 1970*, Unpublished Ph. D. dissertation, University of Wisconsin-Madison.

Littler, Craig, 1985, "Taylorism, Fordism and Job Design," pp. 10–29 in David Knights, Hugh Willmott and David Collinson (eds.), *Job Redesign: Critical Perspectives on the Labour Process*, Aldershot: Gower.

Marglin, Stephen, 1974, "What Do Bosses Do? The Origins and Functions of Hierarchy in Capitalist Production," *Review of Radical Political Economics* 6, 60–112.

Marshall, Alfred, [1923] 1970, *Industry and Trade*, New York: Kelley.

Mendels, Franklin, 1972, "Proto-industrialization: The First Phase of the Industrialization Process," *Journal of Economic History* 32, 241–261.

Messori, Marcello, 1986, "Sistemi di imprese e sviluppo meridionale, Un confronto fra due area industriali," *Stato e Mercato* 18, 403–431.

Minsky, Hyman, 1985, "Review: The Second Industrial Divide," *Challenge* 28 (3): 60–64.

Murray, Fergus, 1983, "The Decentralization of Production – the Decline of the Mass-Collective Worker?" *Capital & Class* 19, 74–99.

Oakey, Ray, 1984, *High Technology Small Firms: Regional Development in Britain and the United States* London: Francis Pinter.

Perrow, Charles, 1981, "Markets, Hierarchies and Hegemony: A Critique of Chandler and Williamson," in Andrew Van de Ven and William Joyce (eds.), *Perspectives on Organization Design and Behavior*, New York: Wiley.

Perrow, Charles, 1986, "Economic Theories of Organization," *Theory and Society* 15, 11–45.

Piore, Michael and Charles Sabel, 1984, *The Second Industrial Divide: Possibilities for Prosperity*, New York: Basic Books.

Pitkin, Donald, 1985, *The House that Giacomo Built: History of an Italian Family 1898–1978*, New York: Cambridge University Press.

Polanyi, Karl, 1957, *The Great Transformation: The Political and Economic Origins of Our Time*, Boston: Beacon Press.

Prais, Sigbert Jon, 1982, "Strike Frequencies and Plant Size: A Comment on Swedish and United Kingdom Experiences," *British Journal of Industrial Relations* 20, 101–108.

Al Rainnie, 1985, "Small Firms, Big Problems: The Political Economy of Small Businesses," *Capital & Class* 25, 140–168.

Ranci, Pippo, 1983, *I trasferimenti dello stato a imprese industriali negli anni settanta*, Bologna: Il Mulino.

Rieser, Vittorio and Maura Franchi, 1986, *Innovazione tecnologica e mutamento organizzativo nell'impresa artigiano: Una ricerca sull'artigianato metalmeccanico di produzione nella provincia di Modena*, Unpublished manuscript along with additional survey results on file with the Confederazione Nazionale dell'Artigianato of Modena.

Sabel, Charles, 1982, *Work and Politics: The Division of Labor in Industry* Cambridge: Cambridge University Press.

Sayer, Andrew, 1986, "New Developments in Manufacturing: The Just-in-Time System," *Capital & Class* 30, 43–72.

Scott, Allan and Michael, Storper, 1985, *Production, Work and Territory: The Geographical Anatomy of Industrial Capitalism:*, London: Allen and Unwin.

Solinas, Giovanni, 1982, "Labor Market Segmentation and Workers' Careers: The Case of the Italian Knitwear Industry," *Cambridge Journal of Economics* 6, 331–352.

Treu, Tiziano, 1975, 1976, *Sindacati e magistratura nei conflitti di lavoro*, Vols. I, II, Bologna: Il Mulino.

Weiss, Linda, 1984, "The Italian State and Small Business," *European Journal of Sociology* 25, 214–241.

Williamson, Oliver, 1975, *Markets and Hierarchies*, New York: Free Press.

Williamson, Oliver, 1985, *The Economics Institutions of Capitalism – Firms, Markets, Relational Contracting*, New York: Free Press.

Comment on "Transactional Calculus and Small Business Strategy" by Mark Lazerson

Felix R. FitzRoy

This interesting paper describes a case study conducted by Mark Lazerson, of 15 small "artisanal" firms in the Modena area of Emilia Romagna in Italy. But it also throws light on the increasing importance of small firms in Italy and elsewhere, and on the much greater relative importance of small firms in Italy compared to the U.S. Lazerson also shows the limited relevance of O. Williamson's transactions cost framework for explaining the growth of small firms in Italy, so the paper should be of general interest to economists who do not usually read more sociologically oriented case studies.

Williamson has frequently argued that small-numbers bargaining and asset-specificity create a situation so vulnerable to opportunism that centralized or vertical hierarchical control should prevail and reduce transaction costs. However he neglects the importance of hightrust personal relationships in attenuating opportunism and *also* reducing the monitoring and information costs of centralized hierarchy.

As Lazerson makes clear, a number of separable factors or influences come together in the contrasting "Emilian model of small highly specialized industrial firms", and contribute to viability. The Italian legal framework favors small firms particularly of the "artisanal" type with essentially a working owner in various ways, including tax, credit and freedom to fire redundant employees. The law also permits artisan-entrepreneurs to form partnerships with other artisanal firms, without losing privileged status. Nevertheless, Lazerson (p. 32) concludes that "artisans receive less support from the state than large industries and state-run firms."

In spite of strong unions in Emilia, Lazerson found that "avoiding unions, paying low wages or firing employees were not policies of small Modena employers" (p. 33). Rather, two major advantages of the system emerge. Flexible specialization in production is facilitated by closely linked artisanal partnerships, and labor relations in each firm are better when the working owner himself supervises and personally knows his employees.

Both dependence on skilled employees and closely linked "satellite firms" specializing in some component of the production process creates a potential "hold-up" problem. Personal contracts and recommendations in hiring and other transactions thus played a major role in creating the high trust relations essential to reduce the risk of opportunism. Extended family networks, more important in the relatively immobile society which still survives in parts of Italy, also played a significant part in providing reliable personal information and reputation effects. The monitoring costs and defensive organization structures of centralized control practised in more mobile societies could thus be economized *without* the hierarchies favored by Williamson.

Z.J. Acs and D.B. Audretsch (eds.), The Economics of Small Firms: European Challenge. 41–42.

Although the Emilian framework is rather special, some quite general lessons do emerge. As Lazerson (p. 38) notes, "there is evidence that the more continuous and long term the exchange relations between economic agents, the less likely is the need to formalize them legally." The challenge for economists and policy makers is to find appropriate institutions in other settings which also encourage the development of specific human capital without opportunism.

3. Firm Performance and Size*

DAVID J. STOREY

I. Introduction

It might have been expected that clearly articulated theories of the relationship between firm size and performance would have been developed. Yet, despite the important role which individual firm performance plays in any economy, and despite the extensive empirical work undertaken in this matter, the relationship remains unsatisfactorily understood.

In almost all theoretical and empirical work, firm performance is expressed in terms of profitability or growth, normally in financial terms and firm size is viewed as a continuum, with large firms at one end of the spectrum. Where they are discussed at all, small firms are viewed as a "scaled-down" version at the other end of the size spectrum. For smaller firms the term "performance" is somewhat wider including not only firm growth in financial and employment terms, but also taking account of failure, ownership change and firm age.

This paper presents an alternative view, by arguing that small firms are not simply "scaled-down" versions of large firms. Instead they have characteristics which are different in type from large firms. The paper recognises that firm size may be viewed as a proxy for market characteristics, financial and/or structure and even location or technological sophistication. It is also keenly aware of the heterogeneity of small firms, yet it argues that there are nevertheless factors which are significantly more relevant to explaining the performance of small firms than large firms.

The paper is in two main parts. The first, covered in sections Two to Five, reviews some of the empirical work which has related firm size to firm performance. Section Two reviews the work on primarily large firms, whilst Sections Three and Four deal with more recent work on smaller firms. These sections demonstrate that, in many dimensions of performance, small firms differ markedly from large or even medium sized firms. For example, whilst size and growth are generally unrelated for medium sized firms they appear to be negatively correlated for small firms. The performance of small firms is also more strongly related to firm age than is the case for larger firms. Finally the issue of firm failure is always central to a discussion of small firms, and is a more ever-present threat than for larger firms.

The second part of the paper, contained in Section Five, is concerned to begin to explore some of the reasons underlying these differences. It is not intended to provide a comprehensive set of explanations for each of these performance differences,[1] but rather to highlight some rarely discussed aspects in which small and large firms differ, other than in the dimension of pure scale. It is hoped that subsequent work will be directed towards estimating the importance of these factors on small firm performance.

Z.J. Acs and D.B. Audretsch (eds.), The Economics of Small Firms: A European Challenge. 43–50.

II. The well established work

There are three well established theories which relate size and growth. The first is that if all firms face identical U-shaped average cost curves then small firms would exhibit faster growth rates than large firms because they were further from the minimum point on their LRAC. This suggests small firms would be expected to grow *faster* than large firms. In imperfect markets, and given the divorce of ownership and control in large firms, there may, however, be a tendency for management in large firms to favour growth at the expense of profitability. In this case small firms would be expected to grow *slower* than large firms. The third, and probably most favoured theory, is that growth should be viewed as a statistical phenomenon resulting from the cumulative effects of the chance operation of a large number of forces each operating independently. In this case firm growth is inferred to be *independent* of firm size – the so-called Gibrat's Law.

Gibrat's Law has been used as the basis for a number of theoretical developments such as those by Lucas (1978), even though its empirical support is not consistently conclusive. Nevertheless the fact that some studies (Hart 1965, Singh and Whittington 1968) find support for Gibrat's Law, whereas others such as Meeks and Whittington (1975) find a positive relationship between size and growth, and Aislabie and Keating (1976) find a negative relationship confirms us in the view that broad support for Gibrat's Law is probably justified.

All these studies, however, examine the applicability of Gibrat's Law to a population of relatively large firms. For example all the U.K. studies used companies that were quoted on the London Stock Exchange. They also measured firm size and performance in terms of Assets and Profitability since this information was most readily available. We now turn to studies which have used data on a wider range of firm sizes.

III. New analyses based on U.S. Dun and Bradstreet data

In recent years there have been several important contributions to the discussion of the relationship between firm size and performance, using Dun and Bradstreet data bases, as amended by the U.S. Small Business Administration. The advantage of this data base is such that it can provide time series coverage of individual firms and establishments in all sectors of the economy. Whilst coverage is not complete, particularly in the small firm sector it is, by any standards, a massive data base. The criteria used for the measurement of size is, however, that of employment, whereas much of the earlier work was both based on the manufacturing sector and used financial, generally Asset-based criteria as a measure of size.

In the United States the data bases have been used primarily to examine the question, initially addressed by Birch (1979), of the contribution to job creation of different sizes of firm (Armington and Odle 1982, Storey and Johnson 1987, Acs and Audretsch 1987). They have provided general support for the Birch view that small firms were a major source of new job creation, but that Birch considerably overestimated that contribution.

These studies have been replicated outside the United States, notably by Colin Gallagher and his colleagues (Gallagher and Stewart 1985, Doyle and Gallagher 1986).

In the present context, however, the study by Evans (1987) is more relevant, since it sets out to test the extent to which the independence of firm growth and firm size (Gibrat's Law) applies in the small firm sector. Evans concludes that Gibrat's Law must be rejected for the small firm sector since growth and size are *negatively* correlated, even allowing for the exiting of slow growth firms.

Evans argues that to fully explain the performance of the small firm sector it is necessary to directly introduce the concept of both age of firm and number of plants. His results suggest that firm growth decreases with firm age for younger firms, but then eventually increases with firm age for older firms. He also finds that the departures from Gibrat's law increase with numbers of plants.

IV. Some results from the U.K. small firm sector

Storey, Keasey, Watson and Wynarczyk (1987) examine the relationship between size and growth in a population of single plant independent manufacturing companies in Northern England. Compared with the U.S. data bases the sample is very modest, with only 636 companies tracked over the 1971–81 period. Nevertheless it is of somewhat larger size than many of the British studies of quoted companies.

The conclusions which the study reaches closely follow those of Evans, even though the U.K. study uses financial criteria for measures of size (Net Assets, Total Assets). It finds that size and growth are negatively correlated for this group of small[2] firms, although the apparent strength of the relationship varies considerably according to the nature of the tests undertaken. Secondly the study showed that when age was included in the regression equations it had a significantly negative coefficient. Thirdly the study of small firm failure showed that rates were negatively correlated with age. Fourthly the performance of the small firm was significantly more volatile, on a year by year basis, than was the case for large firms. Finally the dispersion of growth rates within the small firm population was considerably greater than was the case for large firms.

V. Explaining these differences

The above sections have demonstrated that whilst size and growth may be broadly unrelated for medium and large firms, the same is not true for small firms. The remainder of the paper will be taken up with presenting the case that small firms differ from large firms according to a variety of different dimensions, other than that of pure scale. Indeed, even where there are apparent similarities these can lead to behavioural differences. It is therefore only to be expected that the performance of small firms should respond to very different incentives to that of large, or even medium sized firms.

(a) Firm Formation. Conventional theory has identified the concept of "output entry" (Johnson 1986), defined as "the movement of firms into a market which involves the utilisation of productive capacity not in the market prior to that movement". It has, however, generally failed to distinguish between new firm entry – the formation of a wholly new firm, and cross entry – the diversification of firms already in operation

elsewhere. The role of output entry is to ensure that supernormal profits cannot continue in the long run in a perfectly competitive market. In this sense entrants are seen as passive responders to changes in relative prices.

From our current perspective the key difference between cross entry and new firm entry is that the former is likely to be undertaken by existing firms in the market place, possibly by large or medium sized firms. On the other hand new firm formation is undertaken by individuals. It is here argued that these two groups will respond differently to relative price changes.

In the standard model, increases in post entry profitability in the ith industry will induce entry into that industry. This seems a reasonable proposition where output entry is in the form of cross entry. However it appears to be less justified where output entry is in the form of new firms, and where the decision to enter self employment (start a firm) is made by an individual. As Knight (1921) argued the decision to enter self employment depends upon the expected value of the individuals income working as an employee, as opposed to becoming an employer.

Ceteris paribus, a fall in the expected value of employee income will lead to an increase in self employment. This fall in income could occur where an individual becomes unemployed and is unlikely to obtain work in the immediate future. Given that individuals tend to start their business in the industry in which they were formally employed (Johnson and Cathcart 1979, Cross 1981), then exogenous *reductions* in profitability could lead to job shedding, and hence to increased rates of new firm formation.

Some empirical support for this hypothesis is provided by Storey and Jones (1987), whose cross sectional analysis shows that, ceteris paribus, new firm formation rates were highest in those manufacturing sectors with high labour shedding rates.

Other analyses have been more ambiguous. For example Binks and Jennings (1986) postulate that if these "push" factors for entrepreneurship are important they would expect to find firm formation rates to be higher in the downswing of the trade cycle than in the upswing. Yet, taking data over more than twenty years, they were unable to either conclusively accept or reject the hypothesis. Their view is that whilst "push" factors certainly exist, the downswing of the cycle also coincides with a lowering of aggregate demand and with greater difficulty being experienced by individuals in assembling sufficient resources to start in business. These factors help to offset the "push" factors.

On balance it seems clear that the factors which influence the decisions of an existing firm to enter an industry – cross entry – will differ from those which influence an individual in starting a business – a new firm. Indeed it is even possible that the factors may be diametrically opposed.

(b) The objectives of the small firm owner. Within the economics literature profit maximisation is generally assumed to be the objective of business owners. It has, however, been recognised as not being appropriate in all contexts and so several other objective functions have been proposed (sales maximisation, market share etc.).

For small business owners it is far from clear that the profit maximisation assumption is generally appropriate in a discussion of motivations. Furthermore none of the alternative objective functions, such as sales maximisation or market share, which have been proposed in the economics literature seem any more appropriate for small firm owners. Legions of attitude surveys of such individuals (Scase and Goffee 1981, Curran 1986) have shown that the small firm owner pursues a variety of different objectives in managing his business activities. These will include ensuring a satisfactory flow of income from the business activities, the maintenance of ownership and control, and the derivation of job satisfaction.

In describing these objectives it will be noted that the phrase "business activities" was used, rather than firm or business. In a discussion of small business it is important to distinguish between the business and the entrepreneur.

In this context our studies of entrepreneurs (Storey, Keasey, Watson and Wynarczyk 1987) have demonstrated the importance of two factors. The first is that 79% of owners of fast growth small businesses had an ownership interest in at least one other business, compared with only 38% of owners of non fast growth companies.[3] Interestingly, we also found in an examination of failed firms, that these were *more* likely to have directors with an ownership interest in other firms.[4]

Secondly our studies also demonstrated the variability, between firms, of monies removed from the business in the form of Directors remuneration. It was clear that firm growth was positively associated with the proportion of trading profits which were retained within the business, rather than with the levels of trading profits per se. The monies removed from the business is a decision made by the business owners alone, yet is the clear determinant of whether or not that business grows.[5]

Given both these empirical observations, we are in a position to speculate that the objective of the small business owner is to maximise the time-discounted stream of earnings from a portfolio of business interests, perhaps subject to the constraint of maintaining a satisfactory degree of independence.

Stating objectives in this way helps us to understand several apparently conflicting elements of entrepreneurial behaviour. The first is the apparent conflict whereby individuals who are owners of more than one company are more likely to be owners of both fast growth companies and of companies likely to fail. We should emphasise that it is NOT that the fast growth companies fail, but rather that *other* companies within the Directors portfolio fail. We attribute this to the fact that the entrepreneur has a portfolio of companies, which is constantly adjusting through the formation of new firms and the closure of others.

This, in turn, serves to highlight the distinction between *business failure* and *entrepreneurial failure*. The former occurs much more frequently than the latter and reflects the closure of a firm, whereas the latter occurs when the owner is unable to pay off debts in full and becomes personally bankrupt. There is no reason why a business failure need necessarily be a cause for concern for society providing the resources employed can be costlessly transferred to alternative improved use.

Statistical data, however, tend to be collected at the level of the firm or establishment. Our efforts to identify a relationship between the size and growth of the firm may therefore be thwarted by the fact that, in the small firm sector, the most appropriate unit of account is the entrepreneur rather than the firm or business. The creation and subsequent closure of a firm may merely be part of the small entrepreneurs way of searching out profitable opportunities, analogous to that of the large firm which establishes a new product line. The key difference is that in the case of small firms a new firm is established, whereas for large firms the expansion takes place in-situ.

In several respects these results underline the points made by Nadel (1988) and Lazerson (1989) who shows that the small firm is not an independent autonomous unit as predicated by the perfect competition model.

In one sense therefore empirical studies of small firms have served to demonstrate that small firms are similar to large firms. Certainly those small firms which grow rapidly often do so by spawning and acquiring other small firms, in a manner thought to be characteristic only of large firms.

The motivation for this, often complex, network of ownership patterns, however, differs between large and small firms. The large firm is likely to be acquiring existing firms to strengthen its position in an market, diversifying into new markets, reducing strategic competitive threats etc.

In the case of the small firm, the entrepreneur is much more likely to start a new business than to acquire an existing firm. The entrepreneur is likely to be motivated strongly by uncertainty about the new venture and will establish the new firm as an independent unit which, if it fails, will not jeopardise the viability of the parent firm.

Hence although both large and small firms can have complex ownership structures, with parent organisations controlling a portfolio of satellite firms, the motivations underlying these structures varies significantly between large and small firms.

VI. Conclusion

This paper has presented the case that small firms deserve greater attention from economists who, in the past, have been interested primarily in larger firms.

It is argued that it is unjustifiable to regard the small firm as simply a "scaled-down" version of a large firm. Instead, in several important areas of economics the small firm behaves in a way which is the opposite to that proposed by conventional theory, calibrated upon the large firm sector. For example it is shown that Gibrat's Law does not apply to the small firm sector.It is also argued that entry by new firms does not necessarily take place when profitability in that industry increases.

Given that the small firm sector is becoming of increasing importance in the creation of wealth and employment in most developed countries the paper begins to sketch out the factors which influence the motivations and aspirations of the owners of these businesses and explores their implications for conventional economics.

In particular it discusses the role of multiple ownership of small businesses by entrepreneurs. It argues that this little researched topic requires more investigation by theorists to investigate the factors influencing entrepreneurs decisions on the appropriate portfolio of businesses to be owned.

Notes

* This paper has benefited from the many helpful comments received from Zoltan J. Acs, Hans-Jurgen Ewers and others attending the symposium. The views expressed, however, are those of the author alone.

1. For example the implications of technological change upon firm size is not discussed here. The interested reader should consult either Acs and Audretsch (1988), Dosi (1988) or Diwan (1989).
2. The median employment size of companies in the data base in 1978 was 10 workers.
3. The Directors of Fast growth companies had 4.5 other Directorships, whereas Directors of non fast growth companies had an average of 0.9 other Directorships.
4. Just over one third (33.9%) of failed companies had Directors who were Directors of other companies, compared with only about one fifth (20.3%) of non failed companies.
5. Perhaps it ought to be emphasised that changes in employment are negatively related to Directors remuneration, for a given level of Trading Profit.

References

Acs, Z. and Audretsch, D., 1989, "Job Creation and Firm Size in the U.S. and West Germany", International Small Business Journal, 7(4), 9–22.

Acs, Z. and Audretsch, D., 1988, "Innovation in large and small firms: An empirical analysis", *American Economic Review* 78 (September), 678–690.

Aislabie, C.J. and Keating, G.R., 1976, "Size, Industrial Classification, and the Growth of Australian Factories," *Economic Record* 52 (March), 82–93.

Armington, C. and Odle, M., 1982, "Small Business – How many Jobs?" *Brookings Review*, Winter 1982, pp 14–17.

Binks, M. and Jennings, A., 1986, "Small firms as a source of Economic Rejuvenation" in J. Curran, J.Stanworth and D. Watkins (eds) *The Survival of the Small Firm*, Gower, Aldershot.

Birch, D.L., 1977, "The Job Generation Process," M.I.T. Program on Neighborhood and Regional Change, Cambridge, Mass.

Cross, M., 1981, *New Firm Formation and Regional Development*, 1981, Gower, Farnborough.

Curran, J., 1986, *Bolton Fifteen years on; a review and analysis of small business research in Britain 1971–86*, Small Business Research Trust London.

Diwan, R., 1989, "Small business and the economics of flexible manufacturing," *Small Business Economics* 1(2), 101–110.

Dosi, G., 1988, "Sources, Procedures and Microecomomic effects of innovation," *Journal of Economic Literature*, 26 (September), 1120–1171.

Doyle, J. and Gallagher, C.C., 1986, "The size distribution, potential for growth and contribution to job generation of firms in the United Kingdom, 1982–1984", Research Report No 7, Department of Industrial Management, University of Newcastle upon Tyne.

Evans, D.S., 1987, "The relationship between firm growth, size and age: Estimates for 100 Manufacturing Industries," *Journal of Industrial Economics*, 35, 567–582.

Gallagher, C.C. and Stewart, H., 1985, "Jobs and the Business Life Cycle in the UK", Department of Industrial Management, University of Newcastle upon Tyne.

Hart, P.E., 1962, "The Size and Growth of Firms," *Economica*, 29, 29–39.

Johnson, P.S., 1986, *New Firms: An Economic Perspective*, Allen and Unwin, London.

Johnson, P.S. and Cathcart, D.G., 1979, "The founders of New Manufacturing Firms: A Note on the size of their incubator plants" *Journal of Industrial Economics*, 28, 19–24.

Knight, F.H., 1921, *Risk, Uncertainty and Profit*, Boston, Houghton Mifflin.

Lazerson, M., 1989, *Transactional Calculus and Small Business Strategy*, this volume, pp. 25–41.

Lucas, R.E., 1978, "On the Size Distribution of Business Firms," *Bell Journal of Economics*, 9, 508–523.

Meeks, G. and Whittington, G., 1975, "Giant Companies in the United Kingdom 1948–69", *Economic Journal*, 85, 824–843.

Nadel, H., 1988, "Employment Growth in the French SMES: An Ambiguous Reality", paper given at WZB, International Conference on Small Business Economics, November 17–18, 19.

Scase, R. and Goffee, R., 1981, *The Real world of the small business owner*, London, Croom Helm.

Singh, A. and Whittington, G., 1968, *Growth, Profitability and Valuation*, London, Cambridge University Press.

Storey, D.J., Keasey, K., Watson, R. and Wynarczyk, P., 1987, *The Performance of Small Firms*, London, Croom Helm.

Storey, D.J. and Johnson, S., 1987, *Job Generation and Labour Market Change*, London, Macmillan.

Storey, D.J. and Jones, A.M., 1987, "New Firm Formation – A Labour Market Approach to Industrial Entry", *Scottish Journal of Political Economy*, 34, 37–51.

Comment on "Firm Performance and Size" by David J. Storey

Zoltan J. Acs

Over the past fifty years the growth of the large joint stock company, fueled in part by mass production technologies and organizational innovation, has led economists to single out the large firm for special consideration. A long line of research, starting with the work of Joan Robinson, and including among others, F.J. Hall and C.J. Hitch, Richard Cyert, and Oliver Williamson, supported the view that the large firm was behaviorally different from the small firm. It was perhaps the work of Robin Marris that best articulated the view that managers may have objective functions quite different from entrepreneurs. Once the firm is no longer a price-taker, profit maximization is no longer a valid behavioral assumption.

Many of us here recognize that the creation of new small firms is important for the continued industrial health of a developed economy. Storey's paper is motivated not by the observation that small firms are playing a more important role today, which they are, but by the fact that the small firm is not well understood by economists. He suggests that small firms are behaviorally different from large firms, and are not simple scaled down versions of their larger counterparts. The point goes to the heart of the theory of the firm suggesting that: a particular type of rigorous small-firm theory which has been central to economic analysis for over a century is unable to "handle" the small firm just like fifty years ago, it was recognized that the same competitive model was inadequate to predict the behavior of large firms.

Storey argues that for the small entrepreneurial firms we must differentiate between the firm and the entrepreneur. While profit maximization may be an adequate behavioral assumption for the firm, since profit maximization is not what a firm chooses to do, but what it must do under the penalty of economic death, it is inadequate for the entrepreneur, who is interested in maximizing the discounted stream of earnings from a *portfolio* of business interests. Performance for the small firm must take into account, not only the growth of assets, as for large firms, but also firm *failure* and *ownership* change, something that a joint stock company does not have to worry about. When was the last time that a large firm went out of business?

While large firms predominantly expand via mergers (Kirchhoff, 1989), small firms also have complex patterns of expansion and ownership. However, Storey suggests that the motivation of the two are different. While the large firm expands, to use Lazerson's phraseology, to capture the strategic core – design, marketing, assembly – small firm expansion is a process whereby small firms search out profitable investment opportunities. For the small firm this is almost always done by creating new enterprises as opposed to buying existing firms. This entrepreneurial aspect of firm expansion cannot be easily handled by either the traditional theory of perfect competition nor the choice theoretic versions of the Lucas model, since they are both static in analysis.[1]

However, the direction suggested by Storey does not seem satisfactory either since it ignores innovation. Indeed, incentives for entrepreneurship and incentives for innovation are concepts that may be interchangeable. A more fruitful approach would be to

Z.J. Acs and D.B. Audretsch (eds.), The Economics of Small Firms: A European Challenge. 51–52.

first start with the markets and hierarchies approach of Williamson. As Williamson (1975) himself has pointed out, large companies are becoming increasingly aware of the fact that the bureaucratic apparatus they use to manage mature products is less well suited for innovation.

Finally, an evolutionary theory of the small entrepreneurial firm may be the most promising way to proceed. Here the driving force of the model is what Winter (1984) termed a "technological regime". According to Winter an entrepreneurial regime is one that is favorable to innovative entry and unfavorable to innovative activity by established firms. Recently Jovanovic (1982), building on the work of Lucas, developed a model of – learning by doing – where entrepreneurs learn about their abilities to manage a business. An implication of the model is that firms begin at a small scale and then, if merited by subsequent *performance*, expand either by growing or merging. Pakes and Ericson (1987) build on Jovanovic's model by arguing that firms can actively accelerate the learning process by investing in R&D. This approach may prove most interesting in future research. These points are further developed in Acs and Audretsch (1989).

Note

1. These models are discussed in Reid and Jacobsen (1988).

References

Acs, Zoltan J. and David B. Audretsch, 1989, "Technological Regimes, Learning, and Industry Turbulence," Discussion Paper No. (FS IV – 89–12), Wissenschaftszentrum Berlin.

Jovanovic, Boyan, 1982, "Selection and Evolution of Industry," *Econometrica*, 50, 649–670.

Kirchhoff, Bruce A., 1990, "Creative Destruction Among Industrial Firms in the United States", this volume, pp. 101–116.

Pakes, A. and Ericson, R., 1987, "Empirical Implications of Alternative Models of Firm Dynamics," manuscript, Department of Economics, University of Wisconsin-Madison.

Reid, Gavin C. and Lowell R. Jacobsen, 1988, *The small Entrepreneurial Firm*, Aberdeen: Aberdeen University Press.

Williamson, Oliver E., 1975, *Markets and Hierarchies*, New York, NY: Macmillan Publishing Co.

Winter, Sidney G., 1984, "Schumpeterian Competition in Alternative Technological Regimes," *Journal of Economic Behavior and Organization*, 5, 287–320.

4. The Relationship Between Firm Growth and Labor Demand*

BRUNO CONTINI and RICCARDO REVELLI

I. Introduction

Several American studies have recently estimated models of employment growth from longitudinal data sets of business firms (Evans 1987, Leonard 1986, Hall 1987). By and large, these studies find that the growth rate of employment is inversely correlated with initial size (measured by employment) and with age – young firms tend to grow more rapidly than old ones. These studies have cast considerable doubt on Gibrat's Law, or the assumption of independence between firm size and the rate of growth. However, departures from Gibrat's Law are modest, especially among firms above minimum size. Recently a group of researchers has proceeded along similar lines of investigation using data from a panel of Italian manufacturing firms located in Northern Italy. The purpose of this paper is to compare our results with those obtained for the U.S. and to explore in more detail the soundness of this approach. Our results are similar to the above-mentioned American studies. We find that departures from Gibrat's Law are not large.

II. The basic model

Following Leonard (1986) the basic model – of the stock adjustment family – may be written as follows:

(1) $$s_{i,t} = \alpha X_i + \beta(s_{i,t-1} - \alpha X_i) + e_{i,t}$$

where $s_{i,t}$ is Log (size$_{i,t}$), X_i a vector of firm-specific and time invariant exogenous variables, and β is an adjustment parameter (with $|\beta| < 1$). The length of the interval Δt is determined by the frequency with which the exogenous serially uncorrelated $e_{i,t}$ is assumed to shock the individual firm: one year may be acceptable, anything longer probably not.

The two extreme cases are given by:

a) $\beta = 1$ whence $s_{i,t} = s_{i,t-1} + e_{i,t}$, a pure random walk model implying Gibrat's Law (with unbounded variance, which grows with t);
b) $\beta = 0$ whence $s_{i,t} = X_i\alpha + e_{i,t}$, a fixed effects model.[1]

Both cases exhibit persistence as $\text{var}(e_t) = \sigma_e^2$ becomes smaller. In (1) $s_i \sim N(X_i\alpha, \sigma_e^2/(1-\beta^2))$ if $e_{i,t} \sim N(0, \sigma_e^2)$. One may therefore obtain:

(2) $$E[s_{i,t} - s_{i,t-1} \mid s_{i,t-1}] = E(g_{i,t}) = (\beta - 1)[s_{i,t-1} - X_i\alpha]$$

Z.J. Acs and D.B. Audretsch (eds.), The Economics of Small Firms: A European Challenge. 53–60.

where $g_{i,t}$ is the growth rate of employment. In regressing $g_{i,t}$ on $s_{i,t-1}$ the coefficient is $(\beta - 1)$ and lies between 0 and -1.

Acceptance or rejection of Gibrat's Law is not independent of the length of the period over which the growth rate of employment is calculated. Those who have tested Gibrat's Law observe firms at intervals that may be quite different, depending on data availability. If the observation lag is extended at will, say τ periods, and α is constrained to zero, eq. (1) becomes

$$(3) \qquad s_{i,t} - s_{i,t-\tau} = g_{i,t} = (\beta^{\tau} - 1)\, s_{i,t-\tau} + \sum_{k=0}^{\tau-1} \beta^k e_{i,t-k}$$

The longer the observation lag, the closer to -1 the regression coefficient on lagged log-size.[2] For $\beta = 0.95$, which is very close to the pure random walk model, and an observation interval of 6 years ($\tau = 6$), the coefficient of lagged log-size is –.26. If the observation period were only 2 years ($\tau = 2$), the same coefficient would equal $-.10$.

Equation (3) allows to compare estimation from panels observable at different time-intervals, as is the case in what follows (2).

III. Empirical results

Earlier empirical developments on this issue are those of Hart and Prais (1956), Simon and Bonini (1977), Hymer and Pashigian (1961): all find that size nearly follows a random walk in logarithms (growth is independent of size).

Before turning to recent results, it is appropriate to summarize the nature of the underlying data.

D. Evans' (1987) panel data are drawn from the Small Business Data Base (SBDB): it comprises 42,339 U.S. firms of 100 4-digit industries observed between 1976 and 1980. The large majority of firms has less than 20 employees. Evans' basic regression is as follows:

$$(4) \qquad g_{i,\tau} = a + b\, s_{i,t-\tau} + c \text{ age}_{i,t} + \text{squared terms} + \text{cross products} + u_t$$

the addition of squared terms and interactions carries no particular economic interpretation (it obviously improves fit). In our data the introduction of squared terms leads to unacceptable multicollinearity, which may be present also in Evans' work, although it is not mentioned.

In Evans the problem of sample selection (due to all the firms that are present at the beginning of the observation period but exit the market before its end) is taken care by using Amemyia's simultaneous estimation procedure – the second equation being the probability of survival.

J. Leonard (1986) uses data on 68,690 establishments (with more than 1.6 million employees) located in Wisconsin. He calculates OLS on a regression basically equal to (1): most of the exogenous variables are industry and geographical dummies, others reflect macro variables. His estimates are not corrected for sample selection.

While the vast majority of both Evans' and Leonard's firms are quite small (ours too, as will be explained shortly), B. Hall (1987) works instead on a Compustat data file comprising 1350 large U.S. firms.

Needless to say, in all of those models heteroskedasticity is a problem: the variance of growth rates is much larger among small firms than large ones.[3] If one restricts attention to larger firms the problems becomes less serious (while the results don't look too different), although even B. Hall (1987) reports heteroskedasticity in her sample of large firms.

Table 4.1. The coefficients of log size and age – U.S. and Italian results.

	Coefficient of log		Partial derivatives with respect to log		Implied β estimate
	S_0	Age	S_0	Age	
D.E. Evans (max likelihood), U.S.A.					
1976–80, young firms[a]	–.072	–.034	–.032	–.142	.996
1976–80, old firms[b]	–.033	–.075	–.015	.000	.995
J.S. Leonard (OLS), Wisconsin					
1974–80	–.124				.981
B.H. Hall (OLS), Publicy traded firms, Compustat files					
1972–79	–.0114				.988
1976–83	–.0106				.989
R. Revelli, T. Battagliotti (OLS), Italy, Piedmont region, manufacturing industries					
1977–83, all firms	–.20	–.21			.969
1977–83, larger firms[c]	–.14	–.18[f]			.979
1977–80, all firms	–.09	–.20			.977
1977–80, larger firms[c]	–.04	–.10			.989
1983–86[d], all firms	–.07	–.06			.982
1983–86[d], larger firms[c]	–.11	–.07[f]			.971
1981–83[e], all firms	–.08	–.02[f]			.973
1981–83[e], larger firms[c]	–.07	–.11			.976

Notes:
[a] age less than 7 yrs.
[b] age over 7 yrs.
[c] over 10 employees.
[d] expansion period.
[e] recession period.
[f] not significantly different from zero.

The contrasts of Table 4.1 may be summarized as follows:

a) In Evans, Leonard and Revelli-Battagliotti the estimated β are greater than.9, often just below 1. This is quite in accordance with Gibrat's Law, although there seems to be slight differences between smaller and larger firms. It is among the latter where Gibrat's Law seems a better representation of reality. This is also in line with expectations.
b) According to Evans β is slightly lower among young firms: we too find similar evidence although Evans' result is cleaner, considering that in our sample 1977–83 all firms have at least 6 years of age, while in all three sub-samples 1977–80, 1980–83 and 1983–86 one half of the firms have ages between 3 and 6. This is a meaningful result as it suggests that young firms "have less memory" than the older ones.

c) Evans and Revelli-Battagliotti have age as an important explanatory variable, while Leonard and Hall do not. Again, the results suggest strong similarities: age matters (younger firms grow more rapidly on average); however when the same regression is restricted to "older" firms (more than 7 yrs. in the case of Evans, more than 6 in ours) age looses much of its significance.
d) In the Italian sample estimation yields rather weak results, in the sub-period 1980–83, characterized by deep recession. Evans states explicitly that his estimates do not apply to recession years: the results are not displayed, but the reason must be low significance, as in ours.

Failure of the specified growth model during recession is not unexpected, in view of the fact that Gibrat's Law was meant to explain a feature of long run, steady-state growth.

IV. Some extensions

In a forthcoming paper (Contini and Tenga 1989) we report that small firm expansions and contractions, measured over periods of 3–4 years, are frequently found in alternating sequence, with a high probability that a period of strong growth will be followed by a contraction, and that a contraction will either end in the firm leaving the market, or, if it survives, is likely to lead into sustained growth in the next period.

This suggest that the underlying stochastic process of small firm growth may be autoregressive of second order or possibly higher.[4] We have therefore tried an expanded version of the log growth equation, adding lagged growth rates in the right-hand size.

Estimation was performed (Table 4.2) on the period 1983–86 (with lagged growth rates 1977–80 and 1980–83) and on the period 1980–83 (with lagged growth 1977–80).

Table 4.2. Italy: OLS estimates of growth rate rotation, with lagged growth as regressor.

	Dependent variables						
	Growth rate 1983–86					Growth rate 1980–83	
	All firms			Larger firms [a]		All firms	
Intercept	.14	.50	.38	.29	.68	–.024[b]	.277
log S_{80}						–.083	–.045
log S_{83}	–.07	–.087	–.056	–.109	–.11		
log Age	–.06	–.183	–.134[b]	–.067[b]	–.20	.019[b]	–.110
growth 81/83		–.185	–.165		.25		
growth 77/80			–.088				–.119
Implied β	.982			.971		.973	
Sample size	1013	842	467	351	316	1170	467
F	15.60	32.49	8.1	6.87	3.35	6.50	6.71
R^2	.030	.104	.065	.038	.04	.022	0.40

Notes:
[a] Firms with more than 10 dependent workers.
[b] Not significantly different from zero.

Comparisons with the standard equations on the periods 1983–86 and 1980–83 are not immediate because the sample selection problem is much more serious in the extended observation period: in order to explain growth in 1983–86, with growth lagged all the way back to 1977–80, we had to use the balanced sample 1977–86 which is much smaller than any of the three sub-samples observed on shorter intervals, as it includes only survivor firms, aged at least 9 years.

While the coefficient of lagged size changes only slightly, that of age resents more of sample selection (in the direction opposite than expected): growth lagged one period is quite significant with expected negative sign, but also grow lagged two periods retains significance and negative sign. The surprise comes from a regression that includes only larger firms (i.e. with more than 10 employees): here lagged growth changes sign, suggesting the existence of persistence in growth behavior among other-than-tiniest business firms.

Patterns of time persistence have been found and discussed with regards to profit rates (Mueller 1977, Gerowski and Jacquemin 1988 and Contini 1988), but interpretation in this context is not at all obvious.

The different evidence between small and less small firms may, however, be more apparent than real: if some persistence is common to the population of firms (for which we still lack a good theoretical explanation), g and g_{-1} will exhibit some positive correlation (other things constant), yielding observation as in Fig. 4.1. The cigar-like scatter may actually be observable among the larger firms; among the small ones a very low (negative) g_{-1} and/or g are likely to cause the firm to exit the market.

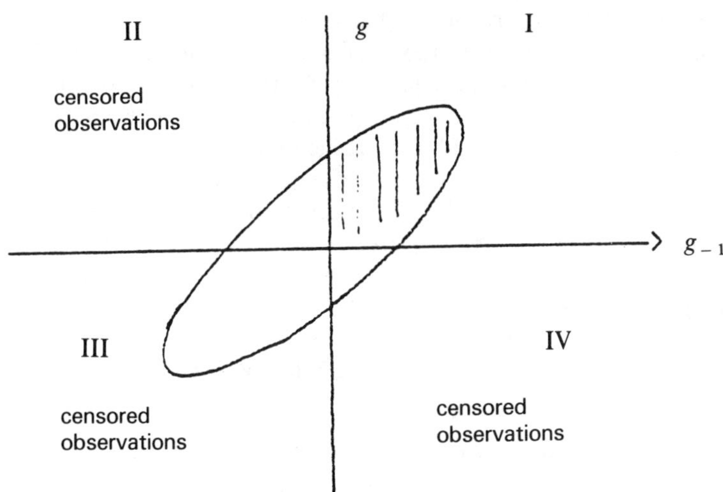

Fig. 4.1. The potential relation between growth and lagged growth.

Thus all firms other than those in quadrant I may be censored from the sample, and the visible observation are those of survivor firms only, located in or near quadrant I (shaded region). Here there is no reason to find g and g_{-1} positively correlated: in fact they may be negatively correlated, explaining the (negative) regression coefficient observed in the sample of the smallest firms.

V. Firm growth and demand for labor

We shall now try to relate these findings to the specification of a labor demand equation. When α is not constrained to be zero as in eq. (2), the stock adjustment equation (1) is one possible specification of the demand for labour, where X is a vector of exogenous variables. A more general formulation may be had extending (1) as follows:

$$s_{i,t} = \delta X_{i,t} + \beta s_{i,t-1} + e_{i,t} \tag{5}$$

and

$$s_{i,t} - s_{i,t-\tau} = g_{i,\tau} = (\beta^{\tau} - 1) s_{i,t-\tau} + \delta \sum_{k=0}^{\tau-1} \beta^k x_{i,t-k} + \sum_{k=0}^{\tau-1} \beta^k e_{i,t-k} \tag{6}$$

which indicates that if τ is the observation lag, the correct specification of the employment growth equation has in the right hand side all the lagged exogenous variables up to $\tau - 1$. The long run impact of the exogenous variables on g is $\delta(1 + \beta + \beta^2 + \ldots + \beta^{\tau-1})$, which tends to $\delta/(1 - \beta)$ as τ increases indefinitely.

In earlier work Contini, Brero and Revelli (1985) estimated (and interpreted as demand for labor) an equation which is fairly close to (6) on a sample of firms observed at four-year intervals (1973–77 and 1977–81), except that the X-variables enter only unlagged (i.e. instead of having x_{81}, x_{80}, x_{79}, x_{78} in the right hand-side of log-growth 1977–81, we retain only x_{81}). Other scholars have used similar specifications. If (6) is the correct specification of labour demand, then estimating Gibrat's Law – coefficient β from (3) may be seriously misleading.

Let us consider same implications of our estimation procedure. The omission of lagged $x_{i,t}$ would not be a major problem if β were close to zero (i.e. if Gibrat's Law did not hold), as the influence of lagged $x_{i,t}$ would rapidly decline and/or if the omitted variables were uncorrelated with the retained regressors.

But experience suggests that this is not the case on either count: firstly β is often close to 1; moreover lagged values of $x_{i,t}$ are likely to be highly correlated with one another (although hopefully not with $s_{i,t-\tau}$). Hence, while the estimate of $(\beta^{\tau} - 1)$ may not suffer too much from the omission, the δ-coefficients will be upward biased in the direction of $\delta(1 + \beta + \beta^2 + \ldots + \beta^{\tau-1})$.

It is therefore of interest to compare our results (Table 4.3) with the estimates of $(\beta^{\tau} - 1)$ and those implied of β, obtained in industry specific equations of labor demand, specified as follows:

$g_{i,4} = f$ (end-of-period firm sales, growth rate of firm output, labor costs, investments, proxies of vertical integration, rate of productivity change, geographical dummies).

While the estimated coefficients of $(\beta^{\tau} - 1)$ are substantially lower than those displayed in Table 4.1 (in that sample the seven industries are pooled together) the implied β roots are only marginally smaller.

In this sample, small (S) businesses are defined as those with less than 100 employees; very few have less than 20. Large (L) firms have employment exceeding 100 units. Therefore the appropriate comparison with Table 4.1 is the sample of firms with at least 10 employees.

Table 4.3. The coefficients of initial size in the estimates of a labor demand equations.

		1973–1977		1977–1981	
		Coefficient of $s_{i,73}$ ($\beta^4 - 1$)	Implied β	Coefficient of $s_{i,77}$ ($\beta^4 - 1$)	Implied β
Industry					
Food (41)	*S*	–.41	.87	–.20	.89
	L	–.34	.90	–.04 [a]	.99 [a]
Beverages (42)	*S*	–.34	.90	–.24	.93
	L	–.12	.97	–.15	.96
Textiles (43)	*S*	–.42	.87	–.27	.92
	L	–.21	.94	–.16	.96
Hide & leather (44)	*S*	–.33	.90	–.31	.91
	L	–.14	.96	–.16 [a]	.96 [a]
Garments (45)	*S*	–.57	.81	–.37	.89
	L	–.25	.93	–.12	.97
Wood & furniture (46)	*S*	–.35	.90	–.11	.97
	L	–.25	.93	–.01 [a]	.99 [a]
Rubber & plastic materials mfg. (48)	*S*	–.44	.86	–.26	.93
	L	–.06 [a]	.98 [a]	–.07 [a]	.98 [a]

Notes:
[a] Not significantly different from zero.
S = less than 100 employees.
L = over 100 employees.

The implied β-coefficient of S-firms is always smaller (often marginally smaller) than that of *L*-firms, as suggested by the theory. On the other hand we find Gibrat's Law to nearly hold in all industries, in spite of the more general formulation in terms of labour demand.

VI. Conclusion

We test the validity of Gibrat's Law on a sample of Italian manufacturing firms. Once the length of the period over which growth rates are calculated is taken into account, our results and all those obtained on U.S. data look very similar. Departure from Gibrat's Law are modest, and age matters as in Evans (1987).

We find evidence that the stochastic process underlying the growth of small firms may be autoregressive of order higher than one. The basic model utilized in all the studies aimed at testing firms's growth characteristics may be viewed as a demand for labor equation with some omitted regressors. When estimation is performed in that framework Gibrat's Law still holds or nearly holds, especially among firms with more than 100 employees.

Notes

* The research was partially funded by a grant of the Ministero della Pubblica Istruzione (fondi 40%, 1986–87) to the Department of Economics, University of Torino. We are grateful to D. Evans for his comments and to T. Battagliotti for her research assistance.

1. Even if β is equal to zero, the regression of $s_{i,t-1}$ on $s_{i,t}$ may yield estimates of β between 0 and 1. If

$$(*) \qquad s_{i,t} = \alpha_i + v_{i,t}$$

where $\alpha_i \sim N(\bar{\alpha}, \sigma_\alpha^2)$, $v_{i,t} \sim N(0, \sigma_v^2)$ uncorrelated with α_i then, from the conditional expectation of log growth given lagged size, one obtains the regression coefficient on lagged size as

$$b = \sigma_\alpha^2/(\sigma_\alpha^2 + \sigma_v^2) - 1$$

The estimated b tends to 0 as σ_α^2 gets large compared to σ_v^2. Thus, for all practical purposes, (*) is a fixed effects model which admits Gibrat's Law if σ_α^2 is sufficiently large. The random variables α_i can be viewed as unobservable characteristics of the firm. For example, in Lucas's (1978) approach the size of the firm depends on the distribution of entrepreneurial abilities which is time-invariant. In this interpretation the α_i's are a fixed effect. B. Hall (1987), too, discusses this special case.

2. As in all AR-models the residuals take the form of polynomials in β which may complicate estimation. We shall not deal here with this problem.
3. Applying White's test, Revelli and Battagliotti (1988) find heteroskedasticity or misspecification in several regression. Usual rescaling techniques do not improve substantially regression results.
4. The autocorrelogram of growth rates over four year-periods confirms this possibility.

References

Contini, B., "Organization, Markets and Persistence of Profits in Italian Industry", *Journal of Economic Behaviour and Organization*, forthcoming.

Contini, B., Brero, A. and Revelli, R., 1985, *The Determinants of Productivity and Labour Demand In Italian Manufacturing*, European Economic Commission, D.G. V, Bruxelles.

Contini, B. and Tenga, S., 1989, "Expansion and Contraction Patterns among Italian Firms", *mimeo*, R&P, Torino.

Evans, D. S., 1987, "The relationship Between Firm Growth, Size, and Age: Estimates for 100 Manufacturing Industries", *Journal of Industrial Economics*, 35, 567–581.

Evans, D. S., 1987, "Tests of Alternative Theories of Firm Growth", *Journal of Political Economy*, 95, 657–674.

Geroski, P. A. and Jacqemin, A., 1988, "The Persistence of Profits: A European Comparison", *Economic Journal*, 98, 375–389.

Hall, B. H., 1987, "The relationship Between Firm Size and Firm Growth in the U.S. Manufacturing Sector", *Journal of Industrial Economics*, 35, 583–605.

Hart, P. E. and Prais S. J., 1956, "The Analysis of Business Concentration: A Statistical Approach", *Journal of the Royal Statistical Society*, 119, Part 2, 150–191.

Hymer, S. and Pashigian, P., 1962, "Firm Size and Rate of Growth", *Journal of Political Economy*, 52 (December), 556–569.

Ijiri Y. and Simon, H.A., 1972, *Skew Distributions and the Size of Business Firms*, North Holland.

Leonard, J.S., 1986, "On the Size Distribution of Employment and Establishments", NBER, Working Paper No. 1951.

Lucas, Robert E., Jr., 1978, "On the Size Distribution of Business Firms," *The Bell Journal of Economics*, 9 (Autumn), 508–523.

Mueller, D. C., 1986, *Profits in the Long Run*, Cambridge University Press.

Revelli, R. and Battagliotti, T., 1988, "Modelli di crescita delle imprese: il caso Italiano", *mimeo*, R&P, Torino.

Comment on "The Relationship between Firm Growth and Labor Demand" by Bruno Contini and Riccardo Revelli

David S. Evans

Professors Contini and Revelli use data on Italian manufacturing companies to investigate the relationships among firm growth, size, and age. In addition to confirming the results obtained by a number of authors for a variety of other countries, they have contributed several interesting insights to this literature. Before discussing their findings it may be helpful to say a few words about why economists should be interested in firm growth.

(1) The earlier studies on firm growth by Hart and Prais and Simon and Bonini were interested in firm growth because of the effect it has on the evolution of the size distribution of firms and ultimately on the concentration of industries. Gibrat's Law implies increasing concentration over time, at least if we ignore the entry of new firms and the development of substitute products.

(2) Another reason to be interested in firm growth is that the patterns of firm growth impose restrictions on theoretical models of industry dynamics. Simon and his colleagues contributed several studies beginning in the mid 1950s that showed that most of the empirical regularities concerning firm growth and the size distribution of firms could be explained by a very simple theory in which growth past some minimum efficient size is determined largely by luck. This theory had little economic content: a virtue to some, a vice to others. Beginning in the late 1970s, a number of economists started examining the economic underpinnings of the size distribution of firms and the dynamics of industries. This theoretical work together with the development of several panel data sets on firms and establishments in the U.S. led to a resurgence in empirical studies of firm growth (most of which are cited in Contini and Revelli).

(3) The claim by David Birch that small businesses generate a disproportionate share of new jobs has also stimulated a considerable amount of research worldwide on the determinants of firm growth. I am less optimistic that these kinds of studies, as practised, have much to say about the role of small firms in job generation. Authors who look at the determinants of employment growth invariably have little or no data on hours of work, pay, job stability, or other variables that would help us understand the role of smaller firms in the labor market. Nor are they tied to the theories that would help us understand why labor market equilibration (the creation of jobs for new workers) necessarily depends on the size distribution of firms.

Professors Contini and Revelli have made a very useful contribution to this literature by extending the results of several recent American studies (including Hall, Dunne, Roberts, Samuelson, and my work) to Italy. The evidence accumulated by all these studies is quite consistent and striking: firm growth decreases at a diminishing rate with firm age and size; for larger firms Gibrat's Law is very close to the mark but not for smaller firms. These authors also find some interesting patterns of firm growth persistence and they present some evidence that this finding is robust to the inclusion

Z.J. Acs and D.B. Audretsch (eds.), The Economics of Small Firms: A European Challenge. 61–62.

of other explanatory variables in the growth relationship. Whether one wants to emphasize these results as confirming Gibrat's Law or as confirming important departures from this Law depends, of course, on why we are interested in the relationship in the first place. If we are trying to say something about changes in industry concentration in the short run, it is certainly true that the departures are small enough to ignore. If we are trying to understand industry dynamics, then it would probably be unsafe to ignore these departures.

5. Small Business in German Manufacturing*

JOACHIM SCHWALBACH

I. Introduction

In recent years, one observes a renaissance of small business research efforts. The stimuli came from different directions. One strand of more policy oriented research concentrated on the impact of small businesses on the creation of new employment opportunities.[1] Another host of studies paid attention to the relationship of innovation productivity of small versus large business.[2] And industrial economics research examined the role of small businesses as actual and potential challengers of larger competitors in a given market.[3] Whatever motive guided this research, it was emphasized that the cumulated knowledge about large business behavior is by far greater than about their small business counterparts.

Among the existing studies on the economics of small business, there is a considerable variance of research efforts across countries. In the Federal Republic of Germany (F.R.G.), there exists a long tradition of public policies which are directed toward support of small and medium-sized business. Part of this tradition is the production of policy oriented research which is mainly performed by the government supported Institute for Small and Medium-Sized Business Research (Institut für Mittelstandsforschung) in Bonn. Like in other countries, in recent years, a lot of attention has been paid to employment effects and to start-up problems by small business. Controversial results can be found to the role of small business in the creation of new job opportunities.[4] And start-ups mainly face, according to a study by Albach (1984), problems like high taxes, high labor cost, and high competitive pressure.[5]

This paper departs from the just mentioned German studies in the sense that it provides some fundamental empirical evidence about the determinants of the size distribution and the importance of small business in the FRG. The adopted explanatory model distinguishes short-run from long-run effects and estimates the rate of adjustment when deviations from the long-run equilibrium level are observed. The chapter is organized as follows: Section II provides some insights into the size distribution of businesses in the manufacturing sector and shows the importance of small businesses over time. Section III presents the empirical model and section IV reports the empirical results. A summary and conclusions are found in the final section.

II. Size Distribution and the Importance of Small Business

The general impression about the development of the number of businesses and its distribution across industry groups is exhibited in Fig. 5.1. In 1980, among the 1,688,690 firms paying value added taxes, 17.2 percent were in manufacturing, 11.1 percent in

Z.J. Acs and D.B. Audretsch (eds.), The Economics of Small Firms: A European Challenge. 63–73.

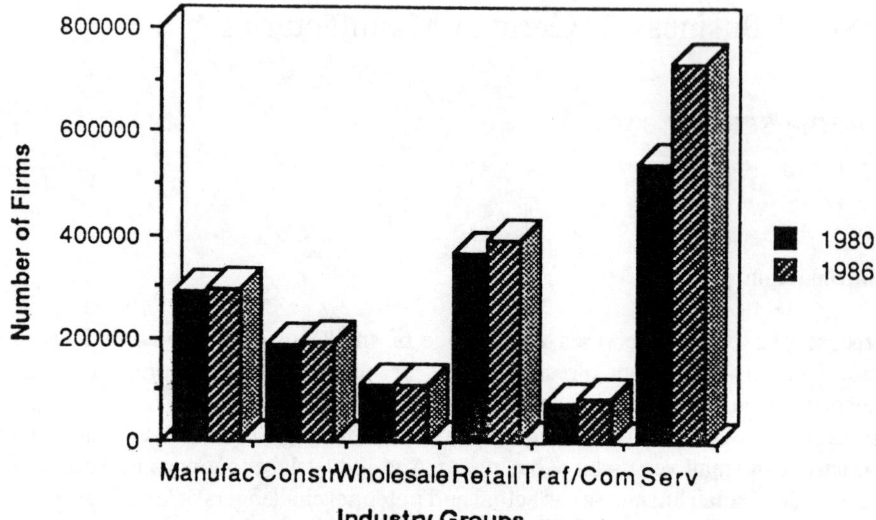

Fig. 5.1. Firms in industry groups.

construction, 6.6 percent in wholesaling, 21.7 percent in retailing, 4.7 percent in traffic/communication, 32.1 in services, and the remaining firms are in other sectors. Figure 1 shows that within the time period 1980-86 the number of firms increased slightly in all sectors, with the exception of services where a significant increase can be observed which corresponds to a share increase to a level of 38.0 percent. A more detailed analysis of the size distribution and the importance of small businesses in each sector can only be performed for manufacturing for which relatively rich census data sets are available. Therefore, the following analysis concentrates on the manufacturing sector only.

Tables 5.1 and 5.2 summarize the extent of the size distribution and the importance of small businesses (firms and plants) in German manufacturing industries in 1986. The tables reveal that the size distributions are highly skewed. For example, 75.7 percent of all plants have less than 50 employees and can be considered small, but only 2.6 percent are large plants with at least 500 employees. The same applies to firms, where 45.7 percent are small (20–49 employees) and only 5.7 percent are large firms (over 499 employees). While the distribution of the share of total number of businesses are skewed to the right, the opposite is observed if the shares of sales and employment are taken into consideration. Large businesses accounted for more than 50 percent of all sales and employment.

Table 5.2 in addition, also shows that within the small size group all plants contributed significantly to the high share of the total number, although plants with either one employee or between 5 to 19 employees had a slightly lower share. If the shares of employment and sales are considered, Table 5.2 indicates, that beside large plants, medium-sized plants with 100 to 199 employees accounted for the third highest share. At the firm level, the relative importance of a size class diminishes with increasing firm size as far as the share of total number of firms is concerned but increases when the shares of employment and sales are considered. Table 5.2, however, shows one excep-

Table 5.1. Firm size distribution in German manufacturing industries, 1986.

	Employment size classes						
	Small firms	Medium-sized firms			Large firms		Total
	20–49	50–99	100–199	200–499	500–999	1000 and more	
Number of firms	15312	8120	4888	3287	1051	860	33499
Share of total number of firms (in %)	45.7	24.2	14.6	9.8	3.1	2.6	100.0
(cumulative share)	(45.7)	(69.9)	(84.5)	(94.3)	(97.4)	(100.0)	
Share of total employment (in %)	7.2	8.2	9.8	14.5	10.4	49.9	100.0
(cumulative share)	(7.2)	(15.4)	(25.2)	(39.7)	(50.1)	(100.0)	
Share of total sales (in %)	5.3	6.4	8.6	13.6	10.0	56.1	100.0
(cumulative share)	(5.3)	(11.7)	(20.3)	(33.9)	(43.9)	(100.0)	

Source: Statistisches Bundesamt, Fachserie 4, Reihe 4.2.1 and own calculation.

tion. In the size class of 500–999 employees the share is lower relative to neighboring size classes. Tables 5.1 and 5.2, therefore, show that the observed plant size distribution does not completely reflect a well behaving function of size distribution.

Table 5.3 reveals the importance of small, medium-sized, and large businesses over the period 1977 to 1986. Considering first the share of total number of plants, it is apparent that the share of small plants increased slightly over time, while the shares of medium-sized and large plants both decreased. Interestingly, the increasing number of small plants did not contribute to a growth of employment and sales shares. Instead, large plants increased their share of employment although fewer large plants were in operation. In addition, Table 3 indicates that the sales of large plants show a positive trend over time. Medium-sized plants, on the other hand, lost shares not only in total number but also in employment and sales.

Only a shorter time period is available for the size distribution of firms. Between 1981 and 1986, the shares of small firms decreased in contrast to medium-sized and large firms. Medium-sized firms increased their sales share as well as their share of the total number, but the employment share stagnated. Large firms, on the other hand, improved their employment share and share in total number, but lost shares of sales. In sum, Table 5.3 reveals that the relative importance of small business diminished over time in the German manufacturing sector, but the overall importance with respect to the total number of businesses is still significant.

III. The Empirical Model

Stochastic growth models and simulation experiments reveal that in the long-run businesses are unequal in size even though they began with the same size.[6] It was argued that stochastic processes generate a size distribution which "... have at their core

Table 5.2. Plant size distribution in German manufacturing industries, 1986.

	Employment size classes												
	Small plants					Medium-sized plants					Large plants		Total
	1	2–4	5–9	10–19	20–49	50–99	100–199	200–299	300–399	400–499	500–599	1000 and more	
Number of plants	8961	15645	12698	13361	16634	9358	5825	2259	1185	701	1326	965	88918
Share of total number of plants (in %)	10.1	17.6	14.3	15.0	18.7	10.5	6.6	2.5	1.3	0.8	1.5	1.1	100.0
(cumulative share)	(10.1)	(27.7)	(42.0)	(57.0)	(75.7)	(86.2)	(92.8)	(95.3)	(96.6)	(97.4)	(98.9)	(100.0)	
Share of total employment (in %)	0.1	0.6	1.2	2.6	7.6	9.1	11.3	7.6	5.6	4.3	12.8	37.2	100.0
(cumulative share)	(0.1)	(0.7)	(1.9)	(4.5)	(12.1)	(21.2)	(32.5)	(40.1)	(45.7)	(50.0)	(62.8)	(100.0)	
Share of total sales (in %)	0.06	0.5	1.0	2.2	6.0	7.7	10.2	7.4	5.4	4.7	14.2	40.6	100.0
(cumulative share)	(0.06)	(0.5)	(1.6)	(3.8)	(9.8)	(17.5)	(27.7)	(35.1)	(40.5)	(45.2)	(59.4)	(100.0)	

Source: Statistisches Bundesamt, Fachserie 4, Reihe 4.1.2, and own calculation.

Table 5.3. Importance of small, medium-sized and large businesses in German manufacturing industries, 1977–1986.[a]

Year		Small		Medium-sized		Large	
		Firms (20–49)	Plants (1–49)	Firms	Plants	Firms	Plants
				(50–499)		(more than 499)	
1977	Number	n.a.	74.4	n.a.	22.9	n.a.	2.7
	Employment	n.a.	12.4	n.a.	38.3	n.a.	49.3
	Sales	n.a.	10.6	n.a.	35.7	n.a.	53.7
1981	Number	47.1	75.2	47.3	22.2	5.6	2.6
	Employment	7.5	12.4	32.5	38.1	60.0	49.5
	Sales	5.7	10.0	27.4	34.0	66.9	56.0
1986	Number	45.7	75.7	48.6	21.7	5.7	2.6
	Employment	7.2	12.1	32.5	37.9	60.3	50.0
	Sales	5.3	9.8	28.6	35.4	66.1	54.8

[a] All figures represent the percentage of the total numbers of employees accounted for by that particular size class.

something like Gibrat's law of proportionate effect – the postulate that expected rate of growth is independent of present size", (Ijiri and Simon 1977, p. 154). What has been observed, therefore, was a frequency distribution which is highly skewed and often represented by log normal, Pareto, or Yule distribution. Although entry by new business and exit of existing ones may affect the size distribution in the short-run, it should not, according to the stochastic process theory, vary the adjustment process toward the long-run equilibrium level.

There is support that the observed size distribution of an industry is not purely a result of mere chance or luck. Market structure and business behavior have been seen as additional important determinants of the size distribution.[7] The existing size distribution of business can therefore be explained by the following model:

$$(1) \qquad S_{it} = \alpha_{0t} + \alpha_{jt}X_{jit} + \mu_{it}$$

where S_{it} represents a measure of size distribution or a section of the distribution in industry i at period t, X_{jit} is a vector of k ($j = 1, \ldots, k$) observable industry-specific variables, and μ_{it} reflects all stochastic variables. In addition, α_0 and α_j are regression coefficients.

If industries i are in long-run equilibrium, we would expect constant and stable regression coefficients, i.e. $\alpha_{jt} = \alpha_{jt+1}$. But if the α_j's deviate over time, we would expect an adjustment process toward the long-run equilibrium level of size distribution in the following way:

$$(2) \qquad S_{it} - S_{it-1} = \lambda(S_i^* - S_{it-1})$$

where S_i^* is the long-run level of size distribution expected by established and new businesses in industry i. The coefficient, λ, represents the rate of adjustment to deviations of the initial, short-run level of size distribution from its long-run equilibrium level. We expect that λ must be greater than zero and less than one. The smaller λ is, the higher will be the speed of adjustment toward the long-run level. The industry is in long-run equilibrium if λ takes on values of zero or one.

S_i^* cannot be observed, but it can be replaced by a proxy which represents industry-specific determinants of long-run size distribution. Substituting these determinants into our dynamic model, we derive the following empirically testable model:

$$(3) \qquad \Delta S_{i,\,t,\,t-1} = \gamma_0 - \gamma_1 S_{it-1} + \gamma_j X_{ji}^* + \varepsilon_{it}$$

where the change in the size distribution is determined by the previous size distribution level and a vector of various industry-specific variables. The intercept γ_0 is equal to α_0 times λ. The estimates of γ_1 reflect the speed of adjustment ($\gamma_1 = \lambda$), and all γ_j's represent values which are equal to λ times α_j, which are the long-run effects of the selected variables. If industry i is in long-run equilibrium, S_{it} is equal to S_{it-1} and, consequently, all γ's are equal to zero. In case short-run equilibrium deviates only slightly from long-run equilibrium, we expect values for all γ's to be close to zero.

IV. Empirical Results

The coefficients of the empirical models (1) and (3) have been estimated for up to 106 four-digit manufacturing industries for the years 1979 and 1985. As dependent variables we alternatively use the entropy measure of size distribution and the share of total employment accounted for by small plants with less than 50 employees. The entropy measure of the size distribution is defined as the sum of the weighted share of each business or group of businesses in industry *i*, where the weights are the logarithm of the inverse of the share. The entropy of the distribution has the useful properties that it is sensitive to very small businesses and, most important, it can be decomposed into within-group and between-group entropies.[8] The decomposition property is relevant for this study, since the available data on the size distribution are presented only for size groups but not for individual businesses. As a consequence, the calculated entropy represents the between-group measure of size distribution. In general, the value of entropy varies between zero and the logarithm of the number of equally sized business. The more unequal the business sizes are, the lower will be the entropy value and, in the one extreme, it takes on a value of zero if one business has a share of one.

The explanatory industry-specific variables used for X_{ji} for models (1) and (3) were selected on theoretical and empirical grounds. Included are measures of economies of scale, product differentiation intensity, R&D intensity, investment intensity, extent of multi-plant operation, degree of specialization, demand growth, exports, and market size. Observations for these variables were available for the years 1979 and 1985 at the four-digit industry level. Detailed information on the measurement of these variables can be found in the appendix.

The estimates of the static and dynamic model are summarized in Table 5.4. Columns (1), (2), (4), and (5) show the results of the static model for each measure of S_{it} for the years 1979 and 1985. Columns (3) and (6) report the results of the dynamic model. By concentrating first on the static model, the results suggest that economies of scale are a very powerful determinant of the presence of small plants and the plant size distribution, independent of time. Thus, the larger the extent of scale economies, the stronger

Table 5.4. Determinants of the size distribution and presence of small plants.

Determinants	Presence of small plants			Size distribution		
	S_i 1979 (1)	S_i 1985 (2)	ΔS_i 1985–79 (3)	S_i 1979 (4)	S_i 1985 (5)	ΔS_i 1985–79 (6)
Economies of scale	– 3.753**	– 2.616**	– 0.043	– 2.126*	– 2.201**	– 0.827*
	(– 5.10)	(– 4.99)	(– 0.81)	(– 1.75)	(– 2.47)	(– 1.77)
Product differentiation	– 0.050*	– 0.060*	– 0.006	0.045	0.074	0.007
	(1.79)	(– 2.20)	(– 1.14)	(0.99)	(1.62)	(0.28)
R & D intensity	– 0.058*	– 0.072*	– 0.001	0.008	0.004	– 0.050*
	(– 1.77)	(2.06)	(– 0.015)	(0.15)	(0.05)	(– 2.15)
Investment intensity	0.009**	0.004**	– 0.001	– 0.017**	– 0.014**	– 0.006*
	(3.10)	(2.35)	(– 1.30)	(– 3.49)	(– 3.73)	(– 2.03)
Multi-plant operation	0.003	0.003	0.002	– 0.093**	– 0.093**	– 0.004
	(0.24)	(0.20)	(0.56)	(– 2.65)	(– 2.62)	(– 0.32)
Demand growth	0.003	0.009	0.008*	0.050	0.014	0.004
	(0.17)	(0.49)	(1.75)	(1.02)	(0.42)	(0.30)
Exports	– 0.478**	– 0.572**	0.005	– 0.060**	– 0.299	0.055
	(– 3.83)	(– 5.13)	(0.13)	(– 3.57)	(– 1.56)	(0.62)
Market size	– 0.083**	– 0.082**	– 0.004	– 0.028	– 0.077**	0.021*
	(– 6.23)	(6.16)	(– 1.20)	(– 0.86)	(– 3.42)	(1.96)
Specialization	0.034	0.050	– 0.014**	– 0.083**	– 0.006	0.034*
	(0.92)	(0.64)	(– 2.87)	(– 2.59)	(– 1.04)	(1.78)
Previous level of S_i	–	–	– 0.047	–	–	– 0.049
			(– 1.59)			(– 1.65)
Constant	1.502	1.536	0.127	0.948	0.741	– 0.166
	(6.79)	(6.69)	(1.64)	(2.60)	(1.90)	(– 0.77)
R^2	0.553	0.545	0.316	0.416	0.363	0.364
F	16.661	18.179	13.731	15.464	16.602	10.912
N	104	106	104	98	106	104

Notes: t-values are given in parentheses;
* significant at the 0.05 level;
** significant at the 0.01 level.

is the incentive to operate plants which are close to the cost efficient size. If that size is large relative to the size of the market, it will be difficult for small plants to survive in the long-run. The result in Table 4, however, is biased upwards since scale economies are proxied by the average size of the plant located at the 50 percent point of the cumulative size distribution.

Table 5.4, furthermore, shows that advertizing and R&D intensive industries account for a lower share of small business but do not favor only large business. The positive, although statistically not significant, coefficients in columns (4) and (5) suggest that medium-sized business enjoy a relatively high and increasing share in those industries. By contrast, Table 5.4 reveals that a high intensity in investments in the production process of goods does not deter small business from entry and survival in that industry. Investment intensive industries, instead, reduce the chance for medium-sized business to remain viable and, thus, exhibit a higher share of small and large businesses.

Industries with a high extent of multi-plant operation seem to be, according to the results in Table 5.4, highly concentrated. Firms in those industries, therefore, operate mainly with large plants but, as the results suggest, also with some small plants. It is worth mentioning that multi-plant operation strategies greatly depend on other industry-specific phenomena. One expects that the extent of multi-plant operation might be influenced by the extent of scale economies in relation to the size of the market and by the segmentation of the market. We tested the expected simultaneity bias but could not find any statistical support.

Table 5.4, furthermore, shows the impact of demand growth on the presence of small business and the size distribution. The coefficients are not statistically significant, but nonetheless indicate that demand growth affects small plants' presence positively and contributes to a deconcentration of the plant size structure of the industry. Larger markets, on the other hand, favor large plants and seem to provide less room for small plants. The results in Table 5.4 are somewhat surprizing, since the conventional belief suggests that larger markets attract new businesses which are predominantly small in relation to the size of incumbents. However, if scale economies are a significant industry-specific factor, one would expect fewer small businesses. This result suggests that large markets are conducive to substantial scale economies and, therefore, provide no profitable market share for small plants.

According to Table 5.4, small business viability is negatively affected by international trade flows. Industries with a high exports intensity are dominated by larger plants, which might be due to the fact that a minimum size is required to exhaust scale economies, and seems to preclude the viability of small businesses in the presence of international competition. Small businesses, instead, are highly specialized in the production and distribution of goods. The results in Table 5.4 show that small plants are predominantly present in those industries in which specialized skills can be developed to exploit cost savings from specialization.

By comparing the coefficients for each explanatory variable for 1979 and 1985, the results in Table 5.4 reveal that the coefficients deviate only slightly for most determinants. For those variables we expect a coefficient close to zero in the dynamic model since the short-run effect deviates only slightly from the long-run effects. The results in columns (3) and (6) indicate that, indeed, most of these coefficients are close to zero, although not all of them are statistically significant. If the short-run and the long-run deviate by a small margin, we expect a rather rapid adjustment process toward the long-run. Table 5.4 shows that the adjustment parameter exhibits a very small value, which indicates that the short-run effects are quite short lived.

V. Conclusions

The study has provided empirical evidence identifying the determinants of the plant size distribution and the importance of small plants in German manufacturing industries. The adopted empirical model distinguishes short-run from long-run effect and estimates the rate of adjustment when a departure from long-run equilibrium occurs. The results show a significant impact of industry-specific factors on the presence of small plants and the size distribution of plants. Foremost, technological factors, like scale economies, limit the prosperity of small business. In addition, industries with a high intensity of investments in advertizing and R&D, and large domestic and foreign output volumes are dominated by large business. The dynamic analysis revealed that departures from long-run equilibrium are only of a very short duration. The last observation is interesting since it shows that any stochastic shocks due to entry, exit, or other events will be absorbed instantaneously.

Appendix

Definition and Measurement of Variables

Economies of scale:	Proxied by the average size of the plant located at the 50 percent point of the cumulative size distribution. For details about alternative measures of scale economies, see Scherer (1980).
Product differentiation:	(0,1)-dummy variable for the extent of advertizing intensity. The value of 1 is assigned to industries with above average advertizing expenditures.
R&D intensity:	(0,1)-dummy variable for the extent of R&D expenditures. The value of 1 is assigned to industries with above average R&D expenditures.
Investment intensity:	Ratio of outlays for investments in machinery and other equipments to number of employees.
Multi-Plant operation:	Average number of plants operated by multi-plant firms.
Demand growth:	Ratio of domestic sales in 1977/1979 and 1979/1985, respectively.
Exports:	Ratio of foreign sales to total sales.
Market size:	Logarithm of domestic sales.
Specialization:	Ratio of sales in the base four-digit industry to total sales.

Data sources

Most data are publicly available from the German Census Bureau (Statistisches Bundesamt) in Wiesbaden and are gathered from the publications of Fachserie 4 for the years 1977 to 1985. R&D data were provided by the Stifterverband für die deutsche Wissenschaft. Advertizing data were gathered from various published sources.

Notes

* I would like to express my gratitude to Stefan Csutor and Sabine Hetebrüg for their assistance in collecting the data. I am also grateful to Zoltan J. Acs, David B. Audretsch, Riccardo Revelli, and the participants of the Small Business Economics Conference, November 17–18, 1988 in Berlin for their very valuable comments.

1. See Storey and Johnson (1987).
2. See Acs and Audretsch (1988).
3. See Baumol, Panzar, and Willig (1982) and Geroski and Schwalbach (1985).
4. For a survey see Fritsch and Hull (1987).
5. See also Albach and Hunsdiek (1985).
6. See Ijiri and Simon (1977) and Scherer (1980).
7. See Jovanovic (1982) and Evans (1987).
8. See Theil (1967).

References

Acs, Zoltan J. and Audretsch, David B., 1988, "Innovation in Large and Small Firms: An Empirical Analysis", *American Economic Review*, 78(4), 678–690.

Albach, Horst, 1984, "Betriebswirtschaftsliche Probleme der Unternehmensgründung", ifm-Materialien No. 14, Bonn: Institut für Mittelstandsforschung.

Albach, Horst and Hunsdiek, Detlef, 1985, "The Financing of Start-up and Growth of New Technology Based Firms in the Federal Republic of Germany", ifm-Materialien No. 27, Bonn: Institut für Mittelstandsforschung.

Baumol, William J., Panzar, John C., and Willig, Robert D., 1982, *Contestable Markets and the Theory of Industry Structure*, New York: Harcourt Brace Jovanovich.

Evans, David S., 1987, "Test of Alternative Theories of Firm Growth", *Journal of Political Economy*, 95(4), 657–674.

Fritsch, Michael and Hull, Chris J., (eds.), 1987, *Arbeitsplatzdynamik und Regionalentwicklung*. Beiträge zur beschäftigungspolitischen Bedeutung von Klein- und Großunternehmen, Berlin.

Geroski, Paul A. and Schwalbach, Joachim, 1985, "Entrepreneurship and Small Firms", WZB Discussion Paper Series, IIM/IP 85–28.

Ijiri, Yuji and Simon, Herbert A., 1977, *Skew Distributions and the Sizes of Business Firms*, Amsterdam: North-Holland.

Javanovic, Boyan, 1982, "Selection and the Evolution of Industry", *Econometrica*, 50(3), 649–670.

Scherer, Frederic M., 1980, *Industrial Market Structure and Economic Performance*, 2nd Edition, Chicago: Rand McNally.

Storey, David J. and Johnson, S., 1987, *Job Generation and Labour Market Change*, London.

Theil, Henri, 1967, *Economics and Information Theory*, Amsterdam: North-Holland.

Comment on "Small Business in German Manufacturing" by Joachim Schwalbach

Riccardo Revelli

Evidence presented in the first part of the chapter shows no change in the size distribution of German manufacturing firms over the period 1977-86. There is in fact international evidence that a reduction in *firms' size* has taken place (and may still be under way). In Italy, for example, between 1978 and 1984 the employment share of firms with less than 20 employees grew from 16.3% to 21%, while that of firms below 100 employees moved from 33.8% to 38.3%. Although centered on self-employment, a paper by Blau (1987) provides international comparisons and some theoretical remarks.

Let me single out three factors that might have contributed to the reduction in average firm size:

- quest for flexibility, as a response to more uncertain markets, which might have led firms to buy products or services, once internally supplied;
- reduced role of economies of scale, due to nature of technogical change (flexible automation);
- market segmentation in consumer goods, related to diversified tastes in affluent societies.

I agree with the author's view that stochastic components ought to be brought into industry supply models to explain distribution of firms by relevant economic characteristics (e.g, size, profits, sales, etc.). The literature on this topic is vast, ranging from early attempts to formulate and test Gibrat's law to more recent and sophisticated models of industry supply embedding entry and exit (Ijiri and Simon 1977, Newman and Wolfe 1960, Lippman and Rumelt 1982, Jovanovic 1982, Hopenhayn 1986).

Roughly speaking, we start with some stochastic process P, which can be made a function of observable or controllable industry characteristics (cost structure, output or factor market specificities, etc.). To each process P there can be associated some long run (or steady state) distribution of firms, provided that the process is ergodic; per se, the presence or absence of entry and exit has no consequences on the nature of the process.

One approach is to estimate the parameters of the stochastic process from flow data, that is from employment changes over time at the firm level and from entry and exit counts. The next step is to see how well the estimated parameters fit observed size distributions. For instance, Gibrat's law is defined by three parameters that can be estimated from firms' flow data; they also define the steady state distribution of firms by size. The outlined approach has some advantage in that it provides more restrictions; however, it requires appropriate panel data that are not always available.

The author appears to choose the route of inferring the determinants of the process from observed distributions. Let $P = p(Xb)$ be a stochatic process, governed by the

Z.J. Acs and D.B. Audretsch (eds.), The Economics of Small Firms: A European Challenge. 74–76.

weighted sum Xb, and let $S^* = s(Xa)$ be the associated steady state distribution, that is the distribution prevailing when the impact of initial conditions faded away; let S_t be the observed distribution at t. S_t diverge from S^* for two reasons:

i) sampling errors
ii) non random components due to the influence of initial conditions (i.e., to the fact that too little time elapsed since the process $p(Xb)$ set in).

Eq. (1)–(3) in section III are somewhat ambigous. It is not clear whether eq. (1) implicitly assumes that the system has reached steady state equilibrium; in fact, first differencing eq. (1) we get a new version of (3), with no adjustment parameter.

Let me take a slightly different approach, which appears to avoid some of these formal difficulties. I would interpret eq. (1) as defining the steady state distribution and define the observed distribution as a weighted average of long run and initial distribution, the weights being δ and $1 - \delta$. Then

(a) $$S_2 = (1 - \delta) S_1 + \delta S_2^* + e_2$$

which is eq. (2) or (3) rewritten; on substituting $X_2 a_2$ to S_2^*

(b) $$\begin{aligned} S_2 - S_1 &= -\delta S_1 + \delta X_2 a_2 + u \\ &= -\delta X_1 a_1 + \delta X_2 a_2 + u \\ &= \delta(X_2 a_2 - X_1 a_1) + \delta X_2 b + u \end{aligned}$$

While the author refers to some adjustment process, δ can be interpreted as a measure of distance. Let me make two quick remarks on the subject. The word adjustment brings to my mind the notion of a reaction function of individual firms to changing environment; there may be no such adjustment and still the system may move towards new equilibria though selection of the fittest firms. In the paper it is twice stated that $\delta = 0$ is equivalent to full adjustment; the term "no adjustment" would seem more appropriate. According to the approach in eq. (a) and (b), $S^*_2 = S_2$ implies $\delta = 1$; $\delta = 0$ corresponds to the case where the system is stuck in S_1, which may or may not be the steady state distribution. Finally, if (a) is the correct specification, then regression (1) and (2) should contain a term identifying the initial distribution.

The author runs two set of regressions, using percentage employment in small firms and entropy measures as dependent variables. The first variable may not be a sufficient statistic for the entire distribution (the same percentage of small firms may be accompanied by different percentages of large ones, across industries). Entropy measures, too, may not completely characterize the size distribution; since entropy is defined by

$$h = -\sum f_i \ln(f_i)$$

the same h can be obtained by interchanging some of the f_i's.

These inadequacies may be at the root of the discrepancies between the two sets of results.

As already pointed out, regressions (1), (2), (4) and (5) seem to be misspecified, or at least incoherent with what appears to be the approach in section III; let us assume that the possible specification errors do not bias coefficients.

Economies of scale (measured by industry median plant size) seem to have reduced their importance in favoring large firms (between 1979 and 1985, see regressions (1) and (2)). This is a very interesting result, in line with qualitative studies on the nature of recent technological changes; however, the result does not survive specification changes (see (4) and (5) where entropy measure is used).

Evidence that open markets favor large dimensions can be found in the negative impact of exports and market sizes on small firms share of employment.

It is not clear how product differentiation is measured and it is therefore difficult to assess the sign of the coefficient; if the variable measures the ability of large firms to differentiate products, then the negative sign could be taken as evidence that survival of firms depends on the existence of exploitable niches.

The positive coefficient of investment is somewhat puzzling, as we would expect highly capitalized industries to show negligible shares of small firms; however, the result may depend on how investments is measured.

The author should explain what is meant by "specialization", whose negative coefficient appears to be the only significant one in regression (3). In this equation the explanatory variables do not account for changes (if any) in the relative importance of small firms. I do not agree with the author's conclusion that the system has fully adjusted: it may not have adjusted at all, as I tried to point out above. Incidentally, there is evidence that movements of firms toward equilibrium are very slow; for example, Contini and Mueller find that profits above and below the norm tend to persist over time (at the individual firm level).

References

Blau, D. M., 1987, "A Time-Series Analysis of Self Employment in the U.S.", *Journal of Political Economy*, 95 (June), 445–467.

Contini, B., "Organization, Markets and Persistence of Profits in Italian Industry", *Journal of Economic Behaviour and Organization*, forthcoming.

Ijiri, Y. and Simon, H.A., 1977, *Skew Distributions and the Size of Business Firms*, North-Holland.

Hopenhayn, H.A., 1986, "A Competitive Stochastic Model of Entry and Exit to an Industry", *mimeo*, November.

Jovanovic, B., 1987, "Selection and the Evolution of Industry", *Econometrica*, 50 (3), 649–670.

Lippman S.A. and Rumelt, R.P., 1987, "Uncertain imitability: an analysis of interfirm differences in efficiency under competition", *The Bell Journal of Economics*, 13 (Autumn), 418–438.

Mueller, D. C., 1986, *Profits in the Long Run*, Cambridge University Press.

Newman, P. and Wolfe, J.N., 1960, "A Model for the Long-Run Theory of Value", *Review of Economic Studies*.

B. ISSUES IN ENTREPRENEURSHIP

6. Some Empirical Aspects of Entrepreneurship*

DAVID S. EVANS and LINDA S. LEIGHTON

I. Introduction

About 4.2 million men and women operate businesses on a full-time basis. Comprising more than a tenth of all workers, they run most of our nation's firms and employ about a tenth of all wage workers. The fraction of the labor force that is self-employed has increased since the mid-1970s after a long period of decline.[1] This paper examines the process of selection into self-employment over the life cycle and the determinants of self-employment earnings using data from the *National Longitudinal Survey of Young Men* (NLS) for 1966–1981 and the *Current Population Surveys* for 1968–1987.

Small-business owners are central to several recent lines of research.[2] First, the static models of entrepreneurial choice developed by Robert Lucas (1978) and Richard Kihlstrom and Jean-Jacques Laffont (1979) have renewed interest in a topic to which the last seminal contributions were made by Frank Knight (1921) and Joseph Schumpeter (1950).[3] David Blau (1985), William Brock and David Evans (1986), and Hedly Rees and Anup Shah (1986) use these models to motivate their empirical work on self-employment selection and earnings. Second, current research on industry dynamics focuses on smaller firms which, because they tend to be younger, have faster and more variable growth, and fail more frequently than larger firms, are a major source of industry changes. For example, Boyan Jovanovic's (1982) model of industry evolution in which heterogeneous entrepreneurs learn about their abilities over time has stimulated empirical work by Timothy Dunne, Mark Roberts, and Larry Samuelson (1987), Evans (1987a, 1987b), and Ariel Pakes and Richard Ericson (1987). These authors analyze entry, exit, and growth of primarily small firms. Third, David Birch's (1979) claim that small firms create a disproportionate share of new jobs has generated much interest in the role of small businesses in the labor market.[4] Many states have programs designed to stimulate small-firm formation. Great Britain, France, Belgium, and the Netherlands have programs that help unemployed workers start small businesses.[5]

While recent studies have enhanced our empirical knowledge of the role of small businesses in the economy, data limitations have forced these studies to sidestep a number of issues that are basic to an economic understanding of firm formation, dissolution, and growth. Several studies (e.g., George Borjas and Stephen Bronars (1987), Rees and Shah (1986), and Brock and Evans (1986)) have used cross-sectional data on self-employed and wage workers to estimate static models of self-employment selection and earnings. But these studies are limited by their lack of data on such important factors as the length of time in business and previous business experience. Recent dynamic studies (e.g., Evans (1987a, 1987b) and Pakes and Ericson (1988)) rely on crude firm characteristics such as size and age but lack information on the entrepreneur himself.[6]

We use longitudinal data that permit a closer examination of some key aspects of entrepreneurship. We focus on white men who comprised 76 percent of all full-time

Z.J. Acs and D.B. Audretsch (eds.), The Economics of Small Firms: A European Challenge. 79–97.

self-employed workers in 1985.[7] Our main source of data is the *National Longitudinal Survey of Young Men* which contains detailed information on a sample of almost 4,000 white men who were between the ages of 14 and 24 in 1966 and who were surveyed 12 times between 1966 and 1981. The self-employed include all sole proprietors, partners, and sole owners of incorporated businesses.

These data permit several innovations over previous research. First, they allow us to track business starts and stops as the cohort of men ages. Second, they enable us to determine the length of time an individual has operated his current business and previous businesses and thereby to distinguish business and wage experience. Third, they permit us to evaluate several theories of entrepreneurship that have been proposed by psychologists and sociologists.[8]

We also use data for about 150,000 white men from *Current Population Surveys* for 1968–1987 as a check on and supplement to our NLS findings. These men were in contiguous years of the CPS March surveys giving us a 2-year panel for each individual. To keep our inquiry open ended – an important consideration given the limited empirical information on this topic – we do not develop and estimate structural models of entrepreneurship in this paper. The reader should exercise caution in placing behavioral interpretations on our results.

We report seven key findings. (1) The probability of switching into self-employment is roughly independent of age and total labor-market experience. This result is not consistent with standard job-shopping models such as William Johnson (1978) and Robert Miller (1984) which predict that younger workers will try riskier occupations first. (2) The probability of departing from self-employment decreases with duration in self-employment, falling from about 10 percent in the early years to 0 by the eleventh year in self-employment. About half of the entrants return to wage work within seven years.[9] (3) The fraction of the labor force that is self-employed increases with age until the early 40s and then remains constant until the retirement years. This relationship results from the process of entry and exit over the life cycle. (4) Men with greater assets are more likely to switch into self-employment all else equal. This result is consistent with the view that entrepreneurs face liquidity constraints.[10] (5) Wage experience has a much smaller return in self-employment than in wage work while business experience has just about the same return in wage work as in self-employment. These differences may reflect some combination of true productivity differences and the results of selection into and out of self-employment over time. (6) Poorer wage workers – i.e., unemployed workers, lower-paid wage workers, and men who have changed jobs a lot – are more likely to enter self-employment or to be self-employed at a point in time, all else equal. These results are consistent with the view of some sociologists that "misfits" are pushed into entrepreneurship.[11] (7) As predicted by one of the leading psychological theories, men who believe their performance depends largely on their own actions – i.e., have an internal locus of control as measured by a psychologist test known as the Rotter Scale – have a greater propensity to start businesses.[12]

The next section describes the data. The third section presents aggregate statistics on self-employment entry and exit over the life cycle and reports estimates of the hazard into and out of self-employment. The fourth section examines the determinants of self-employment earnings. It focuses on the relative returns to business and wage experience and education in self-employment versus wage work. The last section suggests avenues for further research.

II. Data Sources

The *National Longitudinal Survey* is based on a national probability sample of men who were between the ages of 14 and 24 in 1966 and who were surveyed yearly between 1966 and 1971 and in 1973, 1975, 1976, 1978, 1980, and 1981.[13] There were 3918 white men in the initial survey of whom 2731 were still in the survey in 1981. The appendix presents definitions for the variables used in this paper. Because the data are described in detail in Evans and Linda Leighton (1987), we focus on the advantages of these data over those used in previous research.

(1) Using information on employment status and tenure we have calculated total experience in wage work and self-employment for each year of the sample.[14] Previous studies that rely on cross-sectional data have not disaggregated experience. (2) We have found that workers who report themselves as self-employed often have no self-employment earnings and substantial wage earnings which suggests that either the workers are misclassified or their earnings are misclassified. We have found that it is possible to explain most of these inconsistencies using available data on dual jobs, tenure, and incorporation status. Our findings suggest some caution in taking reported self-employment earnings at face value.[15] (3) The panel data on employment status allows us to track entry and exit over time. Previous studies of self-employment selection that rely on cross-sectional data confound the entry and exit decisions. In a cross-section, self-employed workers are workers who entered and remained in self-employment. (4) Data on assets, job changes, unemployment, and some standard psychological test scores enable us to look at a number of issues which cannot be examined with the datasets used by previous researchers. It turns out that these variables are important determinants of self-employment selection and earnings.

One disadvantage of the NLS is that the sample sizes for analyzing self-employment entry and exit are small. For example, the number of entrants into self-employment averages about 50 per year. Another disadvantage is that data are available only for men who are all younger than 40 by the end of the survey. A further problem is that there is substantial attrition – almost a third – between 1966 and 1981. To obtain larger and more representative samples for analyzing self-employment entry and exit we use data drawn from the March Supplement to the Current Population Surveys for 1968–1987. Each CPS survey contains information on the employment status of each respondent for the survey week and for the previous year. About half of all respondents are in contiguous surveys for most survey years.[16] We have matched these respondents for the pairs of years where this was possible. The resulting dataset contains up to 2.33 years of employment information for about 150,000 white men who were between the ages of 18 and 65 at the time of the first observation on them and who were full-time labor-market participants in the first observation year. For each individual, we have information pertaining to the survey week for two years and information pertaining to the longest-held job in the preceding year. We have used the data to calculate entry and exit rates between jobs held as of the survey week and between the longest-held jobs in each year.[17] A deficiency of the CPS data is that individuals who operate incorporated businesses were included with wage workers for the survey-week job in all years and for the longest-held job for the surveys before 1976. For this reason we concentrate on unincorporated self-employment for the CPS data.

III. Entry and Exit

The probability that an individual operates a business T years after entering the labor force equals the probability that he started a business at time t, $t \leq T$, times the probability that he remained self-employed from time t to time T.[18] We examine several aspects of this process of entry and exit over the life cycle in this section. We begin by summarizing the rates of entry into and exit out of self-employment for the NLS cohorts and for the matched CPS data. We show that a simple time-homogeneous Markov model in which entry and exit rates are constant over time provides a helpful first approximation to the cross-sectional relationship between self-employment and age. We then investigate whether the entry or exit rates exhibit duration dependence. We find that entry is time-homogeneous – it is constant in both age and labor-market experience – but that exit decreases sharply with time in business. Finally, we report estimates of the hazard into entrepreneurship that control for a variety of characteristics suggested by social-science theories of the entrepreneur.

An Overview of Entry and Exit

Table 6.1 reports summary statistics on the evolution of self-employment for the NLS white men. The fraction of labor-force participants who enter self-employment exceeds the fraction who exit self-employment thereby increasing the fraction who are self-employed from 3.9 percent in 1966 to 17.7 percent in 1981. Since 1971, when the average

Table 6.1. Self-employment entry and exit 1966–1981.

Survey year	Percent of labor force participants who: Enter self-employment between survey years	Exit self-employment between survey years	Are in self-employment as of the survey year	Percent of self-employed workers who exit self-employment between survey years
1966	1.92	1.49	3.89	30.36
1967	2.78	0.97	4.50	18.03
1968	2.43	1.71	5.54	25.30
1969	2.93	1.41	5.92	19.59
1970	2.35	2.10	7.04	27.50
1971[a]	5.24 (3.67)	1.83 (0.92)	6.64	24.06 (12.86)
1973[a]	4.77 (3.13)	2.91 (1.47)	9.16	26.73 (14.40)
1975	4.22	2.33	10.74	19.09
1976[a]	6.89 (4.82)	3.18 (1.60)	12.00	23.08 (12.30)
1978[a]	6.24 (4.37)	3.76 (1.90)	14.71	20.82 (11.02)
1980	4.04	2.68	16.68	12.93
1981	–		17.73	–

[a] Denotes a two-year transition. We obtained annual rates that are comparable to the one-year transitions under the following assumptions. For entry we assumed that 40 percent of new entrants fail in the first year so that the average annual rate of entry is 1.4 times the two-year entry rate divided by 2. For failure we assumed that the annual rate of survival is s so that the probability of surviving two years is s^2. The annual rate of failure is simply $1 - s$. These adjusted rates are reported in parentheses beside the actual rate.

Source: White males drawn from the *National Longitudinal Survey of Young Men.*

age of the labor-market participants was 25 years, the entry rate – the percent of wage workers who enter self-employment – has been about 4.0 percent per year and the exit rate – the fraction of self-employed workers who return to wage work – has been about 13.8 percent per year. The entry rate was lower and the exit rate was somewhat higher prior to 1971.

A simple time-homogeneous Markov model provides a helpful first approximation to this process. Denote the probability of entering self-employment by e and the probability of exiting self-employment by x. Assume that e and x are independent of time or age. Then the probability that an individual will operate a business T years after entering the labor force is (see, e.g., William Feller (1968, p. 432)),

$$\frac{e}{x + e}\,[1 - (1 - x - e)^T]$$

This simple model has two predictions. The first is that the probability of self-employment increases at a diminishing rate with the length of time in the labor force.[19] The second prediction is that the probability of self-employment converges to a plateau given by $e/x + e$ for older men. We check these predictions with the CPS data which contain many more observations and a broader age range than do the NLS data. The relationship between unincorporated self-employment and age found in the CPS data is displayed in Fig. 6.1 for 150,275 white men who were between the ages of 18 and 65 between 1968 and 1987.[20] The rate of self-employment increases at a diminishing rate with age and approaches a plateau at about age 40 which lasts until about age 60. The average rate of unincorporated business formation (entry into self-employment between successive March survey weeks) was 2.5 percent per year and the average rate of unincorporated business dissolution (exit out of self-employment between successive March survey weeks) was 21.6 percent per year for the CPS sample.[21] The predicted asymptote of 10.4 percent is close to the plateau of about 11.6 percent shown in Fig. 6.1.

The Time-Dependence of Entry and Exit

The Markov model assumes that the probabilities of forming or dissolving a business are independent of time in the labor force.[22] We examined the dependence of entry on time in the labor force in several ways. First, we estimated the probit for entering self-employment as a function of age or labor-market experience for the NLS sample for each year. We can reject the hypothesis that entry depends upon age or labor-market experience at conventional levels of significance for all specifications and years.[23] This finding suggests that the probability of starting a business is independent of age or experience at least until age 40. Second, Table 6.2 and Fig. 6.1 report entry rates by 5-year age categories for the CPS white men. The rate of entry is fairly constant between ages 25 and 50 and then decreases somewhat between ages 50 and 60.[24]

We examined the dependence of exit from self-employment on the length of time in business by estimating the probability that an individual will survive T years in continuous self-employment and the probability of leaving self-employment during the next year given that the individual has been employed for T years. We used data for 460 NLS white men who were observed from the time of entry to the end of the survey.[25] Table 6.3

Table 6.2. Self-employment entry rate by age; white men; ages 21–65.[a]

Ages	Entry rate (percent)	Ages	Entry rate (percent)
21–25	1.7	46–50	2.5
26–30	2.9	51–55	2.4
31–35	2.6	56–60	2.3
36–40	2.8	61–65	3.1
41–45	2.7	21–65	2.5

[a] Entry rate is the percent of men who were wage workers as of the March survey week who were unincorporated self-employed during the March survey week of the following year.

Source: Based on data on 135,752 employed white men from the *Current Population Surveys*, 1968–1987.

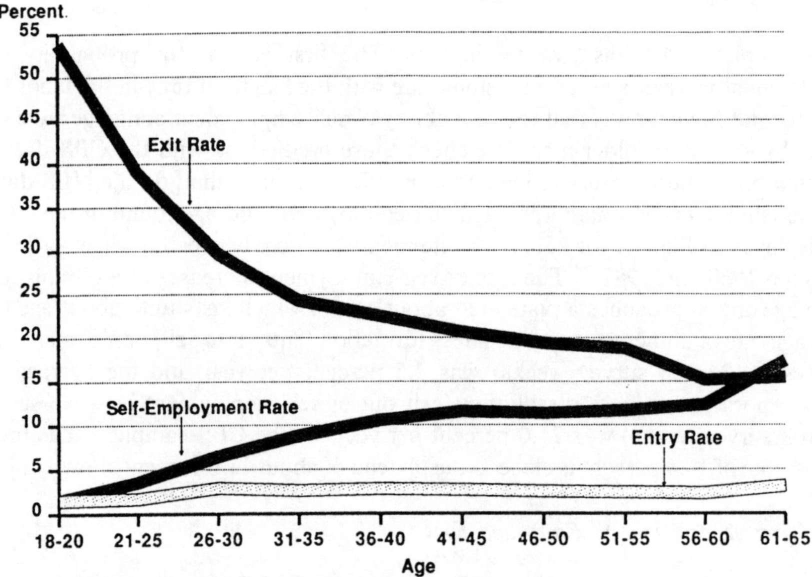

Fig. 6.1. Self-employment rate vs. age; white men; ages 21–65. Based on data on 150,275 employed white men from the *Current Population Surveys*, 1968–1987.

Table 6.3. Estimated survival and hazard rates for self-employment.[a]

Self-employment duration in years	Survival rate (percent)	Hazard rate[b] (percent)
0	100.0	–
2	79.4	10.3
4	61.5	11.3
6	51.4	8.2
8	47.0	4.3
10	41.2	6.2
12	39.9	1.6
14	39.9	0.0

[a] Based on estimates obtained from the Kaplan-Meier procedure using LIMDEP.

[b] Annual hazard rate based on the estimated survivorship function.

summarizes life-table estimates of the survivorship and hazard rates obtained from the Kaplan-Meier procedure.[26] About a third of the entrants leave self-employment within the first 3 years of entry, about a half within 7 years, and about three-fifths within 10 years. The hazard rate decreases with duration in self-employment, falling from about 10 percent in the early years to 0 by the eleventh year in self-employment.[27]

Estimates of the Probability of Entering Self-Employment

Individuals will switch from self-employment to wage work if the expected utility of self-employment exceeds the expected utility of wage work. The difference between these expected values depends upon the difference between expected earnings in the two occupations and upon relative tastes for the two. Expected wage earnings depend upon current wage earnings, education, job tenure, and wage experience. Expected self-employment earnings depend upon education and experience. We therefore conjecture that the probability of switching into self-employment will decline with current wage earnings but may increase or decrease with education and experience depending upon whether these characteristics are more important in self-employment or wage work. Another observable characteristic, which psychologists and sociologists have found to be correlated with selection into entrepreneurship, is the extent to which individuals have an internal locus of control.[28] We measure the internal locus of control by the individual's score on the Rotter test (which was administered in 1976). Finally, an individual will be more likely to switch into self-employment the greater his net worth if there are liquidity constraints as in Evans and Jovanovic (1988). As additional measures of worker quality we include the frequency of job changes (number of changes divided by total labor-market experience), unemployment as a fraction of time in the labor force, marital status, and whether the individual has a health problem.[29]

Table 6.4 reports probit estimates of a basic specification of the determinants of entry into self-employment for 1976–1978, 1978–1980, and 1980–1981 for the NLS. For comparison, we also report linear probability model estimates for the 1968–1986 matched CPS data. The samples consist of individuals who were in the labor force in both survey weeks. Several findings are robust. (1) The probability of switching into self-employment increases with net worth (measured by assets for the NLS and by the difference between family earnings and family income for the CPS). This finding is consistent with Evans and Jovanovic (1989) and suggests that individuals face liquidity constraints.[30] (2) Individuals with low wages are more likely to switch into self-employment. This relationship is highly significant when we control for assets but not for other labor-market characteristics. It remains but is much less statistically significant when we also condition on labor-market characteristics. (3) Wage experience is neither statistically nor substantively significant.[31] Thus, as we found earlier, the hazard into self-employment from wage work is independent of the length of time in wage work. (4) Individuals with longer job tenures are less likely to switch into self-employment.[32] (5) The probability of entry is higher for individuals who have had prior self-employment experience. (6) Individuals who have changed jobs frequently are more likely to switch into self-employment. (7) The effect of previous unemployment on the probability of entering self-employment is not consistent across the years: it is positive and significant for 1980–1981, positive and insignificant for 1976–1978, and negative and insignificant

Table 6.4. Probability of entering self-employment from wage work. *National Longitudinal Survey of Young Men* probit estimates.

1980–1981

Variable	Coefficient	Std. Error	t	Prob. > $\|t\|$	Mean
Enter					.0252039
Tenure	−.0238353	.0081510	−2.924	0.004	43.54411
Tenure^2	.0001638	.0000619	2.645	0.008	3096.182
Income	−.5163689	.2901084	−1.780	0.075	2.063929
Income^2	.0663933	.0541532	1.226	0.220	5.139952
Wage exp.	.0462285	.0285732	1.618	0.106	13.3198
Prev. self	.9107385	.2171792	4.193	0.000	.1030393
Education	.055382	.0434853	1.274	0.203	13.88288
Unemploy	.0478407	.0187881	2.546	0.011	2.361186
Changes	.3698019	.3711313	0.996	0.319	.3244283
Assets[b]	.0985545	.0228677	4.310	0.000	4.645619
Assets^2	−.0010812	.0003849	−2.809	0.005	89.78229
Married	−.5815598	.2076951	−2.800	0.005	.7916976
Urban	.0516553	.2181547	0.237	0.813	.7249815
Handicap	−.0494911	.3936484	−0.126	0.900	.0518903
Constant	−2.909767	.9611979	−3.027	0.003	1

Number of obs = 1349
Log likelihood = −107.94862
chi2(14) = 101.53
Prob > chi2 = 0.0000

F-tests	*F*	*P*-value
Income = 0	2.27	.1041
Asset = 0	11.12	.0000
Tenure = 0	4.28	.0141

1987–1988

Variable	Coefficient	Std. Error	t	Prob. > $\|t\|$	Mean
Enter					.0526658
Tenure	−.0025117	.0060118	−0.418	0.676	37.36151
Tenure^2	.0000356	.0000573	0.621	0.535	2345.797
Income	−.2613197	.234179	−1.116	0.265	1.678607
Income^2	.0327625	.0491364	0.667	0.505	3.379527
Wage exp.	−.0322216	.0197113	−1.635	0.102	11.60596
Prev. self	.6916842	.153986	4.492	0.000	.0838752
Education	.0217275	.0256107	0.848	0.396	13.70546
Unemploy	−.020861	.0155898	−1.338	0.181	2.55832
Changes	.3529475	.2204601	1.601	0.110	.3494789
Assets[c]	.0609102	.0246713	2.469	0.014	1.617229
Assets^2	−.0007327	.0004154	−1.764	0.078	21.10421
Married	−.0153407	.1432351	−0.107	0.915	1.210663
Urban	−.1589805	.1215175	−1.308	0.191	.7041612
Handicap	−.0253471	.2350554	−0.108	0.914	.0643693
Constant	−1.381862	.561222	−2.462	0.014	1

Number of obs = 1538
Log likelihood = −290.4314
chi2(14) = 53.69
Prob > chi2 = 0.0000

F-tests	*F*	*P*-value
Income = 0	1.14	.3215
Asset = 0	3.39	.0338
Tenure = 0	0.26	.7741

Variable	Coefficient	Std. Error	t	Prob. > $\|t\|$	Mean
		1976–1978			
Enter					.0563978
Tenure	−.0188406	.0059464	−3.168	0.002	32.44633
Tenure^2	.0001893	.0000577	3.278	0.001	1783.905
Income	−.0027703	.2210893	−0.013	0.990	1.307402
Income^2	.0148635	.0522132	0.285	0.776	2.088686
Wage exp.	.0282834	.0188645	1.499	0.134	9.883356
Prev. self	.6944128	.1503571	4.618	0.000	.0794421
Education	.0121024	.0245543	0.493	0.622	13.58702
Unemploy	.0036077	.0118607	0.304	0.761	2.796006
Changes	.4891922	.1692598	2.890	0.004	.3675908
Assets	.0787118.	0394622	1.995	0.046	1.52344
Asset^2	−.0023117	.0017761	−1.302	0.193	15.06044
Married	−.3480157	.1239067	−2.809	0.005	.7671316
Urban	.0254816	.1227831	0.208	0.836	.7064888
Handicap	−.1958478	.2220587	−0.882	0.378	.0721649
Constant	−1.976281	.4987808	−3.962	0.000	1

		F-tests	*F*	*P*-value
Number of obs	= 1649	Income = 0	0.19	.8268
Log likelihood	= −324.18232	Asset = 0	2.21	.1105
chi2(14)	= 67.10			
Prob > chi2	= 0.0000			

Current population surveys, 1968–1986; linear probability model estimates; white men, ages 25-60[d]

Variable	Coefficient	Std. Error	t	Prob. > $\|t\|$
Enter				
Income	−7.06372E-06	2.5543E-06	−2.765	.0057
Income^2	5.05253E-05	8.7298E-06	5.788	.0000
Liquidity	7.75240E-07	1.1777E-07	6.583	.0000
Age	−2.42493E-04	3.9411E-04	−.615	.5384
Age^2	2.71727E-06	4.4914E-06	.605	.5452
High school drop	−6.72032E-04	.001328	−.506	.6127
College dropout	.003173	.001376	2.306	.0211
College graduate	.006408	.001628	3.936	.0001
Post graduate	.013793	.001651	8.352	.0000
Urban	−.005001	9.9962E-04	−5.003	.0000
Married	.002432	9.6085E-04	2.531	.0114
Veteran	−.002762	.001019	−2.710	.0067
Constant	.027483	.008177	3.361	.0008

Number of obs	106239
R square	.00286
F-statistic	12.7062

[a] Estimates obtained using STATA.
[b] Assets are for 1981.
[c] Assets are for 1976.
[d] Estimates obtained using SPSSX.

for 1978–1980. But we have found that men who are unemployed are more likely to enter self-employment. For the CPS white men observed, entry rate was 4.7 percent for men who were unemployed (5664 men) as of the initial survey week and 2.4 percent for men who were employed wage workers (126,750 men) as of the initial survey week.[33] (8) There is a negative relationship between the Rotter score and entry for most years but the relationship is generally not statistically significant.[34]

The general message of these results is that relatively poor wage workers – i.e., workers with low wages and a history of instability – are most likely to switch to self-employment holding assets and education constant.

IV. Self-Employment Selection and Earnings

In this section we report cross-sectional estimates of the probability that an individual is self-employed rather than a wage worker and estimates of self-employment and wage earnings for individuals who were self-employed workers or wage workers in 1981. Several other authors report estimates of self-employment selection and earnings models. Borjas and Bronars (1987), Evans (1985), and Brock and Evans (1986) use 1980 Census data, Rees and Shah (1985) use U.K. data on a small cross-section, and Blau (1985) uses data on Malaysian farmers. These previous estimates suffer from two data problems. First, these studies have no information on self-employment versus wage experience. Indeed, all of these studies use proxies for aggregate experience (age less years of education). Second, they have rather sparse information on personal characteristics. The NLS data permit us to estimate a much more refined model and to investigate the effects of wage and self-employment experience on wage and self-employment earnings.

The results reported in this section are primarily descriptive. It is very difficult to place behavioral interpretations on cross-sectional estimates of self-employment selection and earnings. For example, the probability of being self-employed at time T depends upon the underlying probability of switching into self-employment at some previous time and surviving until time T. The cross-sectional estimates confound the determinants of switching and survival. To take another example, the effect of wage experience on self-employment earnings confounds the productivity-enhancing effects of wage experience on business earnings and a variety of potential selection problems, e.g., the possibility that workers who accumulated more wage experience before switching into self-employment had higher opportunity costs of switching into self-employment and therefore must have discovered unusually good self-employment opportunities to induce them to switch.[35] Nevertheless, the results reported here are helpful because they place some restrictions on the behavioral models of entrepreneurial selection and earnings that might be entertained.

The data for the analysis consists of 2,405 white men who were in the 1981 NLS survey, were employed as of the 1981 survey week, and were not enrolled in school full time. To have a clean comparison of the choice between self-employment and wage work, we deleted individuals who held both wage and self-employment jobs. We found a number of possible errors in the self-employment status and earnings information and made several adjustments and deletions to minimize the effects of such errors. Some incorporated self-employed individuals reported wage earnings but no self-employment earnings; we assumed their wage earnings were from their incorporated business. Some individuals switched into self-employment or wage work during the year; we prorated their earnings according to the proportion of the year they spent in the type of job held as of the survey week. Individuals who had inconsistent information – e.g., who reported wage earnings but who were unincorporated self-employed and who had not switched during the year – were deleted. A total of 272 individuals were deleted either because they held both wage and self-employment jobs or because information was inconsistent.[36] A few other individuals were deleted for some of the analyses because of missing information.

Table 6.5 reports probit estimates of the probability that an individual is self-employed rather than a wage worker in 1981. We report estimates both with and without the Rotter score and an indicator of whether the individual's father held a managerial job since there were a substantial number of missing values on these variables. Several findings are notable. First, the probability of being self-employed increases with labor-market experience.[37] This result is consistent with the simple Markov model of self-employment: Individuals who have been in the labor market a longer time are more likely to have switched to self-employment. Second, the probability of being self-employed is higher for individuals who have changed jobs frequently. This finding is consistent with our entry estimates which also indicated that men with more unstable work histories were more likely to enter self-employment. Third, the probability of self-employment is higher for individuals with relatively more unemployment experience. This result is consistent with our earlier finding that unemployed workers are more likely to enter self-employment. Fourth, the probability of being self-employed is higher for more highly educated individuals even after we control for individuals in professional occupations. Fifth, as suggested by psychologists, individuals who have a more internal locus of

Table 6.5. Estimated probability of being self-employed in 1981; white men; probit estimates.[a]

		Model 1			
Variable	Coefficient	Std. Error	t	Prob. > $\|t\|$	Mean
Self-employed					.161165
Urban	−.1845696	.0788463	−2.341	0.019	.7067961
Married	.0705539	.0923126	0.764	0.445	.776699
Divorced	.1504005	.101406	1.483	0.138	.1446602
Handicapped	−.2205851	.1354426	−1.629	0.104	.0859223
Experience	.0631149	.011388	5.542	0.000	14.45653
Education	.0468791	.0159466	2.940	0.003	13.83447
Unemployment	.0008846	.0001591	5.561	0.000	138.5192
Changes	.0129181	.0027347	4.724	0.000	16.87336
Farmer	1.852521	.1674885	11.061	0.000	.038835
Professional	1.318865	.1805655	7.304	0.000	.0286408
Military	.2254239	.1098127	2.053	0.040	.3504854
Mil. exp.	−.0039777	.0032259	−1.233	0.218	9.865049
Constant	−3.077114	.3627388	−8.483	0.000	1

Number of obs = 2060
Log likelihood = −762.87545
chi2(12) = 293.63
Prob > chi2 = 0.0000

Model 2

Variable	Coefficient	Std. Error	t	Prob. > $\|t\|$	Mean
Self-employed					.1618435
Urban	−.2040773	.0838386	−2.434	0.015	.7073955
Married	.0178929	.0986787	0.181	0.856	.7808146
Divorced	.0951484	.1097263	0.867	0.386	.142015
Handicapped	−.2174593	.142506	−1.526	0.127	.0846731
Experience	.0553762	.0123014	4.502	0.000	14.60937
Education	.0179523	.017547	1.023	0.306	13.86549
Unemployment	.0008873	.0001769	5.016	0.000	131.2435
Changes	.013667	.0029617	4.615	0.000	16.71073
Farmer	1.908768.	1732564	11.017	0.000	.0401929
Military	.3334698	.1235012	2.700	0.007	.3494105
Mil. exp.	−.0111616	.0042291	−2.639	0.008	9.019829
Professional	1.364592	.197819	6.898	0.000	.0273312
Rotter score	−.0216171	.0073045	−2.959	0.003	21.8612
Manager father	.3363427	.0962543	3.494	0.000	.1709539
Constant	−2.102342	.442666	−4.749	0.000	1

Number of obs = 1866
Log likelihood = −674.18848
chi2(14) = 303.83
Prob > chi2 = 0.0000

control are more likely to become entrepreneurs. Controlling for the internal locus of control renders the coefficient on education small and statistically insignificant. Sixth, men whose fathers were managers are more likely to be self-employed.

Using the probit selection equation reported above, we were not able to reject the hypothesis that the correlation between selection and earnings is zero; controlling for selection had little effect on the coefficient estimates.[38] On the basis of a Chow test it was also possible to reject the hypothesis that self-employed and wage workers have the same earnings equation at the 1 percent level.

Table 6.6 reports regression estimates of log-earnings equations for self-employed workers and wage workers for our final specification. There are several important differences and similarities in the earnings functions. First, the return to wage experience in self-employment (2.1%) is lower than the return to wage experience in wage work (5.6%) and lower than the return to self-employment experience in self-employment (4.6%).[39] One interpretation of these differences is that human-capital accumulated through wage work is less valuable in self-employment than wage work. Another interpretation is that individuals who switch into self-employment later in their careers (and who have thereby accumulated more wage experience) are relatively poorer wage workers. Second, the return to self-employment experience in wage work (4.5%) is higher than the return to wage experience in wage work (3.1%) although the difference is not statistically significant. This result suggests that workers who fail at self-employment return to wage work at roughly the same wages they would have received had they not tried self-employment.[40] It is not possible to determine the extent to which this result reflects the value of business experience in wage work or the fact that those self-employed workers with the best wage opportunities will tend to switch.

Table 6.6. Estimated log earnings equayions for self-employed and wage workers; regression estimates.[a]

Self-employed workers

Variable	Coefficient	Std. Error	t	Prob. > $\|t\|$	Mean
Log annual earnings					9.722387
Urban	.2984078	.0959255	3.111	0.002	.5886525
Married	.1426724	.1182799	1.206	0.229	.8262411
Handicapped	−.7237983	.1653379	−4.378	0.000	.0744681
Wage exp.	.0212041	.0106104	1.998	0.047	8.838993
Bus. exp.	.1127724	.0267228	4.220	0.000	6.831969
Bus. exp.^{2}	−.0048672	.0012519	−3.881	0.000	78.364
Prev. bus.	.2638763	.1084132	.434	0.016	.2234043
Education	.102862	.0187483	5.486	0.000	13.85816
Unemploy wks	−.0076448	.0023534	−3.248	0.001	12.71631
Changes	−.0019309	.0039824	−0.485	0.628	18.22286
Farmer	.0088565	.1262476	0.070	0.944	.1950355
Professional	.1607639	.1705543	0.943	0.347	.0957447
Military	−.1787064	.122895	−1.454	0.147	.3439716
Mil. exp.	.0065334	.0037604	1.737	0.083	7.723404
Constant	7.547442.3	774288	19.997	0.000	1

Number of obs = 282 $F(14,267)$ = 10.69
R-square = 0.3591 Prob > F = 0.0000
Adj R-square = 0.3255 Root MSE = .71254

[a] Estimates obtained using STATA.

Wage workers

Variable	Coefficient	Std. Error	t	Prob. > $\|t\|$	Mean
Log earnings					9.888144
Urban	.2116573	.0287379	7.365	0.000	.7239521
Married	.2301503	.0304746	7.552	0.000	.7694611
Handicapped	−.180494	.0451322	−3.999	0.000	.0874251
Wage exp.	.0984876.	0198633	4.958	0.000	13.97031
Wage exp.^{2}	−.0024167	.0006396	−3.778	0.000	210.6699
Self exp.	.0447571	.011243	3.981	0.000	.3203938
Education	.0706433	.0054855	12.878	0.000	13.82814
Unemploy wks	−.0042027	.0005479	−7.670	0.000	16.44012
Changes	−.0035781	.0009934	−3.602	0.000	16.32626
Farmer	−.4048178	.1277192	−3.170	0.002	.0101796
Professional	.15914	.1064927	1.494	0.135	.0149701
Military	.0213733	.0400467	0.534	0.594	.3556886
Mil. exp.	.0018262	.0010989	1.662	0.097	10.36886
Constant	7.818336	.1790618	43.663	0.000	1

Number of obs = 1670 $F(13,1656)$ = 49.85
R-square = 0.2813 Prob > F = 0.0000
Adj R-square = 0.2756 Root MSE = .51578

Estimates obtained using STATA.

Table 6.7 Definition of variables for *National Longitudinal Survey of Young Men*.[a]

Variable	Definition
	Categorial variables[b]
Entry	Dummy for individual who was a wage worker in the survey week and self-employed in the next survey week observed
Handicapped	Dummy for individuals who have poor health
Veteran	Dummy for individuals who served in the military
Urban	Dummy for individuals who live within an SMSA
Professional	Dummy for individuals in professional occupations
Farmer	Dummy for individual in farm occupation
Manager Father	Dummy for individuals whose fathers were in a managerial occupation when individual was 14
Married	Dummy for individual who is married
Divorced	Dummy for individual who has been divorced
	Continuous variables
Income	Total Earnings in the previous year
Education	Years of education
Business experience	Years in current business
Previous business	Years in previous businesses
Wage experience	Years of wage experience
Military experience	Weeks of military experience
Tenure	Years in current job
Rotter score	Total score on Rotter Test for 1976
Job changes	Number of jobs held by individual since 1966 divided by wage experience
Unemployment	Weeks of unemployment divided by wage plus unemployment experience times 100.
Unemployment weeks	Weeks of unemployment since 1966
Wage earnings	Wage earnings of wage workers
Self earnings	Self-employment earnings of self-employed workers or wage earnings of incorporated self-employed workers who report wage but no self-employment earnings
Assets	Net worth (assets minus liabilities) of family

[a] Further details are provided in Evans and Leighton (1987).
[b] Dummy equal to 1 if condition holds and zero otherwise.

Third, even after controlling for professional workers, the returns to education are somewhat higher in self-employment than in wage work – 10.3 per year versus 7.1 per year. Fourth, unemployment experience carries a substantially larger penalty in self-employment than in wage work – 0.8 percent per week versus 0.4 percent per week. This result suggests that unemployed workers with the poorest opportunities in the wage sector switch to and remain in self-employment.

V. Conclusions and Suggestions for Further Research

Economists have a lot to learn about entrepreneurship. Our results suggest some avenues to pursue. An interesting finding is that the probability of entering self-employment is independent of age or experience for the first twenty years of employment.

This result is contrary to popular wisdom and inconsistent with imperfect-information models of occupational choice. Behavioral models of entrepreneurial selection that can explain this relationship would be helpful. One possible explanation examined by Evans and Jovanovic (1989) is that individuals face liquidity constraints and have to accumulate assets in order to start viable businesses. Another possible explanation is that it takes time to discover a business opportunity. Older people might be more likely to have identified an opportunity but less likely to choose to exploit it.[41]

Our results suggest that some theories are more consistent with the data than others. The disadvantage theory which views entrepreneurs as misfits cast off from wage work is consistent with many of our findings. People who switch from wage work to self-employment tend to be people who were receiving relatively low wages, who have changed jobs frequently, and who experienced relatively frequent or long spells of unemployment as wage workers.[42] The psychological theory based on the internal locus of control is also consistent with our findings. Self-employed workers at a point in time tend to have a more internal locus of control (a result which is statistically significant) and individuals with a more internal locus of control are more likely to enter self-employment (a result which is generally not statistically significant). The sociological and psychological literature on entrepreneurship contains many insights that economists might consider incorporating in their models.

Notes

* We are grateful to Christopher Flinn, Boyan Jovanovic, Jules Lichtenstein, Edward Starr, Hideki Yamawaki, participants of the International Conference on Small Business Economics held at the International Institute of Management, West Berlin, November 1988, and the referee for helpful comments and suggestions. Portions of our research were supported by the U.S. Small Business Administration under Contract No. SBA-1067-AER-86 to Fordham University and by faculty research fellowships provided by Fordham University to both authors. We retain responsibility for the views expressed below. We will provide a copy of a statistical appendix and the dataset used in this paper on AT-compatible diskettes upon request for one year after the publication date of this paper.

1. See Evans and Leighton (1987), Becker (1984), Haber et al. (1987), and Blau (1987) for details. Evans and Leighton find that self-employment rates peaked in about 1983 and have decreased since.
2. See Brock and Evans (1989) for a review of recent research.
3. See Brock and Evans (1986) for a survey.
4. For criticisms of this argument see Jonathan Leonard (1986) and Dunne, Roberts, and Samuelson (1987).
5. See Mark Bendick and Mary Egan (1987). The U.S. Department of Labor is planning to conduct an experiment in which a sample of unemployment insurance recipients will be given the option to receive business startup funds in lieu of unemployment benefits.
6. For example, taken literally Jovanovic's model assumes that an individual learns about his entrepreneurial ability over time. Firm age is a crude proxy for the duration and intensity of entrepreneurial learning.
7. We concentrate on white males for several reasons. The self-employment rate differs substantially between sex and race groups. The rate for women and blacks is only about a third that for white men. Investigating the source of these disparities would take us too far afield. (See Borjas and Bronars (1987) for a recent analysis of race differences.) Moreover, because blacks and women have low self-employment rates available longitudinal datasets provide too few observations on self-employment entry and exit for these demographic groups.

8. There is an extensive theoretical and empirical literature on entrepreneurship in our sister disciplines. But the empirical work generally does not control for anything more than rudimentary demographic characteristics.
9. This is probably an underestimate because short spells of self-employment (under one year) are underrepresented in the data.
10. See Evans and Jovanovic (1989) for an estimated structural model of entrepreneurship with liquidity constraints using the NLS data.
11. See Pyong Gap Min (1984) for a review of the major sociological theories.
12. An internal locus of control is also a characteristic of individuals who have a high need for achievement which David McClelland (1964) has argued is a key determinant of entrepreneurship.
13. Blacks were oversampled. About 25 percent of the initial respondents were black or other minorities.
14. Some imputations, especially for workers with pre-1966 experience, were necessary. See Evans and Leighton (1987).
15. On the other hand, the fact that most of the individuals who report themselves as being self-employed either report self-employed earnings or report themselves as having an incorporated business suggests that errors in reporting self-employment status are not substantial.
16. The exceptions being 1971–1972, 1972–1973, 1976–1977, and 1985–1986.
17. The construction of these data is described in Evans and Leighton (1987).
18. Note that survival in self-employment is not necessarily equivalent to survival of a business since an individual may remain self-employed as he opens and closes successive businesses.
19. This prediction is consistent with cross-sectional studies by Brock and Evans (1986), Rees and Shah (1986), and Borjas (1987) which find that the probability of self-employment is convex in age. For the NLS men the probability of self-employment increases linearly with age for each of the 12 cross-sections. The lack of convexity is probably due to the fact that these men are all under 40 even at the end of the sample period.
20. The underlying data are reported in the appendix.
21. Entry rates are substantially lower for men under 25 and higher for men over 60 (see below). Excluding these two extremes we obtain a predicted asymptote of 11.0 percent.
22. Because the probability of leaving a job decreases with age, the probability of starting a business conditional upon leaving a job must increase with age. We would like to thank Jacob Mincer for this point.
23. Results are available upon request.
24. It increases after age 60, a reflection of the tendency of older men to switch to self-employment upon retirement. See Victor Fuchs (1982) for an analysis of this phenomenon.
25. There were a total of 396 individuals some of whom entered more than once (i.e., entered, failed, and reentered).
26. We also attempted to control for individual characteristics using parametric hazards formulations. None of the characteristics such as education, wage experience, previous job tenure, marital status was substantively or statistically important.
27. The survivorship function is probably biased upward because short spells of self-employment are underrepresented in our sample since many of our observations are 1-2 years apart. Using the *Current Population Survey* data on the unincorporated self-employed we estimated the failure rate over a one-year period of white men who were wage workers on their longest-held job in the previous year (generally a period of at least six months) and who were self-employed in the survey week. Generally these people would have been self-employed less than nine months as of the survey week. Of these individuals, 41.4 percent were no longer self-employed in the subsequent survey week.
28. See, for example, J. Schere (1982) and Janak Pandey and N. B. Tewary (1979) for empirical studies of the relationship between the internal locus of control and small-business ownership. The hypothesis that entrepreneurs have a high need for achievement is due to McClelland's (1964) pioneering study. Also see McClelland and David Winter (1969).
29. Ivan Light (1979) has argued that these sorts of disadvantages push minorities into self-employment. For a recent study of self-employment of disadvantaged workers see Steven Balkin (1989).
30. Evans and Jovanovic test and reject the alternative hypothesis that high-asset individuals are high-entrepreneurial ability individuals. For further evidence that small firms face liquidity constraints see Steven Fazzari, R. Glenn Hubbard, and Bruce Petersen (1987). For the 1980–1981 entrants we used 1981 assets.

31. The fact that wage experience is not important is consistent with the comparative advantage model since the coefficient on this term reflects the difference in the returns to wage experience in self-employment versus wage work.
32. The coefficients on wage experience are smaller and less significant when we do not condition on job tenure.
33. We get similar results for the NLS men although the sample sizes are very small.
34. Below, however, we report estimates that show that the Rotter score has a statistically significant negative effect on the probability of being self-employed at a point in time–and therefore having entered and survived up to a point in time. The results reported in the text are qualitatively the same when the Rotter score is included.
35. These kinds of problems are analogous to those found in the recent labor-economics literature on the returns to seniority. See Joseph Altonji and Shakotko (1987), Robert Topel (1986), and Katherine Abraham and Henry Farber (1987) for discussion.
36. The probit results reported below are similar when these individuals are included.
37. The second-order term in experience was not significant. We would not expect the concave relationship found by Brock and Evans (1986), Rees and Shah (1986), and Borjas (1987) because our sample only includes individuals under the age of 40 in 1981.
38. The selection correction was performed using Heckman's (1976) Lambda method using LIMDEP. Evans and Leighton (1987) report statistically significant negative selection but also find little effect on coefficient estimates. The difference in the importance of the selection term appears to be the inclusion of blacks in our earlier work.
39. Evaluated at the mean experience levels for self-employed workers.
40. There is a selection bias here too. Workers who leave self-employment for wage work will tend to be workers who were receiving relatively low wages in self-employment or who receive relatively high offers from wage employers.
41. The fact that wage experience carries a higher return in wage work than in self-employment is consistent with this explanation.
42. Of course it is easy enough to restate the sociologist's disadvantage theory in terms of the economist's comparative advantage model. See Table A for the definition of Variables for the NLS Survey of Young Men.

References

Abraham, Katherine and Farber, Henry, "Job Duration, Seniority, and Earnings," *American Economic Review*, June 1987, 77, 278–297.

Altonji, Joseph and Shakotko, Robert, "Do Wages Rise with Job Seniority?" *Review of Economic Studies*, 1987, 54, 437–60.

Blau, David, "Self-Employment and Self-Selection in Developing Country Labor Markets," *Southern Economic Journal*, February 1986, VOL, 351–363.

Blau, David, "A Time Series Analysis of Self-Employment," *Journal of Political Economy*, June 1987, 95, 445–467.

Balkin, Steven, *Self-Employment for Low Income People*, New York: Praeger Press, 1989.

Becker, Eugene H., "Self-Employed Workers: An Update to 1983," *Monthly Labor Review*, July 1984, 107, 14–18.

Bendick, Mark and Egan, Mary, "Transfer Payment Diversion for Small Business Development: British and French Experience," *Industrial and Labor Relations Review*, July 1987, 40, 132–157.

Birch, David, *The Job Generation Process*, Cambridge, Mass.: Center for the Study of Neighborhood and Regional Change, Massachusetts Institute of Technology, 1979.

Borjas, George, "The Self-Employment of Immigrants," *Journal of Human Resources*, Fall 1986, 21, 485–506.

Borjas, George and Bronars, S., "Self-Employment and Consumer Discrimination," University of California at Santa Barbara, unpublished paper, August 1987.

Brock, William A. and Evans, David S., *The Economics of Small Businesses: Their Role and Regulation in the U.S. Economy*, New York: Holmes and Meier, 1986.

Brock, William A. and Evans, David S., "Small Business Economics," *Small Business Economics: An International Journal*, January 1989, 1, 7–20.

Dollinger, Marc J., "Use of Budner's Intolerance of Ambiguity Measure for Entrepreneurial Research," *Psychological Reports*, May 1983, 53, 1019–1021.

Dunne, Timothy, Roberts, Mark and Samuelson, Larry, "The Impact of Plant Failure on Employment Growth in the U.S. Manufacturing Sector," unpublished paper, Pennsylvania State University, January 1987.

Durand, Douglas and Shea, Dennis, "Entrepreneurial Activity as a Function of Achievement Motivation and Reinforcement Control," *The Journal of Psychology*, June 1974, 88, 57–63.

Evans, David S., *Entrepreneurial Choice and Success*, Washington, D.C.: U.S. Small Business Administration, 1985.

Evans, David S., "Firm Growth, Size, and Age: Estimates for 100 Manufacturing Industries," *Journal of Industrial Economics*, June 1987, 35, 567–582.

Evans, David S., "Tests of Alternative Theories of Firm Growth," *Journal of Political Economy*, August 1987, 95, 657–674.

Evans, David S. and Leighton, Linda, *Self-Employment Selection and Earnings over the Lifecycle*, Washington, D.C.: U.S. Small Business Administration, December 1987.

Evans, David S. and Jovanovic, Boyan, "Estimates of a Model of Entrepreneurial Choice under Liquidity Constraints," *Journal of Political Economy*, August 1989, in press.

Fazzari, Steven, Hubbard, R. Glenn and Petersen, Bruce, "Financing Constraints and Corporate Investment," NBER Working Paper No. 2387, Cambridge, Mass.: NBER, September 1987.

Feller, W., *An Introduction to Probability Theory and Its Applications*, New York: Wiley and Sons, 1968.

Fuchs, Victor, "Self-Employment and Labor-Force Participation of Older Males," *Journal of Human Resources*, Fall 1982, 18, 339–57.

Heckman, James J., "The Common Structure of Statistical Models of Truncation, Sample Selection and Limited Dependent Variables, and a Simple Estimator for Such Models," *Annals of Economic Measurement*, Fall 1976, 22, 261–78.

Johnson, William, "A Theory of Job-Shopping," *Quarterly Journal of Economics*, May 1978, 22, 261–78.

Jovanovic, Boyan, "Job Matching and the Theory of Turnover," *Journal of Political Economy*, October 1979, 87, 972–90.

Jovanovic, Boyan, "The Selection and Evolution of Industry," *Econometrica*, May 1982, 50, 649–70.

Kihlstrom, Richard and Laffont, Jean-Jacques, "A General Equilibrium Theory of Firm Formation Based on Risk-Aversion," *Journal of Political Economy*, August 1979, 87, 719–48.

Knight, Frank, *Risk, Uncertainty, and Profit*, New York: Houghton Mifflin, 1921.

Leonard, Jonathan, "On the Size Distribution of Employment and Establishment," NBER Working Paper No. 1951, 1986.

LeRoy, Stephen and Singell, Larry, D. Jr., "Knight on Risk and Uncertainty," *Journal of Political Economy*, April 1987, 95, 394–407.

Light, Ivan, *Ethnic Enterprise in America: Business and Welfare among Chinese, Japanese, and Blacks*, Berkeley, Ca.: University of California Press, 1972.

Light, Ivan, "Disadvantaged Minorities in Self-Employment," *International Journal of Comparative Sociology*, March 1979, 20, 31–45.

Lucas, Robert E., "On the Size Distribution of Business Firms," *Bell Journal of Economics*, Autumn 1978, 9, 508–23.

McClelland, David C., *The Achieving Society*, Princeton, N.J.: D. Van Nostrant Co., 1964.

McClelland, David C. and Winter, David G., *Motivating Economic Achievement*, New York: The Free Press, 1969.

Miller, Robert, "Job Matching and Occupational Choice," *Journal of Political Economy*, December 1984, 92, 1086–1120.

Min, Pyong Gap, "From White-Collar Occupations to Small Business: Korean Immigrants Occupational Adjustment," *Sociological Quarterly*, Summer 1984, 333–352.

Pakes, Ariel and Ericson Richard, "Empirical Implications of Alternative Models of Firm Dynamics," unpublished paper, Department of Economics, University of Wisconsin, December 1987.

Pandey, Janak and Tewary, N.B., "Locus of Control and Achievement Values of Entrepreneurs," *Journal of Occupational Psychology*, February 1979, 52, 107–111.

Rees, Hedley and Anup Shah, "An Empirical Analysis of Self-Employment in the U.K." *Journal of Applied Econometrics*, Spring 1986, 1, 95–108.

Schere, J., "Tolerance of Ambiguity as a Discriminating Variable between Entrepreneurs and Managers," in *Proceedings*, New York: Academy of Management, 1982.

Schumpeter, Joseph, *Capitalism, Socialism, and Democracy*, 3d. ed., New York: Harper and Row, 1950.

Shapero, Albert, "The Displaced, Uncomfortable Entrepreneur," *Psychology Today*, November 1975, 83–88.

Topel, Robert, "Job Mobility, Search, and Earnings Growth: A Reinterpretation of Human Capital Earnings Functions," in: Ronald Ehrenberg, *Research in Labor Economics*, Greenwich, Ct.: JAI Press, 1986.

Wicker, Alan and King, Jean, "Employment, Ownership, and Survival in Microbusiness: A Study of New Retail and Service Establishments," *Small Business Economics: An International Journal*, 1(2), 1989, 137–152.

Comment on "Some Empirical Aspects of Entrepreneurship" by David S. Evans and Linda S. Leighton

Hideki Yamawaki

This paper has contributed to the growing literature on entry, exit, firm growth, and entrepreneurship by presenting first empirical results on several important aspects of entrepreneurship. The empirical findings of this paper are interesting and important, and the use of the new data set is unique and novel. I have three comments that primarily concern the characteristics of the data used in this paper.

Evans and Leighton claim that the result from the probit analysis of entering self-employment from wage work provides some empirical support for the theoretical model of the individual choice between the self-employment and wage states. In particular, the result presented in Table 6.4 shows that relatively poor wage workers with low wages and a history of instability are more likely to switch to self-employment. However, the result also shows that assets or net worth of the individual have a positive effect on entry, implying that those individuals who have large assets are more likely to switch to self-employment. My question then is whether the effects of those seemingly contrasting two sets of variables are consistent. I interpret this result as evidence showing that the data set represents at least two different groups of individuals, namely poor wage workers and those with relatively large net worth. And I wonder whether the second group of individuals has a different behavioral rule from the first group that is well represented by the theoretical model of the paper.

This conjective is reinforced in Table 6.5 which shows the probit result of being self-employed. The authors find from this table that the probability of being self-employed is higher for individuals who have changed jobs frequently, for individuals with more unemployment experience, for highly educated individuals, and for professionals. Thus, the data again show that poor workers who have changed jobs frequently and have been unemployed, *and* professionals with higher education, have switched to self-employment. If the data represent these two groups of individuals as I conjecture, the entry process will be more complex than the model predicts.

My second comment concerns the extent of family-owned business in the United States. As is well known, family-owned business is a major form of organization particularly in small- and medium-sized firms in Japan and European countries. In family-owned business, employees in the firm, say the son or daughter of the owner, are likely to switch to self-employment after he or she inherits the business from his or her parents. I am curious to know whether this sort of entry activity is included in the sample. If it is included in the sample, I would like to know to what extent it accounts for in the whole entry activity. It appears that this type of self-employment process in family business has again a quite different behavioral pattern from that of those poor workers.

The family business story may provide part of the answer to the somewhat puzzling results that the self-employment entry rate is independent of age and experience at least until the age of 40, and is fairly constant between the age of 25 and 50, while the entry

Z.J. Acs and D.B. Audretsch (eds.), The Economics of Small Firms: A European Challenge. 98–99.

rate is determined by net worth or liquidity of the individual. This result implies that age does not matter but liquidity matters to be self-employed. This is at least consistent with the pattern that the young individual who has been employed in a family business inherits the business and switches to being self-employed.

My final comment is on the dynamics. Since the main thrust of the paper is the static analysis of entry, the question on the dynamics is beyond the scope of the paper. However, one may observe some interesting patterns over the three observation periods, 1980–81, 1978–80, and 1976–78. Across these three periods, the estimated coefficients for some variables are not robust in the probit analysis. In particular, the variables such as Income, Unemployment, and Changes have unstable coefficients in Table 6.5. It seems that the instability of the coefficients across different periods is caused by aggregate macro fluctuations or labor market conditions. One conjecture that emerges from this result is that, after the 1975 and 1980 recessions, the individuals who had been unemployed and suffered lower wages chose to be self-employed in the succeeding 1976–78 and 1980–81 periods. Thus, the coefficient for Unemployment for 1980–81 and 1976–78 is positive, but negative for 1978–80, Similarly, the coefficient for Income for 1980–81 and 1976–78 is negative, but insignificant for 1978–80. This is just a conjecture, but there seems to be some dynamic relations between the decision of individuals to be self-employed and aggregate macro fluctuations.

7. Creative Destruction among Industrial Firms in the United States*

BRUCE A. KIRCHHOFF

I. Introduction

There is a growing interest in dynamic modeling of capitalism as recent experience has demonstrated the importance of innovation in shaping the structure and growth rate of capitalist nations. Economists recognize that innovation by its nature describes a dynamic, evolutionary model of capitalism which is inadequately described by the equilibrium models which have dominated economic thought since the 19th century.

Economic interest in dynamic modeling arises from dissatisfaction with explanative powers of textbook comparative static models derived from equilibrium economic theories (Nelson, 1986) and more recently, from empirical research findings which support the importance of innovation in economic growth. Central among these findings are Birch's finding that small, growing firms create most of the new jobs in the U.S. (Birch, 1988) and the other research which shows that small firms are more efficient and productive innovators than large firms (National Science Board 1976, Gellman Research Associates 1976, Acs and Audretsch 1987). Thus, small, innovative firms take on an importance in economic growth not previously recognized. Together, these results indicate that small firms enter existing markets and grow in the way Schumpeter described in his theory of "creative destruction". The economics of new, small firm formation and growth have become significant in understanding overall economic growth in capitalist economies.

Dynamic modeling actually begins much earlier than the emergence of Birch's work but, as yet, linkage between dynamic modeling with small businesses formation and growth empirical research is not evident. Absence of this linkage persists even though dynamic modeling focuses on Schumpeter's theoretical formulation of capitalism as an evolutionary system driven by innovative new firms, nearly all of which start as small firms.

The purpose of this paper is to compare Schumpeterian creative destruction theory to the current dynamic models of capitalism. This review of dynamic models reveals that new firm entry is a required component if long run market concentration and declining innovation rates are to be avoided. Next, this paper provides an empirical analysis of the extent of new firm entry among the largest industrial firms in the U.S. from 1961 through 1980; this analysis demonstrates that evidence of creative destruction is evident even among the largest industrial firms. The paper concludes by noting the vital importance of new firm formation and growth to the vitality and survival of capitalism.

Z.J. Acs and D.B. Audretsch (eds.), The Economics of Small Firms: A European Challenge. 101–116.

II. Schumpeter's Description of Dynamic Capitalism

Schumpeter (1950, p. 83) provides a dynamic model of capitalism in which innovation by new firms provides a pivotal function he titles "creative destruction". At the same time, however, he creates a dilemma for today's economists by perceiving that creative destruction will decline thereby causing capitalism to evolve into socialism (1950, pp. 121–130). This dilemma is important to dynamic modeling because unless such modeling recognizes the pivotal role of new firm formation and entry in creative destruction, such models will fail to model a "sustainable" capitalism.

Schumpeter disagrees that the classical economic model of continuous movement towards equilibrium describes the real world of capitalism. Instead, Schumpeter sees capitalism as a large number of industrial, or market, structures[1] with each made up of one (monopolist) or a few firms (oligopolists) that dictate the operation of the markets under their control. Competition in such a model does not consist of many firms working through a competitive market to achieve an equilibrium price. Instead, Schumpeter perceived competition to be vested in innovation; firms attempt to achieve competitive advantage by creating innovations which other firms do not possess thereby reaping excess rents (1950, pp. 76–81).

Especially important is the "creative destruction" process; entrepreneurs start new firms using innovations to enter existing oligopolistic markets, accumulate market share, and displace existing firms from the market. This growth and displacement process creates new wealth through innovation but also destroys the existing oligopolistic market structure thereby redistributing wealth and resources from the existing set of firms to another set, i.e., the entrepreneurial new firms. Schumpeter argued that innovation by new firms was "creative destruction", creative in that it increased and redistributed wealth and destructive in that it destroyed oligopolistic market structures. Schumpeter believed that capitalist economies were dominated by oligopolies so without entrepreneurial firm entry, oligopolists would not compete in the classical sense and classical equilibrium models are irrelevant. Innovations and changing market structures, not supply and demand equilibrium, are the driving forces of competition (1950, pp. 121–132).

But, Schumpeter did not believe that creative destruction could continue; he concluded that capitalism would irrevocably evolve towards wealth concentration and eventual socialism. This would not happen because of economies of scale in production as described in classical economics. Instead, Schumpeter argued that large firms had the resources to realize economies of scale in research and development (innovation) and could acquire the wealth necessary to buy entrepreneurs out of society before they form new innovative firms. The decline of entrepreneurial entry would allow large firms to grow and accumulate wealth without the threat of "creative destruction" (1950, pp. 132–138). Eventually, only a few large firms would survive, the rate of innovation would decline and socialism would evolve (1950, pp. 136-156). Creative destruction requires new firm innovation and entry.

Schumpeter provides an intuitively attractive model of capitalism; one simply cannot deny that many markets are dominated by a few large firms. Furthermore, few markets can be depicted as "perfectly competitive" or even characterized as "efficient". The assumptions of classical equilibrium competition simply fall short of describing the real world. Nelson and Winter (1982, p. 114) summarize this cogently. "The image of the competitive process presented by Joseph Schumpeter in his *Capitalism, Socialism, and Democracy* has direct and obvious relevance to the economy of today, a straightforward plausibility that the textbook account of competition cannot match."

III. Recent Dynamic Models

Three dynamic models have been created within the last ten years which purport to derive from Schumpeter's theory of competition.

Nelson and Winter's Model

Best known and undoubtedly the most diligent dynamic model builders are Richard Nelson and Sidney Winter. They have evolved a variety of models over the last fifteen years with each model contributing additional insight into the dynamics of capitalism (Nelson and Winter, 1982b). This paper will focus on their last published model since it represents the evolution of their work and incorporates previous models (Nelson and Winter, 1982a).

Nelson and Winter (1982b), justify their journey into dynamic modeling by identifying the weaknesses of "standard textbook economic theory" of both micro and macro economics. These models depend upon defining an equilibrium state and describe change as a movement from one equilibrium state to another, i.e. comparative static analysis. Such models fail to predict or explain the real economic response to changed market conditions. One such change of obvious major importance is technological change, which is never central to conventional comparative static theories. Nelson and Winter set out to model change with technological innovation as a central concept.

Their most recent model focuses "... on the competitive contest among innovators and imitators, on how various technological and institutional conditions, some of which may be subject to influence by government policy, determine the nature of that contest, and on the innovation and price performance of the industry" (Nelson and Winter, 1982b, p. 114). They develop this model by referencing the Schumpeterian hypotheses that, "... a market structure involving large firms with a considerable degree of market power is the price that society must pay for rapid technological advance" (1982b, p. 114). Nelson and Winter have selected a Schumpeter quotation that reflects Schumpeter's concern about the survival of creative destruction within a capitalist system. In this quotation, Schumpeter seems to express his belief that olgopolists will successfully erradicate entrepreneurial entry thereby maintaining and increasing their market power.

Without discussing the mathematical detail of their model, it is evident that they are not modeling Schumpeter's creative destruction process. Their emphasis is on a system wherein there is no entry of new firms, what they call the "endogeneity of market structure" (1982b, p. 119). They define market structure as the degree of concentration of output or capital, but they assume no exogenously determined new entry into the industry.[2]

They separately simulate the outcome of 101 quarters (25 years) of operations of two industries, one made up of four firms and another consisting of 16 firms. Among their conclusions, they find that R&D may be more efficient in a relatively concentrated industry as compared to a less concentrated industry; firms that do innovative R&D experience a declining market share compared to imitators; and, high technical progress industries mature into more concentrated industry structures than low technical progress industries (1982b, pp. 130–131).

These three conclusions agree with Schumpeter's perceptions of capitalism's gradual evolution into socialism. In other words, although Nelson and Winter do not mention it, by eliminating new, entrepreneurial firm entry, they have modeled Schumpeter's capitalism/socialism evolution hypothesis which Schumpeter states is characterized by increasing concentration with diminishing levels of innovation. One must be cautious in drawing policy implications from Nelson and Winter's work because, by assuming no new firm entries into their structure, they have not modeled Schumpeter's competitive capitalism but instead Schumpeter's capitalism/socialism evolution.

On the other hand, one might agree with Schumpeter's evolution hypothesis and argue that capitalism has evolved as Schumpeter predicted and new firm entry is not a dominant characteristic of capitalist economies today. If true, Nelson and Winter's model adequately represents modern day capitalism. This argument is worthy of further examination, which this paper does in a later section.

Futia's Model

Futia modeled Schumpeterian competition with entry wherein entry was restricted to non-innovators, i.e. imitators. He develops a stochastic model of industry dynamics which excludes R&D investment by firms outside the industry, arguing that there are little useful data on the extent of extra-industry innovative efforts and that earlier work did not measure extra-industry innovation. This exclusion allows him to assume a stochastic within-industry innovation process which has a short run equilibrium. This assumption of no extra-industry R&D allows for entry of imitators (Futia, 1980, p. 678).

Futia further assumes that a pure strategy, Nash equilibrium game applies to the competitive industry situation (1980, pp. 682–683). With this model, he demonstrates that the short-run effect of an increase in innovation rate is an increase in the number of firms in the industry, i.e. a decline in concentration (1980, p. 687). But, in the long run, the effect of increasing the number of firms in the industry upon the rate of innovation is ambiguous. It is not apparent whether the innovation rate will increase or decrease (1980, p. 688). Then, by adding an additional assumption, he is able to demonstrate the textbook result that high innovation rates and high barriers to entry result in high levels of long-run industry concentration (1980, p. 690).

Interestingly, Futia's latter finding agrees with that of Nelson and Winter's model, highly innovative industries tend to move towards increased concentration. But, Futia's model includes imitator entry and achieves high levels of concentration when high barriers to entry exist. In a way, Futia is assuming away any entry because the profits associated with imitator entry are low, and if barriers are high, there is minimal incentive and possibly no entry.

New Entry Models Reinganum

Neither Futia's nor Nelson and Winter's models capture the innovative new firm entry which Schumpeter considered so important to creative destruction in capitalist economies. Several other theorists have developed models of industry structure wherein new innovative entry is a component of the model. The most recent of these is Reinganum's which is built upon the single-innovation model of Lee and Wilde (1980) which is a reformulation of a model due to Loury (1979). This paper reports on Reinganum's (1985) work as the more advanced of the three models which includes her review of conclusions relative to the others.

Reinganum perceives an industry where innovative entry can occur and focuses upon an innovation process that is continuous with all firms "racing" to achieve the next innovation. This is a winner-take-all game where the firms that fail to be the first in achieving the next innovation lose all their invested R&D. This she labels a Schumpeterian game. Furthermore, she assumes that the date of success associated with an investment in R&D is stochastically determined. She takes a dynamic programming approach to solve this game and assumes that a Nash equilibrium exists for the game (Reinganum, 1985, pp. 83–89).

Her first conclusion is that the current incumbent's (the firm owning the most recent innovation) rational decision is to invest less in R&D than each challenger, which makes it likely that it will lose the race for the next innovation. She next concludes that all firms prefer to be the incumbent rather than the challenger (1985, pp. 89–90).

She then creates a comparative static model to examine the effects of this model. She notes that an increase in the number of firms results in an increase in the rate of expenditure by each firm. This means that the pace of innovative activity is faster as the number of challengers increases (1985, p. 94). Thus, where innovative entry is allowed, Reinganum's model suggests that innovation and concentration are negatively correlated.

One explanation of this negative correlation arises from her observation that anticipation of additional future innovations reduces the value of incumbency, tends to enhance the value of being a challenger, and tends to depress investment on the current innovation (1985, p. 97). Thus, anticipation of innovation draws more firms into the race and as more firms enter, the rate of innovation rises.

Summary of Dynamic Models

Reinganum's results suggest that new innovative firm entry is indeed a significant factor in modeling Schumpeterian creative destruction. Exclusion of new firm entry as done by Nelson and Winter and Futia results in models which show market concentration increasing with innovation. This does not agree with Schumpeter's creative destruction hypothesis; these models do, however agree with Schumpeter's capitalism/socialism evolution hypothesis. Thus, policy makers who believe in durable capitalism should not take policy prescriptions from the authors of these models. Reinganum's model shows the importance of new innovative entry and supports Schumpeter's creative destruction hypothesis.

The question that remains unanswered is whether new innovative firm entry as assumed by Reinganum is a factor in contemporary capitalism. As mentioned earlier, new small firm entry and growth has been identified in empirical research. But, can such small firms challenge the entrenched large firm oligopolists in a market structure destroying contest? Popular wisdom, led perhaps by Galbraith's (1971) description of *The New Industrial State* focuses on large firm activity, ignoring small firms. When measured through conventional crossectional statistics, large firms dominate economic activity in the U.S. and large firms make up the significant oligopolistic markets. If creative destruction is occurring among the largest firms, it must begin with the formation of small firms because entrepreneurial firms rarely begin business as large firms. But, by the time entrepreneurial firms are sufficiently successful to be recognized by competitors and economists, they are "cross-sectionally" large thereby contributing to the popular perception that only large firms are of importance. The dynamics of small firms entering and growing to large firms are simply ignored.

IV. Confirmation of New Entry

Considerable empirical evidence exists to demonstrate that new firm entry is an ongoing growth phenomenon within capitalist economies.[3] All such references note that firms are small at the time of formation, most with less than 100 employees, and little has been done to trace whether such small firms ever emerge as major firms in market structure. If none of these new small firms grow into position as a monopolist or oligopolist, then one must ask whether Schumpeter's creative destruction is a meaningful phenomenon in capitalist economies.

Lacking a rigorous mathematical model that is not fraught with the problems encountered by Nelson and Winter, Futia, and Reinganum, I will not attempt to make a rigorous test of creative destruction. If, as Schumpeter suggests, capitalism is dominated by creative destruction, it should not be difficult to find evidence of firm entry and growth. Thus, rather than a rigorous proof, I propose to explore the data for overwhelming evidence.

New Source of Data

Recognizing the limitations of federal statistics,[4] it is necessary to find data that identify individual firms, i.e., "micro data". Such data are available from the Industrial COMPUSTAT file published by Standard and Poors Inc. The COMPUSTAT data file contains detailed financial information and employment data for the "largest and most significant firms" whose stock is traded on the New York, American, and Regional Stock Exchanges. This includes Canadian and foreign headquartered firms. This file contains twenty years of data on each firm.

In addition, COMPUSTAT also provides an "over-the-counter" file which contains the same financial and employment information on those firms whose stock is traded over-the-counter and which command "greatest investor interest" as determined by number of institutional holders, volume traded, price movement, earnings growth, regional and/or economic importance. This file also has twenty years of data.

The COMPUSTAT files are continuously updated as firms release more current data. This is done by adding current year information to the file and dropping the oldest or earliest year from the file. Also, firms which are merged, acquired, or otherwise no longer meet the criteria for inclusion in the files are dropped from the files as their eligibility expires. However, since 1970, COMPUSTAT has placed data on existing firms, including any history of their operations after 1969 into a "research file". This Research Data File is a separate file and contains annual financial and employment data on firms that were in the COMPUSTAT industrial file in 1970 or after but which were deleted from the file sometime after 1970.

These files offer "micro-data" on over 4000 firms in the U.S. for twenty years. Thus, they were selected for use in testing propositions about creative destruction.

Two problems exist with the use of these files. First, they are enterprise files and most enterprises of large size operate in more than one market. Yet, if this analysis can show that there is movement of new firms into the ranks of large industrial corporations while other large firms decline and exit, this result can be used as a surrogate for creative destruction in individual markets. The second problem is that new firms do not enter the files until they are of sufficient age and size to become publicly traded. Rarely do new, small firms achieve this status in the first few years of their life. Thus, we cannot trace small firms from their formation but only from the date they become publicly traded.

An advantage of the files is that movement of firms into and out of the files due to changes in primary industry classification of any one firm is not a component of the change measured here. COMPUSTAT firms are classified by their SIC code in the last year of the file, i.e. 1980, or when they exited the file due to acquisition or termination. This means that some firms which were "industrial" firms in 1970 but became "service" firms (through acquisitions or growth) before 1980 are not listed as industrial firms in the file at all. For this reason, COMPUSTAT's 500 largest industrial firms in 1970 differ from those listed by *Fortune* magazine's 1970 listing. It also means that the degree of change measured by COMPUSTAT is free of SIC industry re-classification as a cause of exit from the file.

V. Propositions to be Tested

Schumpeter's creative destruction hypotheses can be restated in testable form. First, if creative destruction is working, there should not be any evidence of increasing wealth concentration over time among the largest industrial corporations. Wealth concentration is used as a surrogate for market concentration in the absence of clear market boundaries among multi-establishment large firms.

This leads to Proposition 1.

- Proposition 1: Total assets of the largest 500 industrial firms will not increase as a percent of total industrial assets over the 1970-80 time period.

Second, the model of creative destruction will be tested by examining the dynamics of entry and exit from the ranks of the 500 largest industrial firms. If creative destruction is taking place, a major portion of the 500 should change within a ten year period as new firms grow into the 500 and old firms decline.[5]

- Proposition 2: At least a fifth of the firms within the ranks of the 500 largest industrial firms will exit from the group and be replaced by other firms.

Furthermore, if firms grow and enter as hypothesized by Schumpeter, then their growth rate must eventually decline as they become vulnerable to entrepreneurial entry. If this cycle of growth and decline exits it should be possible to measure a difference in growth between new, innovative firms as they cnter the 500 and after they become members of the 500.

- Proposition 3: The rate of growth of entering firms will be greater than their growth after entry has been achieved.

Several assumptions have been imposed upon these propositions. First, a period of ten years has been selected arbitrarily for testing these propositions. There are twenty years of data so I simply divided by two; there is no other standard by which the appropriate time can be selected. Second, the time period 1961 through 1980 has been selected for study since this was the time period when (a) most economists believed that large firms dominated economic activity; and (b) merger/acquisition activity had not begun substantial expansion as under the reduced anti-trust enforcement policies of the Reagan Administration. Third, proposition 2 assumes that one fifth of the firms is a "major" measure of inter-class movement. This is "intuitively" appealing in the absence of any statistical test for this dynamic analysis. After all, a fifth means that 100 firms exit and 100 firms enter, a total change of 200 firms. And, fourth, I have assumed that the 500 largest firms are an appropriate group for analysis of industrial concentration. Some might choose fewer, say 100. Others might choose more. But *Fortune* magazine has made "500" magic so I chose 500.

Assembly of the Project Data File

Since the objective of this research is to analyze 20 years of data on the largest corporations in the U.S., it was necessary to combine the three COMPUSTAT files (Industrial, Over-the-counter, and Research) into a single Project File. This was done by reading the COMPUSTAT data files (tapes) and writing the firms along with the necessary financial data on each into a new file thereby combining the three files into a single Project File. This resulting Project File includes all firms that exist or existed in the COMPUSTAT files from 1970 through 1980. And, the file also contains up to 10 years of historical data on all firms that existed in 1970.

Modifying the Project File

COMPUSTAT includes several types of firms which complicate attaining the objectives of this research project. First, it includes all firms publicly traded in the U.S., regardless of country within which they are headquartered. Foreign firms had to be deleted from the file. A list of foreign headquartered firms was obtained from COMPUSTAT and these firms were identified and coded as foreign firms within the Project File. Hereafter, all analysis on the Project File excludes these foreign firms.

Second, the file contains some non-industrial firms; COMPUSTAT includes some banking, utility, life insurance, railroad, and other firms in its files. Since all firms are coded with Standard Industrial Classification (SIC) number, the SIC numbers were used to sort out the non-industrial firms. Only those firms with SIC numbers between 1000 and 1500 (mining) or 2000 and 3999 (manufacturing) are included in the file. However, COMPUSTAT only records the SIC number once per firm; thus, the SIC number assigned to each firm is the number that identifies the firm's major business activity in 1980 for firms in the Industrial and Over-the-Counter files and the last year of inclusion for those firms in the Research file. In other words, any firm that changed its major business activity during the 1961–1980 period will be identified with its most recent business activity. For example, if a chemical manufacturing firm would acquire a large steel manufacturing business in 1979, the chemical firm's business activity might change into a steel manufacturing SIC number. Thus, all previous years of chemical manufacturing activity would appear as steel manufacturing in the COMPUSTAT file. This is not important unless a major service of financial firm acquires an industrial firm (or vice versa) and suddenly has its entire business activity reclassified into (or out of) the industrial sector. Throughout the analysis that follows, I routinely listed out the firms that enter and exit the industrial categories to identify such unusual activity. I made repeated references to the *Fortune* 500 listings to assist in this routine checking. There are differences but, if anything, since the firms are listed with only one SIC number, the analysis reported here understates the movement into and out of the Fortune 500.[6]

As noted earlier, since the COMPUSTAT Research file was not begun until 1970, firms that were in the COMPUSTAT file prior to 1970 but lost their eligibility prior to 1970 are not in the Project File at all. Thus, a firm that was in the file from 1960 through 1969 but was acquired by another firm in 1969 (i.e. the firm's stock was no longer traded publicly) was dropped from the COMPUSTAT file in 1969, was not put in the Research file and is lost from the COMPUSTAT files and the Project File forever.

The Project File is a rectangular file consisting of 21 records per firm; 3216 firms have basic descriptive data such as name, industry identification, and Cusip number on the first record. Then there are twenty records, each of which is the annual financial data for one year from 1961 to 1980. Some firms have one or more blank records; blank records mean that these firms were not in the COMPUSTAT file for one or more of the years between 1961 and 1980. For example, some firms do not enter the COMPUSTAT file until after 1961 and others exit the file before 1980. However, there are no missing records; for every year that a firm existed and was eligible for inclusion in COMPUSTAT, it has a record in the file. Furthermore, COMPUSTAT clearly labels when and why a firm exits its file. Thus, once a firm enters the COMPUSTAT files, it remains there unless its record of activity is clearly labeled as to when and why it departs.

Data Analysis

The Project File is set up as a SPSSX System file so that it can be read and manipulated with SPSSX instructions. The first step taken was to rank order all firms separately in each year. For example, the value for total assets in 1961 was read for all firms in 1961. Then, the firms were ranked from greatest total assets in 1961 down to the smallest total assets in 1961. Firms that had zero assets (no record for that year) were assigned the largest rank numbers in alphabetical order. The ranks were recorded as an additional variable for all firms in that year. This procedure was repeated for each year, 1962 through 1980. As a result, all firms have one additional variable added to each of their 20 annual financial records; this additional variable defines the size rank of each firm for each year.

By accessing the rank variable in each year, it is possible to identify the largest and smallest firms in the file for that year. Thus, each firm's movement up and down the ranking is traceable year by year. But, since the file does not contain all firms for the 1961–1969 period, it is not possible to know the exact ranking of all industrial firms during that nine year period. However, beginning in 1970, all significant industrial firms are in the file because COMPUSTAT's Research file has been included in the Project File. Thus, for 1970 through 1980, the exact rankings of all firms can be reliably determined.

VI. Testing the Propositions

Three propositions have been offered for testing. These will be examined in the order they were proposed.

Testing Proposition 1

Proposition 1 states that concentration as measured in total assets of the largest 500 industrial corporations will not increase as a percent of all corporate assets over the ten years studied. To test this proposition, using traditional comparative static methods, the 500 largest firms in 1970 were selected and their assets were summed to a total in 1970. Then, the 500 largest firms in 1980 were selected and their assets were summed. Total assets for all corporations were then obtained from the Internal Revenue Service's annual reports of corporation income tax returns. The results of this comparison are shown in the top half of Table 7.1.

The 500 largest firms in 1980 (determined by assets) held 16.55 percent of all corporate assets, a slight, probably not significant, decline from the 16.82 percent held by the 500 largest firms in 1970. In other words, on a comparative static basis, concentration of industrial assets is unchanged from 1970 to 1980.

Table 7.1. Relative size of the 500 largest industrial corporations based on assets (000 omitted).

	1970	1980
TOTAL ASSETS ALL CORPORATIONS	2,635,000	7,617,000
Total assets 500 largest industrial corporations	443,163	1,260,709
Number of firms	500	400
500 as percent of total	16.82%	16.55%
TOTAL ASSETS OF ALL INDUSTRIAL CORPORATIONS	636,886	1,836,420
500 as percent of total	69.58%	68.65%

Since there has been a shift in business activity from manufacturing into services, it is possible that the above results are influenced by the disproportionate growth of assets within service businesses. To examine this, the assets of the 500 largest firms were compared to total assets for all industrial firms as reported by the Internal Revenue Service. This is shown in the bottom half of Table 7.1. Note that in 1970, the 500 had 69.6 percent of all industrial firm assets; their share dropped slightly to 68.7 percent by 1980. Although no evidence of increased concentration is apparent in either comparison, there is also no strong evidence of declining concentration of assets.

Other Observations

Only 414 of 1970s 500 largest firms were still among the 500 largest in 1980. One must be curious about what happened to the 86 firms that disappeared from the list and how this might affect asset concentration. Eighty six firms either were acquired or had significant decline in assets relative to the other firms during this ten year period. Firms that were acquired and did or did not suffer declining assets are still among 1980s 500 largest firm simply because acquisition necessarily results in one firm equal in size to the sum of the previous two firms, i.e., larger than the largest of the two. Thus, some of the change in composition is due to the acquisition of the missing firms by other firms which are among 1980s 500 unless there has been a significant decline in assets among both the acquired and acquiring firms.

At the same time, acquisition activity among the largest firms provides a bias towards increased asset concentration when measured by a rank ordering of the 500 largest firms. When 1970-500 firms are acquired by other firms already in the 1970-500, there will be a net increase in the size of the surviving firm; this will also delete the acquired firm from the 500 list. Such deletion makes room for a new firm to enter the ranks of the 500. The combined total assets of two 1970-500 firms (now one because of acquisition) plus the addition of a new firm to the 500 would lead, ceritus paribus, to increased total assets and asset concentration. And, if a 500 firm is acquired by a firm that is not already within the 500, a larger firm emerges within the 500 even though a firm is not removed from the 500. Either way, acquisition activity within or among the 500 tends to increase total assets of the 500.

But, increased assets concentration does not occur as shown in Table 1. One must conclude that other factors are eroding the asset base of the 500 largest even as the size of firms effectively increases due to acquisition/merger activity among them.

Testing Proposition 2

Proposition 2 states: "At least a fifth of the firms within the ranks of the 500 largest industrial firms will exit from the group and be replaced by other firms." As noted, from 1970 to 1980, 86 of the 1970-500 left the ranks of the 500. This is not one fifth but 17 percent. Furthermore, although the Project File does not allow determination of the 500 largest firms in 1961, analysis does indicate than no more than 418 of 1970-500's firms were among the largest 500 in 1961.[7] Thus, at least 16 percent of the 1961-500 were displaced from the 1970-500.

Sixteen to seventeen percent displacement every ten years is a rather respectable amount given the widespread perception that market concentration changes little over time. And, historically, economic growth has been largely attributed to large firms.

Furthermore, 41 of 1970s 500 firms did not exist in the 1961 COMPUSTAT file, i.e., they were not publicly traded. Some of these 41 are well known new, high growth firms of the 1960s – Digital Equipment Company, Control Data Corporation and Iowa Beef Processors, Inc. are good examples. A few were large, closely held firms which chose to go public – Occidental Petroleum is a good example. But, the question of greatest importance is whether the new entries had high growth rates that declined when they matured.

Testing Proposition 3

Proposition 3 states that the rate of growth of entry firms will be greater during entry than after entry is accomplished. The first step in this analysis was to calculate the annual change in assets for each firm in each year. This annual change was then computed into a percent change by dividing the year to year change by the assets in the first year. For example, for each firm, change in assets for 1962 was calculated by subtracting total assets in 1961 from total assets in 1962. This was then converted into a percent by dividing by 1961s assets and multiplying by 100.

Several other factors affect annual changes in assets measured in this manner. Overall economic activity, average industrial growth and even international trade activity can affect whole industries. Thus, annual changes in assets are adjusted to average industrial activity measures to remove the effect of such exogenous variables. I chose to standardize the annual changes computed above to the mean of the annual changes for the entire list of industrial firms in the Project File. This was done by computing a mean and standard deviation of annual percent change in assets for all industrial firms in the Project File. Annual asset change for each firm was then standardized with the mean and standard deviation of all industrial firms.

Table 7.2 shows the normalized percent change in assets for the 82 firms that entered the 500 between 1961 and 1970. Note that between 1962 and 1970, these firms averaged above the growth of all industrial firms. But, beginning in 1971 and every year thereafter, these firms showed an average growth below all industrial firms. Clearly, something significant happened to these firms in 1970 that changed their growth rate for the next ten years.

How did the growth of the 418 firms differ from before 1970 to after 1970? The year by year results are also shown in Table 2. On average, these 418 firms had growth

Table 7.2. Normalized growth in assets of 500 largest industrial firms.

	Average annual percent change in assets	
Year	82 new firms Percent	418 existing firms Percent
1961–1980	0.12%	–0.13%
1961–1970	0.42%	–0.13%
1971–1980	–0.15%	–0.13%

rates slightly below the average for all industrial firms in every year recorded. The average across all 19 years is – 0.13 percent. The average for 1962 through 1970 is also – 0.13 percent, as is the average for 1971–1980. And this average growth rate is very similar to that for the 82 entry firms after 1970.

These results clearly show variation in rates of growth based on size of firm, a rejection of Gibrat's law. As such they agree with Evans' (1987) findings which also reject Gibrat's law.

Disaggregating the Components of Growth

It is possible to 'crudely' disaggregate the year changes in assets of each firm by use of the notations in the COMPUSTAT file. Footnotes label each year of financial data for each firm with a specific note if the firm's financial data has been affected by a merger/acquisition or a dissolution during the year. The absence of a footnote means that the year was unaffected by such activity thereby indicating that change in asset value is due to internal growth. Thus, annual changes in assets can be allocated to years when merger/acquisition or dissolution activity occurred.

Allocating each year's change in assets to internal growth, merger/acquisition growth and dissolution growth yields the results shown in Table 7.3. For the 82 firms the period of 1962 through 1970 shows 62.3 percent of their growth due to merger/acquisition and 37.3 percent due to internal growth. This merger/acquisition activity is far above the average for all industrial companies while the internal growth is slightly above. However, beginning in 1971, the extent of merger/acquisition declines significantly so as to provide only 32.6 percent of their growth while internal growth provides 65.3 percent. At the same time, their merger/acquisition growth remains above the average for all industrial firms (.21%) while their internal growth (– .12%) falls below.

These 82 firms show a merger/acquisition growth and internal growth about equal to that of the 418 firms during the 1971–1980 time period as shown in Table 7.4. Note that for the 418 firms over 19 years, 71.9 percent of total growth in assets was due to internal growth, 27.4 percent was due to merger/acquisition growth, and 7 percent was due to dissolution growth. On a normalized basis, internal growth was below that of all industrial firms while merger/acquisition growth was above. This is true for the entire 19 years.

This analysis suggests a negative correlation between size of firm and asset growth rates due at least in part to different rates of merger/acquisition growth. Consistently over the 19 years studied, the 418 firms show growth rates below the average for all industrial firms. The 82 new entry firms show higher growth rates during the time before they enter the 500; but once they become large, their growth rates taper off to be similar to that of the 418 firms. This agrees with Schumpeter's hypothesized creative destruction process. Firms enter, grow and become large; once large, their growth rate declines as they experience entry of new entrepreneurial competitors.

However, since the decline in growth rates of the 82 firms is most pronounced in their merger/acquisition growth, it is possible that U.S. antitrust enforcement policy serves as a brake on this growth opportunity. Once firms become large enough to draw attention to their merger/acquisition activity, further activity may be discouraged by antitrust enforcement. Antitrust policy is not a component of Schumpeterian theory but perhaps it is necessary to insure creative destruction.

Table 7.3. Twenty years of assets growth for the 82 firms in 1970s but not in 1960s 500 largest firms.

	Annual Dollar change in assets – (000,000 omitted)							
	Total growth		*Merger/acquisition*		*Internal growth*		*Discontinuances*	
Year	Dollars	Percent	Dollars	Percent	Dollars	Percent	Dollars	Percent
1962–1980	66,599.7	100.0%	26,504.0	39.8%	38,947.4	58.5%	1,148.2	1.7%
1962–1970	16,204.1	100.0%	10,094.2	62.3%	6,041.7	37.3%	68.2	0.4%
1971–1980	50,395.6	100.0%	16,409.8	32.6%	32,905.7	65.3%	1,080.0	2.1%

Table 7.4. Twenty years of assets growth for the 500 largest firms as measured by total assets in 1970.

	Annual Dollar change in assets – (000,000 omitted)							
	Total growth		*Merger/acquisition*		*Internal growth*		*Discontinuances*	
Year	Dollars	Percent	Dollars	Percent	Dollars	Percent	Dollars	Percent
1962–1980	1,051,845.7	100.0%	288,588.4	27.4%	755,896.9	71.9%	7,360.4	0.7%
1962–1970	256,477.2	100.0%	75,258.8	29.3%	180,946.5	70.6%	272.2	0.1%
1971–1980	795,368.5	100.0%	213,329.6	26.8%	574,950.4	72.3%	7,088.2	0.9%

On the other hand, the evidence on the 82 entering firms suggests that merger/acquisition activity is a common mechanism, perhaps a necessity, to achieving membership within the 500 largest firms. In 1967, 47 percent (33 of 70) of the firms reported merger/acquisition activity. And, the number of firms involved in such activity each year suggests that most, perhaps all, firms are involved. This may be a Schumpeterian innovative response to market structures. Perhaps firms find their innovative effect on markets enhanced by the acquisition of other new innovative firms in the same or ancillary industries, e.g. backward integration of manufacturing or raw materials supply, and/or forward integration into distribution. Further research is required to understand the role of merger/acquisition activity in the growth of new, innovative firms.

VII. Conclusions

Current dynamic models of capitalism confirm Schumpeter's belief that capitalist economies require new firm entry and growth to assure that innovation does not become the mechanism of increased concentration of industrial activity. Creative destruction is necessary to maintain capitalism.

Entry and growth of new small firms may well be indicative of creative destruction in contemporary capitalism. Analysis of a data set created from the COMPUSTAT data file reveals that evidence of creative destruction appears among the 500 largest industrial firms from 1961 through 1980. Specifically, there is no evidence of increasing concentration, there is a firm displacement rate of 16 to 17 percent every ten years, and new entries grow very fast until they become large at which time their growth rate declines significantly.

On the other hand, small business research on new entry, even when combined with this paper's analysis of evidence of creative destruction among large firms, does not adequately define the dynamics of entrepreneurial entry and growth in the U.S. economy for policy purposes. We know that small firm formation is an active part of U.S. capitalism, and that entry and exit are important phenomena among the 500 largest industrial firms. But we do not know what happens in between these two measured limits. For example, the results reported here show clear evidence that merger/acquisition activity is an important component of new firm growth from small to very large but what about those that do not grow into the 500 largest? Is it because they shun merger/acquisition? Or do their markets develop entrepreneurial entry so early that their growth is stunned by competition? Additional empirical research is required to understand this.

There is no doubt that one policy emphasis emerges from the existing models and empirical research reviewed herein – *new firm entry is a necessary requirement of sustainable capitalism.* Just as Schumpeter hypothesized almost 50 years ago, new firm formation, entry and growth is an active component of capitalism's competitive process. The focus of economic policy should be upon the formation, entry and growth processes.

The concept of 'barriers to entry' takes on new importance in a Schumpeterian economy. Deregulation, for example, removes regulatory constraints from entry and results in the formation of new firms. Examples abound in the U.S. trucking and airline industries which were deregulated in the late 1970s.

Industrial policy, on the other hand, formulated by a "panel of experts" drawn from government and industry is not likely to reduce barriers to entry. Professional planners see an orderly industrial structure as preferable to a disorderly structure. New entry is disorderly and will no doubt be discouraged under such industrial planning.

Antitrust policy may be an important component of sustainable capitalism. The data analysis reported here shows a large amount of merger/acquisition activity contributing to rapid growth of new firms. But, among the largest industrial firms, the rate of merger/acquisition activity is much lower, thereby contributing to the negative correlation between growth rate and size of firm. Decline in growth rate of the largest firms is a component of Schumpeter's creative destruction theory. Yet the emergence of merger/acquisition activity as a major component of this decline suggests that antitrust policy enforcement may be a cause. This raises the question of whether such decline would occur without antitrust? Perhaps the experience of the 1980s will eventually answer this question since antitrust policy was weakly enforced during the Reagan years.

Notes

* The research reported herein was funded with grants received from the University of Nebraska at Omaha Faculty Research Committee. The author is especially indebted to Robert E. McAuliffe, Jr., Babson College, for his assistance, and Roy Thurik, Erasmus Universiteit Rotterdam and Zoltan J. Acs, WZB, for their helpful comments on earlier drafts.

1. Schumpeter used the term "industrial structure" to denote what in current economics is referred to as "market structure". Hereafter, the term market structure will be used in this paper. He also used "monopolist" to designate any market where concentration of suppliers made the market imperfect. Current terminology uses monopolist for a single supplier and oligopolist for the general case of two or more suppliers.
2. This assumption also appears in their earlier work (1978, p. 527).
3. See for example: Acs and Audretsch (1989), Armington (1986), Kirchhoff and Phillips (1988), and Storey and Jones (1987).

4. U.S. Government published statistics cannot be used to measure firm movement from formation to dominance within a specific market because individual firm information is not available from such sources. Thus another source of data is required.
5. This and the third proposition are contrary to Gibrat's law since they assume firm rate of growth is negatively correlated with firm size. Some empirical research on Gibrat's law shows such correlation. See: Contini and Revelli, 1989.
6. Early in the analysis, I discovered that the 500 largest COMPUSTAT firms are different than the *Fortune* 500. A firm by firm check of the differences revealed satisfactory reasons for these differences. For example, the most common difference is that *Fortune* includes "co-operatives" in its list, but since co-operatives are not publicly traded, they are not in COMPUSTAT. And some firms that were industrial in 1970 are service firms in 1980.
7. Since the COMPUSTAT file contains all firms that existed in 1970 and thereafter, firms that discontinued prior to 1970 are not recorded in the file. Therefore, it is not possible to compute with accuracy the rank order of all firms in 1961; some firms may be missing. But, the rank order of all firms in the file was computed and only 418 firms appear among the 500 largest in the 1961 project file.

References

Acs, Zoltan and Audretsch, David, 1986, "Innovation, Market Structure, and Firm Size," *Review of Economics and Statistics*, 69, 567–515.

Acs, Zoltan and Audretsch, David, 1989, "Small Firm Entry in U.S. Manufacturing," *Economica*, 56, 255–266.

Armington, Catherine, 1986, "Entry and Exit of Firms: An International Comparison." An unpublished paper prepared for the U.K. Conference on Job Formation and Economic Growth, London, England.

Birch, David, 1988, *Job Creation in America*, New York, Wiley and Sons.

Contini, B., and Revelli, R., 1989, "The Relationship Between Firm Growth and Labor Demand," this volume, pp. 53–60.

Evans, David S., 1985, "The Relationship Between Firm Size, Growth and Age: U.S. Manufacturing 1976–82," unpublished research report for the U.S. Small Business Administration, Washington, D.C.

Futia, Carl A., 1980, "Schumpeterian Competition," *Quarterly Journal of Economics*, 94(4), 675–95.

Galbraith, John Kenneth, 1971, *The New Industrial State*, New York: New American Library.

Gellman Research Associates, Inc., 1976, *Indicators of International Trends in Technological Innovation*. An unpublished report prepared for the National Science Foundation.

Kirchhoff, Bruce A. and Phillips, Bruce D., 1988, "The Effect of Firm Formation and Growth on Job Creation in the United States," *Journal of Business Venturing*, 3(4), 261–272.

Lee, Tom and Wilde, Louis L., 1980, "Market Structure and Innovation: A Reformulation," *The Quarterly Journal of Economics*, XCIV, pp. 429–436.

Loury, Glenn C., 1979, "Market Structure and Innovation," *The Quarterly Journal of Economics*, XCIII, 395–410.

National Science Board, 1977, *Science Indicators, 1976, Report of the National Science Board*, Washington, D.C.: U.S. Government Printing Office.

Nelson, Richard R. and Winter, Sidney G., 1978, "Forces Generating and Limiting Concentration Under Schumpeterian Competition," *The Bell Journal of Economics*, 9, 524–548.

Nelson, Richard R., 1986, "Evolutionary Modeling of Economic Change," as published in: *New Developments in the Analysis of Market Structure*, eds. Joseph E. Stiglits and G. Frank Mathewson, Cambridge, MA: The MIT Press, 450–474.

Nelson, Richard R. and Winter, Sidney G., 1982a, "The Schumpeterian Tradeoff Revisited," *The American Economic Review* 72(1), 114–132.

Nelson, Richard R. and Winter, Sidney G., 1982b, *An Evolutionary Theory of Economic Change*, Cambridge; MA: Harvard University Press.

Reinganum, Jennifer F., 1985, "Innovation and Industry Evolution," *The Quarterly Journal of Economics*, C, 81–99.

Schumpeter, Joseph A., 1950, *Capitalism, Socialism and Democracy*, New York: Harper and Row.

Storey, David and Jones, A.M., 1987, "New Firm Formation – A Labour Market Approach to Industrial Entry, "*Scottish Journal of Political Economy*, 34(1), 37–51.

Comment on "Creative Destruction among Industrial Firms in the United States" by Bruce A. Kirchhoff

Roy Thurik

Professor Kirchhoff's paper deals with two questions: first, is there a process of increasing concentration of wealth among firms; and second, is there a significant shift of wealth of one group of firms to another? Theoretical hints concerning this question can be found in the work of Schumpeter, who presents the concept of creative destruction. Professor Kirchhoff studies these two questions using American data material of the top 500 firms of the period 1960–1980. He mainly uses COMPUSTAT-data on individual firms. A huge amount of data handling preceded his analysis.

I would like to organize my discussion of Professor Kirchhoff's paper by asking several questions. Both questions put forward by Professor Kirchhoff are more or less equivalent to the question whether there is a relation between growth and size of firms. If there is a positive relation, concentration is expected to increase and wealth is not expected to shift from one group of firms to the other.

If there is a negative relation between growth and size, no a priori propositions on the development of concentration and wealth distribution can be made.

So I wonder why Professor Kirchhoff doesn't use his data material on the micro level and create a panel data set of about 500 or less (that depends on the set-up) firms for a period of about 20 years and study the relation between growth and size. Clearly, there are a lot of factors affecting growth but using panel data econometric one can correct for omitted or neglected variables in the sense that unbiased results may obtain. Furthermore, systematic industry or time effects may be detected. No information is lost using micro instead of aggregate variables. Some work has been done in this area: Birch (1979), Javonovic (1982) and Hommes and Van Leeuwen (1987) find or predict a negative relation, Singh and Whittington (1975) a positive relation, and Hall (1987) warns that the relation may depend upon the size of the firms: she predicts a negative relation for smaller and a positive relation for large firms. I refer to the contribution of Contini and Revelli in this issue, and particularly to the discussion of Evans for a survey of studies in the area of the relation between growth and size.

My second question has to do with the findings of Hall and is partly due to my limited knowledge of Schumpeter's work. If Schumpeter talks about creative destruction, doesn't he rather mean a process which takes place at the lower and of the size distribution of firms, where there is a continuous fight for entry and survival, in which new ideas of products, markets etc. play a crucial role. I think, there is enough difference in size even among the top 500 so that the influence of size on the relation between growth and size can be studied.

My third question relates to the variables chosen: value of assets is chosen, but what is the reason behind this choice? Would sales, value added, employment, etc. be reasonable alternatives and are the results expected to be different?

My fourth remark relates to the way propositions 2 and 3 are defined. First, "at least a fifth of the top 500 firms will be replaced". This is a very speculative proposition

Z.J. Acs and D.B. Audretsch (eds.), The Economics of Small Firms: A European Challenge. 117–118.

without a frame of reference. I would propose to study the phenomenon of exit using differences in growth rates of individual firms, which could be clearly defined once the relation between growth and size is established. Second, "the growth rate of entry firms exceeds that of existing top 500 firms". I wonder whether this is a tautology? Shouldn't the question be whether firms are entering the top 500 because of their own growth or because of the decline of others. And if they enter because of growth, you have an implicit answer to proposition 1.

Are the results dependent upon the choice of the "magic" 500 or would they be different in case of the top 100?

My sixth question is one based upon sheer curiosity: are there firms which climb the charts without mergers and acquisitions?

I realize that most of my questions are of the "why didn't you do something else"-type, which are very difficult to answer in economics. Unlike physics, chemistry, etc, economics lacks central paradigmata, which are broadly accepted, so that these questions may very well lead to abstract discussions.

Nevertheless, Professor Kirchhoff's answer may lead to a connection between his and Contini and Revelli's (1990) paper and this connection again may lead to a better understanding of growth and concentration processes.

References

Birch, D.L., 1979, *The job generation process*, Cambridge, MIT Press.

Contini, Bruno and Revelli, Riccardo, 1990, 'The Relationship Between Firm Growth and Labor Demand," this volume, pp. 53–60.

Hall, B.H., 1987, *The relationship between firm size and firm growth in the U.S. manufacturing sector*, Journal of Industrial Economics, 35. June 583–606.

Javanovic, B., 1982, Selection and the evolution of industry, *Econometrica* 50, 649–670.

Singh, A. and Whittington, G., 1975, The size and growth of firms, *Review of economic studies*, 52, January, 15–26.

Hommes, G.H. and van Leeuwen, G., *The relation between firm growth and firm size in Dutch manufacturing in the period 1972–1984*, Central Bureau of Statistics, Voorburg, Netherlands. Mimeo in Dutch.

8. Investment and Capital Diversity in the Small Enterprise*

WILLIAM C. DUNKELBERG and ARNOLD C. COOPER

I. Introduction

Competitive markets are driven by the decisions of business owners and consumers' responses to those decisions. The efficiency outcomes of these decisions in response to known prices and technologies have been extensively examined. However, in a world in which future prices and technologies are unknown and are revealed incompletely in a time-dependent process through "market experimentation", the role of the "firm" or the owner of the firm is supplanted by the role of the "entrepreneur". Entrepreneurs are economic agents that must make resource allocation decisions in the context of risk, uncertainty and imperfect information, and market imperfections not faced by the business automatons of textbook markets (Herbert and Link, 1989).

In this context, issues of human capital and less-than-perfect capital markets take on important roles in the making of resource allocation decisions. With constantly changing technologies, business owners must become entrepreneurs, taking risks, resolving uncertainty (there is no such thing as "no decision"), and adjusting to ("capitalizing on") the opportunities revealed in evolving economic disequilibria. This paper presents extensive information regarding the nature of the human and financial capital inputs into the creation and development of new businesses. The data presented reveal both the diversity and the magnitude of the inputs and to what degree certain inputs can be substituted in the "entrepreneurial process".

Capital adequacy is often cited as a major factor affecting the success of a new enterprise. A shortfall of equity capital can affect a new firm's prospects for success in a number of ways. Insufficient funding may precipitate a need for borrowing, difficult for a new venture, time-consuming, and often insufficient to meet the firm's needs. Borrowing strains the operation of the firm with interest payments which reduce cash flow. This increases the vulnerability of the firm to adverse changes in the economic environment. Suppliers of equity capital must wait for a return on monies invested, but banks do not wait for interest payments. Inadequate capital may influence the firm's initial decisions and policies in ways that diminish prospects for success. A poorly financed venture may be forced to start with a poor location, inadequate professional advice, or insufficient inventory. Finally, capital provides a "cushion" for mistakes and the time needed to adjust policies in response to feedback from the marketplace. Sufficient capital gives the firm time to learn from its mistakes and become stronger and better managed.

Less emphasized, but perhaps more important is the human capital available to the firm. "Managerial inadequacy" is often cited as the major reason for failure. Judicious use of financial capital requires smart management. Poor decisions about strategy or operations can squander large amounts of capital, risking the financial base of the

Z.J. Acs and D.B. Audretsch (eds.), The Economics of Small Firms: A European Challenge. 119–134.

company. If the founder devotes too little time to the business, then others must be hired to do the work or provide the management. This raises costs and may rob the firm of the enthusiasm and the entrepreneurial skills needed for success. It is difficult to hire individuals with the same motivations as the entrepreneur. If critical skills are absent, they must either be hired (a drain on capital) or the firm must face the financial implications of poor decisions or actions that result from the lack of these skills. This skill shortage increases the initial amount of capital needed by the firm and high-lights the importance of education in the entrepreneurial process.

There exists a potential substitution between these two factor inputs – human and financial capital. Good management will stretch scarce capital, while sufficient capital can cover management mistakes. It is the objective of this paper to document the magnitude and diversity of these capital inputs and to seek evidence of their substitutability or complementarity.

This paper analyzes data collected from 2994 new firms (under 18 months old) over a four year period beginning with 1985. The data were generated from the membership files of the National Federation of Independent Business (NFIB), a national organization of over 500,000 firms. The membership is quite representative of the population of small firms in U.S.[1]

II. Financial Capital Inputs

This section deals with the size of the initial capital investment and the relative importance of different sources of capital. Some simple examinations of the relationship between financial capital inputs and human capital inputs are presented in bivariate tables.

Much of the popular writing on the financing of new firms has focused on high-technology ventures, a minor fraction of new business starts in the U.S. The NFIB studies, however, cover a broad cross-section of new small businesses. Because of the risky nature of new ventures, most of the financial capital, not surprisingly, is supplied by the entrepreneur, the one with the "inside" information about the venture, most knowledgeable about the company to be formed and the biggest "winner" should the firm succeed. The median firm started with about $ 20,000 in financial capital (Table 8.1). A surprising 32% of all firms started business with financial investments of less than $ 10,000, making clearer the importance of the financial value of the human capital inputs discussed in the next section.

Firms were asked to estimate the actual percentage of their initial funds that came from each source. The results are shown in Table 8.2. For all firms, 72% used personal savings to start their firms, with this source providing an average of 56% of all funds when used. Forty-four percent secured funding from a financial institution, which provided an average of 65% of total capital invested when used. Only 1% used venture capital firms for any capital, and 3% obtained funding from a government sponsored program (such as the SBA). Although exciting and well-covered by the news media, venture financing affects very few new firms started in the U.S.

A 1979 NFIB study of 890 founders of new firms (regardless of how many years the firm had been in business) indicated that for 40 percent of small firms, only one major

Table 8.1. Financial capital inputs.

Amount	Percent of firms
Under $ 5,000	18%
$ 5,000–9,999	14%
$ 10,000–19,999	16%
$ 20,000–49,999	25%
$ 50,000–99,999	15%
$ 100,000–249,000	8%
$ 250,000 or more	2%
No answer	2%
All firms	100%

Question: What was the total amount of capital invested in your business by the time you made your first sale?

Table 8.2. Percent of capital from each source (average for owners using this source).

	Percent of total capital	Percent using this source
Personal savings	56%	72%
Friends, relatives	47%	28%
Individual investors	56%	8%
Lending institution	65%	44%
Venture capital	58%	1%
Suppliers	31%	6%
Former owners	51%	8%
Government	61%	3%
Other	65%	2%

source of financial capital was used (Table 8.3). Twenty-three percent utilized personal savings as their only source of funds, and 73 percent overall used personal savings as their only or a major source of capital. Institutional sources of funds (banks, other savings institutions, insurance companies) provided capital in some form (loans or investments) in 46 percent of the cases. Friends and relatives provided capital in 21 percent and "outside individual investors" provided capital in five percent of the starts. Professional venture capitalists and the government together helped to fund only about one percent of this broad cross-section of small businesses. These data did suggest that institutional sources of capital are becoming more frequent participants in the establishment of new firms (see Dunkelberg and Cooper,1981, for a more detailed discussion of financing entry).

III. Human Capital Inputs

Although "financial" issues seem to get the most attention, the "human capital" inputs to a firm are probably the most important, both as the major determinant of success or failure and of future growth. Financial capital can "cover" mistakes made by management, but few new firms have sufficient amounts of financial capital to negate the impact

Table 8.3. Source of capital for small business starts.[a]

One major capital source	Percent
Personal savings	23
Friends; relatives	2
Institutional lenders	7
Individual investors	3
Venture capital	*
Government	1
Other source	4
	40%
Two major sources[b]	
Savings and:	
institutionallender	23
friends; relatives	11
individual investors	2
Friends; relatives and:	
personal savings	3
institutional lender	2
Lender and:	
personalsavings	11
friends; relatives	3
	55%
Other pattern; no answer	5%
Total	100%

[a] Firms that were started by their owners, not purchased or inherited.
[b] Most important source listed first.
* Less than .5%.
Source: *How small businesses begin*, National Federation of Independent Business, 1979. Figures are based on 890 founders of firms, part of a sample of 1805 businesses that included firms regardless of when it was started.

of weak management. Indeed, the high rates of return attributed to years of schooling (Thurow) in part reflect the improved quality of decision-making associated with educational experience.

There are two important dimensions to human capital inputs – quantity and quality. Although these two dimensions possess some substitutability, working extra hours cannot easily make up for a deficiency in specific skills (such as accounting or legal advice) needed by the firm (unless extra hours are spent acquiring these skills). Human capital inputs occur in many forms:

1. Hours worked by the business owner.
2. Hours worked by unpaid family members.
3. Support provided to the entrepreneur by members of the immediate family working outside of the business.

4. The hours and skills contributed by partners.
5. Education, training and experience possessed by the entrepreneur.
6. Employees.
7. Independent contractors.

In some instances (e.g. employees, independent contractors), needed human capital inputs are paid for explicitly by the firm. In other instances (e.g. partners, owner, owner's family), the firm trades ownership (claims to future income) for needed inputs. The next several sections of the paper present basic data on the quantity, quality and diversity of the human capital inputs present in the entrepreneurial process, factor inputs not widely analyzed in the literature to date.

Hours worked

Entrepreneurs are known for their hard work and tenacity. Starting a new firm requires tremendous amounts of time for most entrepreneurs. Normal business activities require substantial time, particularly if funds are limited for hiring other employees. In addition, substantial time must be devoted to the special problems associated with starting a firm (or taking over an existing one), such as identifying and becoming acquainted with suppliers, lenders, and potential customers. And, as noted earlier, extra hours may be required to accomplish tasks that the entrepreneur is not properly trained to do. Time is also required to "undo" mistakes made by the entrepreneur.

Table 8.4 shows the distribution of hours worked by entrepreneurs in their first year or two of business. It is notable that only 8% worked less than 40 hours per week, while 52% worked 60 hours or more. Clearly, most entrepreneurs make an enormous investment of personal time and talents in their business endeavors. Sixty hours per week for fifty weeks produces an annual investment of 3,000 hours. Valued at the wage foregone by the entrepreneur, this represents a substantial sum invested in the company.

Table 8.4. Hours worked.

Hours	Percent
No ans	2%
Under 40	8%
40–49	15%
50–59	23%
60–69	28%
70 or more	24%
Total	100%

Question: About how many hours per week do you work for the firm?

Unpaid Family Members

An additional source of human capital is the family of the entrepreneur. Family members can work for "no pay" in the company, providing raw hours of time as well as specific skills (if available). Such actions reduce the "break-even" point of operation on a cash flow basis and reduce the amount of capital needed by the firm. New ventures financed by established corporations will have relatively more financial capital, but less commitment on the part of employees to put in the long hours invested by entrepreneurs and their family members.

In 1982, 25% of a cross-section sample of 2030 firms reported using unpaid family workers. Of those, 20% received 40 hours or more per week of service from unpaid workers. The 1985 NFIB study presented an interesting contrast to those figures, with 48% of the firms (all in their first 18 months of business) reporting unpaid family workers in the firm (Table 8.5). It appears that unpaid workers are most likely to be found in newer companies. Thirty-five percent of these new firms received 40 hours or more per week of effort from these unpaid family members.

The contributions of these unpaid workers are substantial. For example, 20 hours per week for 50 weeks valued at $ 5 per hour is worth $ 5,000 to the firm in reduced cash outlays. Thirty-two percent of the firms started with less than $ 10,000 in initial financial capital, making a $ 5,000 saving in cash outlays a very substantial contribution to the capital of the firm.

Table 8.5. Total unpaid family hours worked per week.

Percent with unpaid family workers:	48%
Number of workers	Percent of firms
None	51%
One	25
Two	15
Three or more	9
All firms	100%
Hours per week	Percent of firms
1–9	25%
10–19	19
20–39	21
40–49	9
50 or more	26%
All firms	100%

Question: How many unpaid family members are there that work for the firm? (Include children that are paid some type of small payment.) How many hours per week in total do these unpaid family members work?

Working Family Members

Instead of working in the newly established firm (with or without pay), family members can work outside the firm where the value of their contribution is presumably higher since the individuals would choose to work in the new firm were that not the case. These family workers supplement the cash flow available, permitting the entrepreneur to work more hours at a lower wage. These funds can directly support the entrepreneur's family or be made available to the business.

Fifty percent of all firms reported family members with outside jobs (Table 8.6). Most of these were held by a spouse working full-time (70%) or part-time (22%). Once again, valued at market, these contributions represent substantial investments in the firm.

Table 8.6. Outside employment by family members.

	Percentage of firms
Spouse	
Full-time	35%
Part-time	11%
Other family member	4%
No family member with an outside job	34%
No spouse	13%
No answer	3%
All firms	100%

Question: In your first year of business, did/does your spouse or other adult family member residing with you have a job other than working for your firm?

Partnerships

One way to acquire certain specialized human capital inputs is through forming partnerships. Partners increase the number of raw hours of time available to the company, and usually represent a diversity of human capital. It is not unusual for partnerships to be formed based on complementary human capital skills. Partners provide psychological support and provide a "sounding board" for ideas regarding the firm's growth and development. Partners also reduce the dependence of the firm's success on the health or commitment of a single individual, making the company less risky from a lender's or investor's point of view.

The total amount of initial financial capital invested appears to increase with the number of partners (Table 8.7). The presence of one partner has little impact on the amount of initial capital invested.[2] However, with two or more partners, the percentage with more than $ 100,000 in initial capital more than doubles. Thus, the addition of one

Table 8.7. Number of full-time partners and initial capital investment.

Number of partners		No ans	Capital invested in the firm at start: Under $ 10K	$ 10–$ 49K	$ 50–$ 99K	100K +
No answer	1%	5%	31%	39%	10%	15%
None	70%	1%	33%	41%	15%	10%
One	20%	2%	31%	42%	15%	10%
Two +	9%	2%	24%	38%	15%	21%
All	100%					

Question: What was the total amount of capital invested in your business by the time you made your first sale?

partner may represent additional human capital rather than additional financial capital for the firm. Any substitution of partner skills for financial capital could be outweighed by other factors, such as a larger initial size for the new venture and the improved opportunity to raise capital from all sources associated with the presence of partners.

Firms with partners may start on a larger scale and more easily attract financial capital. The percentage of initial capital coming from outside sources (particularly unrelated individual investors) rises with the number of partners (Table 8.8). Initial employment also rises with the number of partners (Table 8.9), indicating that firms with partners begin on a larger scale. Thus, it may well be true that for a given level of initial employment or sales, partners reduce (are substitutes for) financial capital requirements. However, these firms appear to take advantage of available capital to start at a higher level of endeavor, or perhaps at a better location, or with more inventory etc. than would otherwise be possible.

Table 8.8. Source of capital and the number of full-time partners.

	Average percent of funds invested came from:								
No. of partners	Pers. saving	Friend relat.	Indiv. invest	Fin. inst.	Vent cap.	Trade credit	Former owner	Gov't	Other
No answer	37	9	7	19	2	1	3	4	2
None	44	12	2	30	*	2	4	2	1
One	34	16	7	27	1	2	5	2	3
Two +	31	14	14	29	2	3	3	1	2
All	40	13	4	29	1	2	4	2	1

Question: Of the above amount, please indicate approximately what percentage of the funds invested in your firm came from (the following sources):

Table 8.9. Initial employment by number of full-time partners.

	Total employment					
No. of partners	1	2	3	4	5	6 +
No answer	23%	8%	23%	5%	8%	33%
None	17	29	19	12	7	17
One	9	25	19	12	10	25
Two +	7	14	15	14	11	39

(The entrepreneur and all partners are counted in the number of employees at the firm.)

Education, Training, Experience

The quality of human capital is another important dimension of the capital inputs to the firm. Given the natural abilities of the entrepreneur, skills can be enhanced in a number of ways:

1. Formal education.
2. Specialized training.
3. On-the-job experience
4. Experience in a variety of jobs or positions.

The distributions of these various dimensions of training are shown in Table 8.10. These entrepreneurs were better educated than the general public, with 26 percent having at least a bachelor's degree and 59 percent reporting some college education. Sixty-three percent reported taking at least one business course and 43 percent took three or more. Fifty-seven percent had some type of technical or vocational training. Twenty-five percent received some type of certification from a formal program. Forty percent took a specialized course related to their business undertaking, enhancing either their general business abilities, or providing skills specific to the business they engaged in.

"On-the-job" training represents another important dimension of human capital that bears directly on the success of the venture. Twenty-six percent of the owners reported receiving some type of "on-the-job" training (Table 8.10).

Experience from prior employment provided both industry knowledge and management experience (Table 8.11). Thirty-five percent reported having five or more jobs prior to the founding of their current venture. A number of the entrepreneurs (26 percent) had already owned or started a firm. Sixty-five percent had general supervisory experience and 11 percent had supervised other managers. The sum total of this diverse experience represents a substantial capital value to the new venture, easily translating into dollars saved, thereby contributing to the capital base. This experience also reduces the probability of management error which wastes scarce financial capital.

Table 8.10. Education and skills of entrepreneurs.

Formal education	Pct.	Number of business classes	Pct.	Technical training	Pct.
Didn't finish HS	7%	None	38%	Any...[a]	57%
High school	33	1 or 2	23	License[b]	25
Some college	26	3 to 6	18	Vocational[c]	9
Associates degree	8	7+	19	Military[d]	7
College, BA, BS	16	No ans	2	General[e]	19
Advanced work	9[a]			Specific[f]	24
No answer	1			On-site:	
	——		——	General[g]	10
All firms	100%		100%	Specific[h]	16

[a] Five percent reported MBA or equivalent degrees.
[b] Structured program: certificate, degree, license.
[c] High-school vocational courses.
[d] Military vocational training.
[e] Occasional courses with general applicability.
[f] Occasional courses with firm-specific spplicability.
[g] On-site employer training – general applicability.
[h] On-site employer training – specific applicability.

Table 8.11. Job-related experience.

Prior number of jobs	Pct.	Similarity to prior business	Pct.	Management experience	Pct.
One	10%	Same product	31%	Supervised:	
Two	16	Similar product	11%	No one	19%
Three	20			Workers	39
Four	15	Same customer	29%	Managers	11
Five	12	Similar customer	12%	Own business	26
Six	8			Other	1
Seven	4			No answer	1
Eight	3				
Nine +	8				100%
None or No ans.	4				
Total	100%				

Another dimension of the value of experience and the transfer of skills and knowledge from the "incubator" to the new firm is the very high percentage of entrepreneurs that dealt with the same products and customers as in their prior jobs. This clearly reduces the cost of establishing relationships with customers and suppliers, and should lead to more soundly-based decisions about business strategy. Thirty-one percent of the new firms studied reported selling the same product or service, and 29 percent were dealing with the same customers as the firm which the entrepreneur left. An additional 11 percent dealt with similar products and 12% with similar customers. Since many entrepreneurs entered businesses similar to those that they left, this "specific" human capital was not lost (Table 8.11).

One way to acquire some of the specific human capital needed is through a franchise arrangement. Twenty-seven percent of the firms reported some percentage of "franchise" sales, with 10% reporting 75 percent or more of their volume as franchise sales. Entry into a franchise business usually requires substantial financial capital outlays. In exchange, the entrepreneur receives name recognition, advertising services and generally receives pre-structured management and financial packages that the entrepreneur may not have the skills or the financial support to develop.

In total, it is clear that the value of the human capital investments in the firm far exceeds the value of financial capital in the typical new firm. Financial capital is most commonly provided by the entrepreneur and is in very short supply, leading the entrepreneur to attempt to substitute human capital for financial capital where possible. The nature and magnitude of these substitutions are examined in the next section.

IV. Multivariate Findings

Several types of potential substitutions are obvious: (1) entrepreneurs with relatively more human capital will need less financial capital to start a firm (of a given size and type); (2) entrepreneurs will substitute on several different "margins" to get the human capital needed by the firm (e.g. entrepreneurs with less formal education will more often engage in specialized training, are more likely to work with the same products and/or customers as in their previous jobs etc.); (3) less well educated entrepreneurs will work more hours to supplement their human capital deficiencies.

With a large number of possible "inputs" in the investment process, identifying the substitutions and complementarities potentially present poses a complex empirical task. One possible approach would apply a production function framework to the inputs, with firm sales as a measure of output. For new firms in the short run, however, the presence of substantial "excess capacity" may present a problem. Initially, even a very small number of employees or small facilities may be very large relative to realized sales. Just how fast sales will rise to economically justify the commitment of space, inventory, staff and other such inputs will depend on the strength of the local economy. The presence of these exogenous differences in "output" for given sets of inputs will confound the estimation of substitution parameters.

An alternative approach would compare each firm's level of capital input for each factor with a "typical" level for all new firms starting under identical circumstances (the same industry, initial employment etc.). In a crude sense, specification of the industry (e.g. professional services) and a level of employment identifies a production function (for the industry) and the level of operation on that production function for the firm (employment). For each input, I_i^*, an expected or "typical" level can be estimated for a firm in a given industry with a given level of initial employment and other conditioning variables. The difference between the "typical" value, I_i^*, and the actual value, Ii, provides a measure of the deficiency or surplus of the ith capital input relative to typical firms with the same production function. Once these deviations are estimated, they may be used to determine substitution and complementarity among the various capital inputs. For example, firms that have invested more financial capital than comparable firms may invest fewer hours of work in the enterprise (i.e. be observed to work fewer hours). Such an approach represents an adaption of the partial adjustment model discussed in Nadiri and Rosen and developed in more detail in Dunkelberg and Stafford.

The capital inputs identified for analysis include:

FC: Financial Capital
ED: Education (quality of human capital)
HW: Hours Worked (quantity of human capital)
SE: Spouse Employment
UH: Unpaid Family Hours

Conditioning variables for each capital input were the following:
- Industry
- Initial Employment
- Age
- Race
- Sex
- Number of Partners
- Percent of Business Owned
- Whether Purchased or Started the Firm

Each of the five capital inputs was regressed on the conditioning variable set (Table 8.12). These regressions were used to construct the expected or typical levels of input for each firm (denoted with an *) based on the specific values of the conditioning variables. The expected value of each variable was then subtracted from the actual value for each firm, creating a measure of the excess or deficiency for each capital input.[3] These differences represent the deficiency or surplus (relative to "typical" firms) for each capital input. These "disequilibria" were then incorporated in the following equation to measure complementarity and substitutability with total hours worked:

$$(HW - HW^*) = f(FC - FC^*, ED - ED^*, SE - SE^*, UH - UH^*)$$

Most of the variables are "dummy variables". In the case of Industry classification, the category "Retail" was omitted from the regression. In all other cases, the omitted groups are clear. As a consequence, the coefficients on the dummy variables should be interpreted as deviations from the omitted category. Mean values for each variable are shown in the Appendix.

Although the first set of regressions is used only to create the "expected" or "typical" levels of the various capital inputs, there are some interesting results worth pointing out. Retailers and farmers clearly put in the longest hours. Every industry coefficient in Column 3 is negative save that for farmers. The use of unpaid family members in manufacturing, construction, and the financial and professional services is substantially lower than in other industries (Column 5). Retailing (the omitted category) apparently lends itself to this practice. Minority entrepreneurs were better educated on average,

Table 8.12. Regression results.

Predictor	[1] Years of education	[2] Financial capital	[3] Owner hours	[4] Dummy: Spouse employment	[5] Unpaid hours
Industry:					
Const.	−.19	−.77*	−2.37*	−0.1	−10.88*
Mfg.	.39*	−.06	−.86	−0.8	−10.96*
Transp.	−.20	−.22	−3.49	−0.6	−7.36
Whole.	.00	−.09	−4.05*	.01	6.02
Retail	–	–	–	–	–
Agric.	.87*	.53*	1.27	−.27*	−2.48
Financial	.81*	−.80*	−2.87*	−.02	−13.84*
Services	−.25*	−.55*	−2.00*	.02	−6.70*
Profess.	2.32*	−.03*	−7.78*	−.00	−13.84*
Age	−.002	.013*	−.072*	.004*	.182*
% Own	−.087*	−.210*	−.357	−.002	1.770*
Race	.326*	−.050*	3.246*	−.035	5.160
Sex	−.175*	−.452*	−5.812*	.492*	.174
Started	−.120*	−.587*	.034	.051	2.867
# Partners	−.012	.014	.189*	−.003	−.119
Employment	.010*	.044*	.081*	−.008*	.649*
Constant	4.626	4.219	61.487	.588	1.848
R2	.12	.15	.03	.06	.03

* Significant at the ten percent level, two tail test.

while female owners had less education. Initial employment was positively associated with the level of the financial investment, the level of formal education, the use of unpaid family members and the number of owner hours worked. Only the probability of the spouse having an outside job was negatively associated with initial employment size. Those starting their firms from scratch had less financial and human capital than those purchasing a firm and they relied much more heavily on unpaid family help.

Table 8.13 presents the relationship between deviations from expected levels for each of the capital inputs and all other "disequilibria". These results indicate that the higher the quality of human capital invested (measured by education), the fewer hours the entrepreneur worked per week. Each year of education reduced average weekly hours by.8 hours. This reduction is attributable to both efficiencies in decision-making due to education as well as the presence of specialized training (see Schultz 1975, 1980) for a more elaborate discussion of the value of general skills for dealing with "disequilibria").

Not surprisingly, unpaid hours supplied by other family members also resulted in a reduction of time invested by the entrepreneur. Twenty hours of unpaid help reduced average owner hours by. 4 hours per week.

Having a spouse employed outside the business also reduced the hours worked by the owner. Although the coefficient failed significance at the 10% level, its magnitude indicated a reduction of .6 hours per week on average for the owner when the spouse was employed outside the firm. A working spouse and high levels of human capital quality were associated with lower usage of unpaid family members.

Larger amounts of financial capital were associated with additional rather than fewer hours worked by the owner (the proportion of the firm owned by the entrepreneur was accounted for in the first stage of estimation). Thus, it does not appear that in practice larger financial capital investments are a substitute for human capital inputs. The initial capital investment is represented by categorical data (coded 1 to 9) rather than actual dollar amounts. Thus the coefficient cannot produce "per dollar" estimates of the impact of additional capital on hours worked, but the variable is a sufficiently robust instrument to capture the impact of additional capital on hours invested. The larger the investment relative to expected levels, the more hours the owner worked. Financial capital appears to be a "complement" to hours invested. Perhaps with more at stake, the owner puts more effort into the enterprise. Or, investments beyond typical or expected levels may occur for firms that require larger than typical (given the crude industry definitions used) inputs of hours which the conditioning variables were unable to capture.

Table 8.13. Coefficients for disequilibrium estimation.

Predictor	Dependent variable HW–HW*	FC–FC*	ED–ED*	SE–SE*	UH–UH*
HW–HW*	–	.008*	–.007*	–.001	–.148*
FC–FC*	1.052*	–	.143*	–.017	.445
ED–ED*	–.798*	.128*	–	.011	–1.057*
SE–SE*	–.574	–.053	.040	–	–4.191*
UH–UH*	–.022*	.000	–.001*	–.002*	–
R2	.02	.03	.02	.01	.01

* Significant at the ten percent level, two tail test.

V. Conclusion

The findings presented here make it clear that human capital inputs or "investments" in new firms are substantial, the equivalent of tens of thousands of dollars of financial capital. These "investments" come from the entrepreneur, from their families and from partners (and presumably their families).

The data indicate that many small firms start with very little financial capital. Entrepreneurs provide the bulk of the financial capital as well as the human capital invested in their firms.

There are many ways to "capitalize" a new firm, involving various combinations of human and financial capital. The importance of these human capital inputs has been neglected even though many observers attribute the high failure rate among small firms to deficiencies in human capital (e.g. poor management). Since management ultimately determines how effectively financial capital is employed in the enterprise, more attention should be given to this dimension of entrepreneurial activity.

The results from this study indicate that there is a quantity-quality substitution for hours worked by the entrepreneur. Well educated owners worked fewer hours per week than similarly situated less educated counterparts. Less clear was the impact of a spouse working outside the business. The results suggest that a working spouse reduces hours worked by the entrepreneur (rather than making it possible for the entrepreneur to work longer hours). Financial capital and human capital investments were observed to be "complements", as hours worked were higher for firms with higher than typical financial capital investments. Thus, in spite of the complexity of arrangements and the diversity of capital inputs, logical patterns of capital substitution appear to be present in the new enterprise formation.

The relationship of these inputs, their quantity, quality, and how well they are managed, to the success of the firm is the subject of current research by the authors. This issue is complex, requiring a definition of "success" based not only on sales, employment growth, or profitability, but also the complex objectives of the "entrepreneur." Equally interesting is the impact of the "external environment." The best capitalized and managed firm can fail in the face of adverse economic developments in the market served by these smaller firms, typically geographically small in size and thus "risker" in terms of potential variance in demand. This work promises to provide substantial insight into the probable successfulness of government policies designed to promote small firm growth and development.

Appendix

Predictor	Mean	Standard deviation
Industry		
Construction	.07	.26
Manufacturing	.08	.27
Transportation	.02	.15
Wholesale	.04	.20
Retail	.47	omitted
Agriculture	.02	.14
Financial	.05	.22
Services	.19	.39
Professional	.06	.23
Age	36.15	9.78
% of company owned	4.31	1.17
Race(1-0)	.06	.24
Sex (1-0)	.22	.41
Started (1-0)	.64	.48
Initial employment[a]	4.69	7.37
Number of partners	6.68	3.53
Hours worked per week	56.51	18.09
Years of education[b]	4.19	1.80
Family unpaid hours	16.15	46.68
Spouse employed (1-0)	.80	.92
Capital invested[c]	3.40	1.74
Number of firms: 2915		

[a] Includes the owner.

[b] Included in categorical form:

1. Less than high school
2. Some high school
3. High school graduate
4. Some college education
5. Associates degree
6. Bachelors degree
7. Some graduate school
8. MBA degree
9. Other advanced degree

[c] Included in categorical form:

1. Under $ 5,000
2. $ 5,000–$ 9,999
3. $ 10,000–$ 19,999
4. $ 20,000–$ 49,999
5. $ 50,000–$ 99,999
6. $ 100,000–$ 249,999
7. $ 250,000–$ 499,999
8. $ 500,000 or more

Notes

* The authors wish to thank the NFIB Foundation, the National Federation of Independent Business, and American Express Travel-Related Services for invaluable support of this project.

1. See "Report on the Representativeness of the National Federation of Independent Business Sample of Small Firms in the United States" by William C. Dunkelberg and Jonathan A. Scott, 1979, for the Small Business Administration.
2. It is possible that respondents included their spouses as partners in this question. To the extent that this occurred, we would observe no increase in financial capital reported where single partners are in fact spouses.
3. These "disequilibria" are simply the residuals from the five equations estimated to determine "typical" levels of each capital input.

References

Cooper, Arnold C. and Dunkelberg, William C., 1986, "Entrepreneurship and Paths to Business Ownership", *Strategic Management Journal*, 7, 1, 53–68.

Cooper, Arnold C., Dunkelberg, William C. and Woo, Carolyn, "Entrepreneurship and the Initial Size of Firms", forthcoming, *Journal of Business Venturing.*

Cooper, Arnold C., Dunkelberg, William C. and Woo, Carolyn, "Entrepreneurs' Perceived Chances for Success", forthcoming, *Journal of Business Venturing.*

Dennis, William J., Dunkelberg, William C. and Van Hulle, Jeffrey S., 1988, *Small Business and Banks: The United States*, The NFIB Foundation, Washington D.C.

Cooper, Arnold C. and Dunkelberg, William C., 1981, "A New Look at Business Entry: The Experience of 1805 Entrepreneurs", in *Frontiers of Entrepreneurship Research*, Boston, Babson College, 1–20.

Dennis, William J., Dunkelberg, William C. and Scott, Jonathan A., 1980, *How Small Businesses Begin*, National Federation of Independent Business, San Mateo, California.

Dunkelberg, William C. and Scott, Jonathan A., 1984, "Rural vs. Urban Bank Performance: An Analysis of Market Competition for Small Business Loans", *Journal of Bank Research*, 15, 167–178.

Dunkelberg, William C. and Stafford, Frank P., 1971, "Debt in the Consumer Portfolio", *The American Economic Review*, 61, 598–613.

Herbert, Robert F. and Link, Albert N., 1989, "In Search of the Meaning of Entrepreneurship", *Small Business Economics*, 1, 39–50.

Nadiri, Ishag M. and Rosen, Sherwin, 1967, "Interrelated Factor Demand Functions", *The American Economic Review*, 57, 457–491.

Oi, Walter Y., 1962, "Labor as a Quasi-Fixed Factor", *Journal of Political Economy*, 70, 538–555.

Schultz, Theodore W., 1980, "Investment in Entrepreneurial Ability", *Scandinavian Journal of Economics*, 82, 437–448.

Schultz, Theodore W., 1975, "The Value of the Ability to Deal with Disequilibria", *The Journal of Economic Literature*, 13, 827–846.

Shull, Bernard, 1981,"Studies of Small Business Financing", Inter-Agency Task Force on Small Business Finance, Washington, D.C.

Thurow, Lester, 1970, *Investment in Human Capital*, Wadsworth Series in Labor Economics and Industrial Relations.

Comment on "Investment and Capital Diversity in the Small Enterprise" by William C. Dunkelberg and Arnold C. Cooper

David B. Audretsch

Thomas Kuhn (1962) observed that very little scientific research is done on questions such as "Does God exist?" This is not because these are unimportant questions to humans. Rather, because research efforts devoted towards such worldly questions typically fail to produce satisfying answers, they usually give way to more mundane research topics, which may be inherently less central to human existence, but at least can provide some value added to the stock of human knowledge. And this has, I think, been the reason for the paucity of research efforts devoted towards understanding entrepreneurship in the economics literature. This scarcity of research should not be misinterpreted as a lack of interest in the subject. In fact, most economists would probably agree that entrepreneurship is *the* most important question in industrial economics and perhaps even in the study of market economies. Rather, this lack of research on the subject reflects the difficulty of the subject and the lack of data or ability to say anything intelligent and not a lack of interest.

Thus, Professors Dunkelberg and Cooper make an important contribution in their paper by analyzing one of the few and best data sources available on entrepreneurs – the rich data base assembled by the National Federation of Independent Business (NFIB). Most economists in Europe have not yet heard of the NFIB data bases; I think that within several years this situation will drastically change. Because these data are able to provide us with information about entrepreneurs and the process by which firms enter, survive, and exit, that has previously been unavailable.

The fundamental question Professors Dunkelberg and Cooper raise in the paper is, "To what extent are human capital inputs substitutable for financial capital inputs?" They conclude that there is no empirical support that they are, in fact, substitutable inputs. In view of a rich literature in financial economics, and particularly in the financing of small business, this is a substantial conclusion, with significant policy implications. While there have been numerous calls for the public subsidization of new firm formations (Greenbaum et al., 1984) to compensate for credit rationing and other difficulties experienced by small firms in obtaining funds in the public equity market, the findings of Dunkelberg and Cooper's paper suggest that (1) the labor input, and especially the quality of that labor input or human capital is by far the most decisive input for small firms, and (2) the bulk of the financial capital input is typically supplied by the entrepreneur himself or herself. This would cast at least some doubt on the necessity of public programs subsidizing, at least financially, small firms.

In fact, these results using the NFIB data are reinforced in a recent study by Reid and Jacobsen (1988) based on a survey of new small firms established in Scotland. Like Dunkelberg and Cooper, Reid and Jacobsen find that obtaining external funds does not play a major role in the establishment of new firms. Similarly, the important role contributed by both family members and partners in new firms which Dunkelberg and Cooper find is consistent with similar results reported by Wicker and King (1989) based on a large sample of retail and service firms.

Z.J. Acs and D.B. Audretsch (eds.), The Economics of Small Firms: A European Challenge. 135–137.

Future research using the NFIB data may strengthen the validity of Dunkelberg and Cooper's conclusions by applying a slightly different methodology. In particular, they conclude that "Larger amounts of financial capital were associated with *additional* rather than fewer hours worked by the owner... Thus, it does not appear that in practice larger financial capital investments are a substitute for human capital inputs." However, this inference is based upon the relationship between deviations of each firm's level of financial capital input from an empirically derived "expected" level of input and the deviation in the firm's level of human capital and the "expected" level of input. Since the level of output of the firm is not controlled for in the estimating equations, firms with greater output might be expected to utilize greater levels of not only financial and human capital inputs, but, in fact, all types of inputs. That is, the positive association between the financial and human capital inputs inferred by Dunkelberg and Cooper may reflect that both are inputs in a production function

(1) $$Q = f(K, L, i)$$

where K represents financial capital inputs, L represents human capital inputs, and i represents all other inputs required to produce output, Q. Figure 8.1 demonstrates how an entrepreneur may choose to increase Q by increasing either L, K, or both, holding i constant, or $i = \bar{i}$. In fact, as Lucas (1978) points out, entrepreneurs with greater endowments of human capital may be able to manage or utilize a greater amount of physical and therefore financial capital. Thus, a statistical analysis that does not hold constant the level of output of the entrepreneurial firm is likely to capture the tendency of firms with greater output levels to utilize both greater amounts of labor inputs, including human capital, and financial capital inputs. Only by holding the firm level of output in a production function model can the extent of substitutability between factor inputs be correctly inferred. Thus, Professors Dunkelberg and Cooper may be measuring a shift from A to B^1 rather than to B.

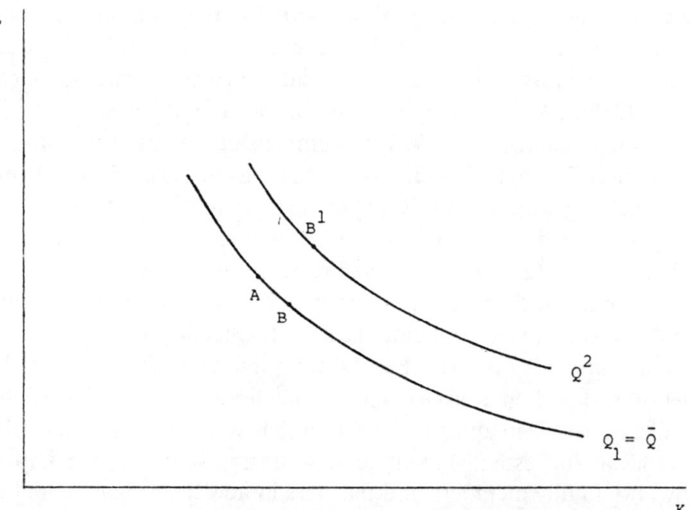

Fig. 8.1. Substitutability between human- and physical capital.

An important step in their research agenda could be to estimate the production function

(2) $$Q = \alpha \mathrm{HW}^{\beta_1} \mathrm{FC}^{\beta_2} \mathrm{ED}^{\beta_3} \mathrm{SE}^{\beta_4} \mathrm{UH}^{\beta_5} \mu$$

which can be made tractible through

(3) $$\ln Q = \ln \alpha + \beta_1 \ln \mathrm{HW} + \beta_2 \ln \mathrm{FC} + \beta_3 \ln \mathrm{ED} + \beta_4 \ln \mathrm{SE} + \beta_5 \ln \mathrm{UH}$$

In fact, estimating industry or at least sector-specific production functions could reveal that the substitutability between financial capital and human capital inputs is sector- or industry-specific.

Finally, I would like to emphasize that the papers by David Evans (1990) and Dunkelberg and Cooper are the pioneering studies on the empirical analysis of entrepreneurship. There are several intriguing discrepancies as well as some consistencies in the findings in these papers. For example, while Evans finds that the hazard rate of entering into self-employment is independent of age, at least for the first twenty years of employment, Dunkelberg and Cooper's results reveal that age is a substitute for hours worked, suggesting that age is an important input for entrepreneurship. Similarly Evans finds that the returns to education are somewhat higher in self-employment than for wage work, which Dunkelberg and Cooper conclude that the possession of a college degree is no substitute for the number of hours worked by the entrepreneur. However, the results in Evans' study suggest that human capital accumulated through wage work is less valuable in self-employment than in wage work, which is consistent with Dunkelberg and Cooper's finding that management experience or specialized training are not substitutes for hours worked. While the inconsistencies are not surprizing, given that Evans' data sample is restricted to white young men and Dunkelberg and Cooper's is not, they do suggest the importance and promise of future research on the questions and determinants of entrepreneurship.

References

Evans, David S. and Leighton, Linda S., 1990, "Some Empirical Aspects of Entrepreneurship", this volume, pp. 79–97.

Greenbaum, Stuart I., Kanatas, George and Deshmukh, Sudhakar D., 1984, "Credit Rationing and Small Business Financing", in Paul M. Horvitz and R. Richardson Pettit (eds.), *Small Business Finance: Problems in the Financing of Small Businesses*, Greenwich, CT: JAI Press.

Kuhn, Thomas S., 1962, *The Structure of Scientific Revolutions*, Chicago, IL: The University of Chicago Press.

Lucas, Robert E., Jr., 1978, "On the Size Distribution of Business Firms", *Bell Journal of Economics*, 9, 508–523.

Reid, Gavin C. and Jacobsen, Lowell R., 1988, *The Small Entrepreneurial Firm*, Aberdeen: Aberdeen University Press.

Wicker, Alan W. and King, Jeanne C., 1989, "Employment, Ownership and Survival in Microbusiness: A Study of New Retail and Service Establishments", *Small Business Economics*, 1 (2), 137–152.

C. TECHNOLOGY, STRATEGY, AND FLEXIBILITY

9. Flexibility, Plant Size and Industrial Restructuring*

ZOLTAN J. ACS, DAVID B. AUDRETSCH and BO CARLSSON

I. Introduction

Throughout the twentieth century there has been a general movement towards larger minimal optimum plant size. Sands (1961) found that average physical output per plant increased between 1904 and 1947 by about 3 percent per annum. Blair (1972) found the share of industry sales originating in the eight largest plants declined from 1947 to 1958 thereby concluding that this seeming reversal of past trends was attributable to fundamental changes in the direction of technological advances away from centralizing innovations and towards decentralizing technologies.[1] Shepherd (1982) found a substantial increase in the scope of competition within the four-digit Standard Industrial Classification (SIC) industries between 1958 and 1980 confirming the trend identified by Blair. Also, Carlsson (1989a) showed that both firm and plant size decreased between 1972 and 1982 in manufacturing as a whole and especially in metalworking industries in several industrial countries. He hypothesized that the emergence of new computer-based technology has improved the quality and productivity of small and medium scale production relative to standardized mass-production techniques which dominated previously. According to Piore and Sable (1984) the emergence of this new technology represents, in fact, an "industrial divide" where firms and society are confronted with a choice of technological modes.[2]

In our 1988 paper (Acs, Audretsch and Carlsson) we provided the first empirical test of the Piore and Sable (1984) thesis that flexible production will tend to promote the relative viability of small firms. We concluded that there is substantial evidence supporting the hypothesis that at least certain flexible technologies have promoted the viability of small firms. An implication of our 1988 paper is that if small firms are growing relative to large firms and accounting for an increased share of sales in the engineering industries, the mean plant size in these industries would be expected to decrease over a similar period. Similarly, if the relative growth of small firms is related to the application of flexible technologies as we found, the expected decline in plant size would also be expected to be related to the application of flexible technologies. The purpose of this paper is to examine plant data from the Bureau of the Census to test whether the shift in mean plant size is also related to the application of flexible technologies using the model from our 1988 paper.

In the second section of this paper we examine the historical relationship between technological change and minimum efficient scale. After developing the model in the third section, we test the hypothesis that changes in mean plant size are positively related to the application of flexible technologies in the fourth section. Finally, in the last section a conclusion and summary are provided. We find that the mean plant size has tended

Z.J. Acs and D.B. Audretsch (eds.), The Economics of Small Firms: A European Challenge. 141–154.

to decrease the most in those engineering industries where there has been the greatest application of programmable robots and numerically controlled machines. Thus, we conclude that there is substantial evidence supporting the hypothesis that flexible technologies are related to a decrease in mean establishment size.

II. Historical Background

From 1920 through 1970, and especially during the post-War years, the mass production mode was at its zenith, engineered by the scientific management within the corporation, protected by government regulation of the external environment, and supported by the prevailing social institutions. This was the world of countervailing power so aptly described by Galbraith (1957), where virtually every major institution in society acted to reinforce the stability needed for mass production. In fact, Piore and Sabel (1983) attribute the unprecedented economic growth from mass production during this period less to technology than to social and political forces.

Wheelwright (1985, p. 30) describes the corporation during this phase as being in a "responsive mode". Management sought to reduce costs through automating those tasks previously performed by labor. Such capital substitution enabled increases in the minimum efficient scale (MES), and the essence of efficient production was to attain efficiencies through *scale* rather than through innovation.[3] The large bureaucracy was the most efficient organization at managing the scale of enterprise rendered necessary through long production runs of standardized goods. Since rivalry among firms existed mostly through cost reductions via capital substitution, products remained remarkably standardized throughout the period.

This was also the period when the organization of industry most closely resembled the visions of Berle and Means (1932) and Bain (1956); manufacturing markets typically were moderately-to-highly concentrated, dominated by a few large firms, and characterized by an absence of price competition. Since the large enterprise was best suited to mass production, both concentration within markets and aggregate concentration – the share of manufacturing industries controlled by the largest 200 firms – grew during this period.[4] Despite the Great Depression, 1920 through 1970 was a period of extraordinary stability for the large corporation. Only 14 of the 278 largest U.S. companies were liquidated during this time. And all but 5 of the largest 50 manufacturing corporations in 1972 were included among the largest 200 in 1947. Similarly, the same industries dominated manufacturing for over fifty years – petroleum, rubber, machinery, food products, chemicals, primary metals, and tobacco (Shepherd, 1985).

Mass production in America was made possible by the fusion between organizational innovation and new technology, especially in the machine tool industry. Machine tools have been an integral part of the industrial growth process ever since the industrial revolution in Great Britain in the latter part of the 18th century. While certain machine tools existed long before then, there is no doubt that the development of modern machine tools is closely linked to the first several decades of the industrial revolution. With a much higher degree of precision being applied to machine tools, the demand for them grew enormously.

At the end of the 1920s there emerged a major new technology that affected the machine tool industry, the transfer machine. Transfer machines consist of a number of smaller machines or work stations, each performing a separate operation such as drilling or milling, organized to work together in such a fashion that a workpiece is automatically put in place at one work station and then transferred automatically to the next work station. Work is performed simultaneously at all work stations, and several operations may be performed simultaneously at each work station (Carlsson, 1984).

After the Second World War there was an increased use of mechanization in mass production. The first large-scale application of automation was at the Ford engine plant in Brook Park, Ohio. Ford tied together several large stationary transfer machines (ST) into a continuous system. The system inspired a succession of improved engine plants in the United States and became known as "Detroit Automation" or "Fordism". While the development of automation continued into the early 1970s, the most important technological progress in the last 30 years appeared in an entirely different direction.

With the advent of numerical controls in the late 1940s, the potential emerged for reversing the 150-year technological trend in machine tools favoring large-scale production. The original developments in numerical controls started around 1949, when the U.S. Air Force began new methods of machining in the aircraft industry that could produce highly complex parts. The new methods were not only more accurate than the conventional methods, but also less expensive. Using the financial support from the U.S. Government, John Parsons and the Servomechanisms Laboratory at MIT developed the first prototypes by 1951. The first commercial numerically controlled machines were displayed in 1955 at the National Machine Tool Builders' Association show.

Perhaps the relatively high cost of numerically controlled (NC) machines in more conventional applications explains both their slow rate of diffusion and the bias in diffusion rates towards large firms. Although the major technical inventions for NCs occurred by the end of the 1950s, NC machine tools did not become widely applied commercially until the late 1960s (Nabseth and Ray 1974). By the end of the 1960s, the production of NCs accounted for about one-fifth of the U.S. production of all machine tools. In fact, this share declined in the early 1970s and did not exceed 20 percent until the end of the decade. As Carlsson (1989(b)) notes, the extensive diffusion of NCs did not really begin until 1975, when the microcomputer began to be used as the basis for the numerical control unit, enabling the use of computer numerical control.

There is some evidence that the diffusion rate of NCs has varied between large and small firms. Romeo (1975) examined a sample of 152 firms from 20 manufacturing industries and found that the rate of adoption by 1970 was positively related to firm size. In the same year, a study by Globerman (1975) employed a survey of 90 Canadian firms to confirm the earlier findings by Mansfield et al. (1971) that the probability of a firm adopting NC technology is positively related to size. There are three major reasons why the diffusion rate was observed to be higher for larger than for smaller firms. First, the amount of equipment and machinery used tends to be positively related to large firms. Because more equipment is depreciated and needs to be replaced in the larger firms, they tend to introduce new types of machinery earlier than do their smaller counterparts. Second, the scope of production, in terms of product lines, tends to be greater in large than in small firms. Thus, large firms are more likely to be producing some product, or set of products, that are particularly conducive to application of the new technology. Finally, the financial resources available to large firms exceed those at the disposal of small firms, enabling the larger firms to more easily finance a new capital investment and survive should that risky investment fail.

Despite this evidence that the diffusion rate of large firms exceeded that of small firms in the adoption of NCs in the 1960s, there is substantial evidence that such machines were available and used by small firms in the late 1970s and early 1980s. For example, Northcott and Rogers (1984) found that of 1200 factories with at least 20 employees in the United Kingdom, 23 percent used computer numerically controlled (CNC) machine tools in 1983 and they predicted this would rise to 30 percent by 1985. Most significantly, they found that the share of large firms that had adopted CNC technology was 31 percent, and declined only slightly with decreasing firm size, so that 22 percent of the firms with between 200 and 499 employees and 21 percent with between 20 and 199 employees used CNC technology. Similar results were found in a 1982 survey, which identified that one-fourth of all adopters of NCs had fewer than 50 employees (Dodgson 1985).

A massive 1985 survey of 6000 firms in the Netherlands revealed similar results. Koning and Poutsma (1989) found that about 55 percent of the plants with at least 200 employees had adopted CNC technology, while about 40 percent of the plants with between 50 and 199 employees used this new technology. Thus, considerable evidence exists that, despite their slower rate of adaption of the new technology in the 1960s and early 1970s, by the early 1980s the use of NC machines had clearly spread to small firms as well as large firms.

There are at least some indications that smaller firms employ different strategies in implementing NCs than do their larger counterparts. For example, using the same survey for the Netherlands previously described, Poutsma and Zwaard (1989) found that the operator is much more likely to program a CNC machine in smaller than in larger firms and when the batches are of a smaller lot. Similarly, the machines were more frequently programmed directly at the location of the machine for small firms, but more likely either somewhere else on the shop floor or elsewhere in the plant for larger firms. Similarly, Dodgson (1985) found that the percentage of cost savings tended to be greater for the smaller than for the larger firms which had adapted NC technology.

The group of industries most reliant upon the application of machine tools comprises the metalworking sector. The metalworking sector consists of non-electrical machinery, electrical machinery, transportation equipment, and instruments. Historically these industries have had the greatest application of mass-production technology and large-scale firms have tended to dominate the industry. If flexible technologies have been a catalyst for small-scale production, this should be reflected more intensively in the metalworking sector than elsewhere in the economy (Mills and Schumann 1985).

In fact, as shown in Fig. 9.1, firms with fewer than 100 employees in the metalworking industries accounted for 15.6 percent of total sales in 1976. This was just slightly above the average for all U.S. manufacturing industries of 14.9 percent. The share of sales accounted for by small firms in the metalworking sector subsequently increased, and accounted for 22.5 percent of total sales by 1986. The increase in the presence of firms with fewer than 500 employees during this time period was even more dramatic, rising from a share of 30.1 percent of sales in 1976 to 39.7 percent of sales by 1986.

At the same time that the tradeoff between scale and flexibility is changing, there seem to be at least two reasons for adapting flexible production. These arise primarily

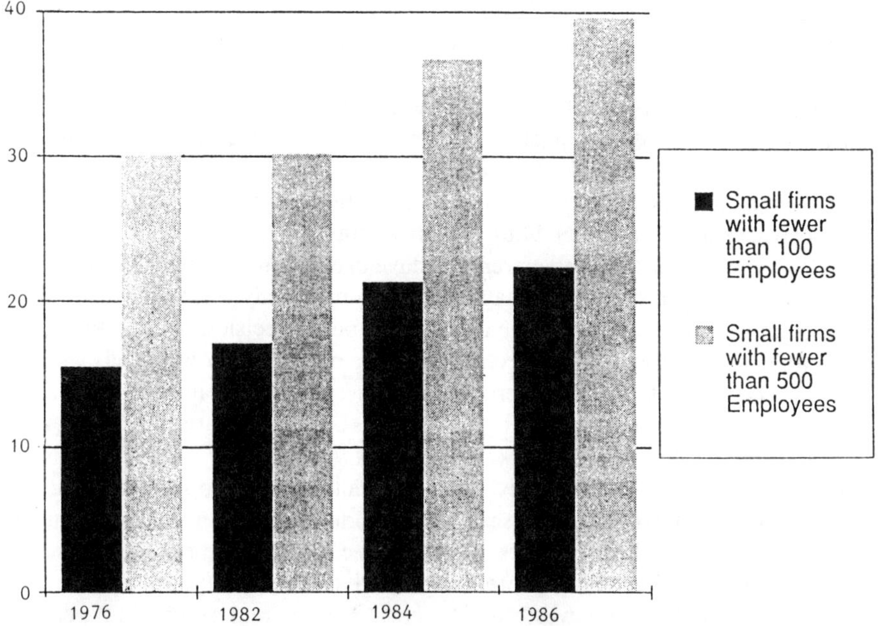

Fig. 9.1. Small-firm share of sales in the metalworking industries, 1976–1986.

because of changes in the character of competition resulting from the internationalization of markets (Audretsch, Sleuwaegen and Yamawaki, 1989).

First, the increased international competition exposed consumers to a greater variety of products. To the extent that consumer tastes are destandardized, mass-production enterprises may no longer maintain a market advantage. When consumers preferred a standardized product at the lowest possible price, firms with a scale large enough to attain the MES prevailed. But with the advent of demand proliferation, mass-production firms faced the loss of consumers to an array of differentiated custom-produced substitutes.[5]

Second, greater competitive pressure and turbulence has reduced profitability and has forced companies to reduce the amount of capital tied up in their operations.[6] For example, while mass-production (integrated) firms in the steel industry would build capacity for years in advance, tying up capital and depressing profits, the minimills build just enough capacity for present needs.[7] In spite of what the term implies, minimills are not a miniature version of an integrated plant. *Their smaller size does not imply that they must operate at a higher level of average cost despite a smaller scale.* Rather, the cost curves differ between mass-production and flexible-production firms, enabling the smaller-scale firms to actually attain lower costs (Barnett and Schorsch 1983).

The same factors precipitating the "breakdown" of the mass-production system also formed the incentives for the evolution of newly structured enterprises. The flexible-production firm thrives on the very factors that were debilitating to the traditional mass-production firm. Flexible producers view innovation as a never-ceasing process. Rather than trying to control and direct the path of change, as had their predecessors – the mass-production corporations – flexible producers accommodate continual change from both the demand and supply sides of the market. The firm consciously strives to create new market niches by continuously redesigning its product to satisfy consumer tastes. Where the mass-production firm succeeded by achieving a size large enough to exhaust scale economies, the flexible producer succeeds from a process of continuous product differentiation.

Changing institutional and technological conditions appear to have altered the balance between assets and liabilities of small firms. In general, the liabilities have become less of a burden while the strengths have become increasingly important. The vertical hierarchy was a superior management instrument only when there existed clear and continuous feedback, and homogeneity in the types of decisions made. But, because flexible production demands that effective decisions be made at lower levels within the firm – those closer to the production process – the hierarchical organization is becoming a burden while the smaller horizontal organization is becoming more efficient (Lazerson 1989; Carlsson 1989(b)).

Similarly, the historical scale disadvantage of small firms is disappearing. According to Friedman (1983), flexible enterprises reduce production costs through productivity growth by utilizing skilled workers. Also, the capacity to produce specialized, customized goods is becoming more effective than the ability to manufacture a standardized product at the lowest possible cost. That is, real product differentiation creates enough of a product niche and sufficiently lowers the cross-price elasticity to negate the scale advantage of larger rivals. Thus, production cost advantages do not map precisely onto market advantages, as was the rule during the era of mass production.

Abernathy et al. (1983) argue that the existence of a dominant design and lumpy technology during the era of mass production were conducive to market concentration. Conversely, continual technological change in the form of product modification fosters real product differentiation and niches, leading to deconcentration. The advent of flexible production also creates an erosion of what were formerly entry barriers. There is an increased potential for technologically based entry because "... a shift in core concepts destroys the competence of established competitors at the same time that it allows other producers to gain market share by introducing new concepts. Market preference for new technical configurations removes the advantage enjoyed by industry leaders as a result of their investments and places a premium on technical capabilities that they do not have" (Abernathy et al. 1983, p. 133). Because flexible production has advantages over mass-production, the market positions of the dominant, traditional firms are being eroded by flexible producers, which leads towards increasing competition. Therefore, as the optimal size of plant and firm declines and entry occurs by small-scale-flexible producers, a noticeable shift towards decentralization and deconcentration may also occur (Acs and Audretsch 1989).

As noted earlier, observations on changes in mean plant size, mean firm (enterprise) size, number of establishments, number of firms, and employment in the 106 four-digit Standard Industrial Classification (SIC) engineering industries in the U.S., between 1972 and 1982, strongly support the deconcentration thesis, and suggest a structural change in the engineering industries has taken place. Both the plant and firm sizes are measured in terms of employment. Not only did the mean plant size of all 106 engineering industries decline by 12.7 percent, but the average plant size declined in 79 out of the

106 four-digit SIC engineering industries. While the mean plant size declined by more than 50 percent in ten of the industries, the decrease was 50 percent and 25 percent in 25 industries, and between 25 percent and 0 percent in 44 industries (Carlsson 1989(a)).

The mean firm size in the engineering industries declined by 13.4 percent between 1972 and 1982. Similarly, in 78 industries the average firm size declined. The distribution of mean firm size changes across the engineering industries closely resembles that for the changes in mean plant size described above. A second striking aspect of the data is that while the mean plant and firm sizes have been decreasing in the engineering industries, there has generally been an increase in both the number of plants and the number of companies, as indicated by the simple correlation of 0.97 between the two variables in Table 9.1. For the entire group of engineering industries the number of plants increased by 27.5 percent between 1972 and 1982. There was an increase in the number of establishments in 86 of the 106 four-digit SIC engineering industries. As shown in Table 9.1, the changes in plant size are strongly and *negatively* correlated with the changes in the number of plants and with the number of firms but positively correlated with the other variables. These trends of a decreasing mean establishment size and mean firm size accompanied by increases in the number of plants and firms are consistent with the shift in the firm-size distribution towards an increased presence of small firms (measured by share of sales) observed in our 1988 paper (Table 9.1). Finally, the trends towards smaller plants and companies cannot be attributed to a decrease in overall employment. Rather, employment increased by 11.3 percent for the entire group of engineering industries between 1972 and 1982. All but 49 of the industries experienced at least some employment growth over the period.

The impact of technical change on scale economies has perhaps been best summed up by Shepherd (1982, p. 624) who concluded that, "It is possible but unlikely that MES increased broadly in U.S. industries while the degree of monopoly was declining so markedly. The opposite process – a broad decline of MES in a variety of industries – is much more likely to have occurred... The present findings suggest two alternative inferences about the role of scale economies. Competition would have risen as broadly as it has only if (1) MES were already well below actual market shares in many industries, and/or (2) MES has declined compared to market size during the period, especially since 1968. It seems probable that both conditions occurred in some degree."

Table 9.1. Correlation matrix for 106 four-digit SIC industries.*

	Change between 1972 and 1982 in:				
	No. of establ.	No. of companies	Establ. size	Company size	Gross output
Change in number of companies	0.971				
Change in establishment size	−0.248	−0.267			
Change in company size	−0.192	−0.263	0.940		
Change in gross output	0.525	0.448	0.537	0.589	
Change in value added	0.521	0.448	0.555	0.594	0.938

Source: U.S. Department of Commerce, Bureau of the Census, *Census of Manufacturing*, 1972–1982, Washington D.C. 1986.

* For a list of the engineering industries, see Carlsson (1989(a)).

III. The Model

In our 1988 paper we followed the theory posited by Dasgupta and Stiglitz (1980), among others, that specific characteristics of technology and knowledge determine the size distribution of firms. We found that the small-firm share of industry sales in any given period, t, is determined by factors representing the state of technology (T) and knowledge (K), along with the extent of what were termed structural barriers to entry (BE), so that

$$(1) \qquad SFP_t = f(T_t, K_t, BE_t).$$

Using the standard linear assumption for tractability leads to a cross-section regression model

$$(2) \qquad SFP_1 = \beta_0 + \beta_1 T_1 + \beta_2 K_1 + \beta_3 BE_1 + \mu_1 .$$

An implication of Dasgupta and Stiglitz' (1980) theory is that an industry firm-size distribution would remain constant over time as long as these basic underlying determinants remain invariant. That is, the small-firm presence (*SFP*) would not be expected to change unless there was a change in T_1, K_1, or BE_1. Piore and Sabel (1984), Piore (1986), Carlsson (1984), Dosi (1988), and others, have argued that technology has evolved in such a way as to shift the firm-size distribution promoting the growth of small firms relative to that of large firms. In particular, flexible manufacturing systems, and the implementation of numerically controlled machines and programmable robots represent this new technology.

If small firms are growing relatively to large firms and accounting for an increased share of sales in the engineering industries, the mean plant size in these industries would be expected to decrease. That is, if the relative growth of small firms is related to the application of flexible technologies, the expected decline in plant size would also be expected to be related to the implementation of flexible technologies.

To empirically test the hypothesis whether a shift in the mean plant size is related to the application of flexible technologies we estimate the model

$$(3) \qquad CPS = B_0 + \beta_1 NC + \beta_2 PR + \beta_3 MP + \beta_4 ST + \beta_5 AA + \beta_6 K/L + \\ + \beta_7 RD/S + \beta_8 SKILL + \mu$$

where *CPS* is defined as the change in the mean plant size between 1972 and 1982. The first five explanatory variables are specific measures of technologies used in the production process. The first two represent flexible technologies. The share (%) of the total number of machines accounted for by numerically controlled machine tools is represented by *NC*. In 1983, numerically controlled machine tools accounted for an average of 3.64 percent of machine tools. These machines are conducive to flexible production, batch production and short production runs. It is hypothesized that the application of numerically controlled machine tools should promote smaller plant sizes, and therefore a negative relationship between *NC* and *CPS* is expected.

The share (%) of the total number of machines accounted for by programmable robots is represented by PR. Using programmable robots rather than mechanical devices to connect various machines to each other enhances the flexibility of numerical machine tools. A negative relationship is expected with *CPS*. The next three variables represent technologies that favor mass production. *AA* represents the share (%) of the total number of machines in 1983 accounted for by automatic assembly machines. The greater the extent to which a production process relies upon a highly mechanized production of commodity-like-goods, the greater will be the share of total machines accounted for by assembly machines. Since assembly machines reflect a mass-production technology, it should be positively related to plant size. Similarly, *ST* represents the share (%) of the total number of machines accounted for by transfer or station-type machines in 1983. The transfer machine represents the most intensive use of mass-production technology. Since transfer machines are related to the extent of mass production, they are expected to exert a positive effect on plant size.

The most pervasive machine tool used in the engineering industries is the mechanical press (*MP*) accounting for 6.65 percent of all machines used. Since mechanical presses are used predominantly for mass production, B_3 is expected to be positive.[8] The machinery data were obtained from the American Machinist.[9]

To represent changes in knowledge in the industry, the 1982 *R&D*-sales ratio from *Science Indicators* (*R&D/S*) and a measure of skilled labor (Skill), defined as the share of total employment accounted for by non-production employees in 1982 from the U.S. *Statistical Abstract* are included as explanatory variables. However, these two variables may affect the relative plant size growth differently. While industries in which the evolution of knowledge has been more dependent upon *R&D* have tended to present a barrier for the viability of small firms (Acs and Audretsch, 1989), Winter (1984) has argued that smaller firms are more likely to prosper in industries in which the evolution of knowledge emanates more from skilled labor and high levels of human capital.[10]

According to White (1982, pp. 42–43), "... higher capital-labor ratios tend to be associated with higher MES. Capital equipment tends to come in large lumps. Larger machines tend to be more efficient (e.g., more specialized, and at full rates of utilization, have lower costs per unit of output) than smaller machines. Thus, the more capital-intensive the basic processes in an industry, the higher the *MES* and the less likely that small business will flourish." White (1982), who argued that such a measure of capital intensity is superior to measures of the *MES* in a study estimating the share of an industry accounted for by the smallest firms, found the capital-labor ratio to exert a negative influence on his measure of the extent of small firms. To control for such barriers, we include the capital-labor ratio (*K/L*), defined as the total capital stock divided by total employment (thousands of dollars) from the *Annual Survey of Manufactures*. *K/L* is expected to exert a positive effect on the change in the mean plant size. Finally, μ represents stochastic disturbance.

The model has been specified with respect to technical economies of scale. It does take into account *R&D* expenditures and heavy capital costs. The estimation procedure does not take into account economies (and diseconomies) in finance, marketing or management. The evidence on this, as exists, is that management factors usually favor small firms and plants, while finance and marketing favor large scale. On balance, according to Silberston, (1972, p. 386) "In relation to other types of economies, however, such scanty evidence as there is suggests that technical economies will often be dominant."

IV. Empirical Results

In our 1988 paper we found that the implementation of flexible technologies was positively related to the relative growth of small firms, or the increase in the relative growth of small firms (or the increase in the share of industry sales accounted for by small firms over time). To test the hypothesis that the changes in mean establishment size are related to the application of flexible technology we use the model developed in our 1988 paper. Using the percentage change in the mean plant size between 1972 and 1982 as the dependent variable, the regression model was estimated for 68 four-digit SIC industries for which there were comparable data.[11] The results are shown in Table 9.2. These results are in general consistent with our 1988 findings that flexible technologies promote smaller firms and mass-production technologies promote larger plants. As shown in equation (1), the negative and statistically significant coefficient for programmable robots and numerically controlled machines implies that flexible technologies promote the presence of smaller plants. Similarly, the positive and statistically significant coefficient for transfer machines implied that mass-production technologies promote larger plants.

Table 9.2. Regression results for change in mean establishment size, 1972–1982 (*t*-ratios listed in parentheses).

	(1)	(2)	(3)	(4)	(5)
PR	– 0.0823 (– 3.0271)**	– 0.0729 (– 2.1619)**	– 0.0831 (– 3.0848)**	– 0.0811 (– 2.4576)**	– 0.0858 (– 3.1611)**
NC	– 0.1164 (– 2.0115)**	– 0.1232 (– 1.8567)*	– 0.1214 (– 2.1630)**	– 0.1252 (– 1.8920)*	– 0.0966 (– 1.7908)*
MP	– 0.0450 (– 1.4590)	– 0.0441 (– 1.3251)	– 0.0445 (– 1.4541)	– 0.0457 (– 1.4034)	–
ST	1.3368 (1.8679)*	1.1985 (1.7095)*	1.4311 (2.1287)**	1.4347 (2.1143)**	1.3791 (2.0360)**
AA	0.0372 (0.4061)	0.0820 (0.9701)	–	–	–
K/L	0.0277 (0.8582)	0.0239 (0.7133)	0.0303 (0.9690)	0.0297 (0.9215)	0.0279 (0.8831)
RD/S	– 9.0212 (– 0.9477)	–	– 10.6460 (– 1.2409)	–	– 5.8674 (– 0.7338)
SKILL	–	0.0058 (0.6062)	–	0.0011 (0.1097)	–
Intercept	6.5205 (2.6249)**	5.5986 (2.4579)**	6.6405 (2.7110)**	6.6134 (2.6647)**	3.4335 (3.1931)**
R^2	0.201	0.194	0.199	0.193	0.171
F	2.161**	2.067**	2.528**	2.134**	2.565**

* Statistically significant at the 90% level of confidence, two-tailed set.
** Statistically significant at the 95% level of confidence, two-tailed set.

As implied by the positive coefficient of K/L, the more capital intensive an industry the larger will be the plant size, although the coefficient is not statistically significant. The knowledge environment as implied by the coefficient of *SKILL* is positive, where higher levels of human capital promote larger plant sizes, although the coefficient cannot be considered statistically significant. Because the simple correlation of 0.74 between RD/S and *SKILL*, these variables are not included in the same equation. The strongest results are in equation three as indicated by the *F*-ratio, where only two measures of mass production are used.

There are two differences between these results and our 1988 paper. First, we found industries that had a high level of *R&D* expenditure *hindered* small firms while here *R&D* promotes small *plants*. Second, while programmable robots promoted the growth of large firms, here they fostered the growth of smaller plants. One explanation for these disparate effects has been provided by Pratten (1987, p. 110) who concluded that, "computers and robots have greatly increased labour productivity. These changes have certainly reduced the number of employees required to produce a given output of many products. They have also reduced the *MES* of plants in many industries where the size of plants is measured in terms of numbers of employees, but this is an unsatisfactory measure in any case. These changes have not necessarily reduced the economies of scale for large output of products."

In our 1988 paper we were able to carry out the statistical analysis to 1986. However, because the Census data are not available past 1982, the most interesting period, 1982–1986, is missing from this analysis. Therefore, the results, while consistent with our earlier paper, should be interpreted with caution.

V. Conclusion

In this paper we have examined the hypothesis that the application of flexible technology affects the mean plant size in the metalworking industries. We find that the mean plant size has tended to decrease the most in those engineering industries where there has been the greatest application of programmable robots and numerically controlled machines. Inflexible technologies characterized by transfer machines have tended to promote larger plant size. Thus, we conclude that there is substantial evidence supporting the hypothesis that flexible technologies are related to a decrease in mean establishment size.

These results are consistent with our 1988 paper where we find that the application of flexible technologies has increased the viability of smaller firms. The causes of this resurgence of small scale and its impact on markets is an active area of research. We appear to be in the midst of a period of "creative destruction", the process by which entrepreneurs develop new products and processes that displace the traditions of the past (Acs and Audretsch 1988b). If the development and growth of small firms is due to the development of new products, then history teaches us that, over time, only a handful of the firms in these new industries will survive. However, if technological change has reduced optimal firm size, diseconomies of scale may be here to stay. Only time will tell.

Notes

* We wish to thank Jianping Yang for his computational assistance. All errors and omissions remain our responsibility.

1. For a test of the Blair hypothesis see Geroski and Pomroy (1987).
2. For a survey of the literature see Silberston (1972), Scherer (1980), Pratten (1987), and Dosi (1988).
3. According to Silberston (1972, p. 376) "If the sum needed were large in relation to the internal or external resources of any one firm in an economy under study, then in some meaningful sense the economies of scale could be said to be important: a plant of M.E.S. would cost so much to build that this would constitute a serious barrier to entry into the industry."
4. For an analysis of trends in concentration in individual markets, see Shepherd (1982).
5. While such a splintering of demand is more obvious with consumer-oriented goods and services, it has also occurred with intermediate goods and services for producers. For example, telecommunications earlier consisted primarily of just one type of service, which was provided by AT&T. However, with the development of computers, the demand for telecommunication services has proliferated to many different types of products that must be manufactured specifically for the use by the individual customer.
6. As manufactured products became sufficiently standardized and evolved towards the latter life-cycle stages, a skilled labor force and high level of technology no longer guaranteed the competitive advantage since it could easily be copied. The internationalization of markets also militated against large scale by creating an uncertain environment. According to Scherer, "The problem is aggravated when the firm operates in a rapidly changing and uncertain environment, for it is the non-routine decisions associated with change that press most heavily upon top managers' capacities (Scherer 1980, p. 85)." To put it another way, bounded rationality limits scarce managerial ability and time.
7. In 1978, the capital cost of a greenfield plant was between $ 1,296 and $1,514 per ton. A minimill of 400,000 tons could be built for between $ 154 and $ 320 per ton (Acs 1984, p. 102).
8. As was pointed out in our 1988 paper, it should be recognized that these five different types of machine tools cannot at all be considered to be homogeneous. That is, one programmable robot is not the equivalent of one mechanical press. Rather, these are very heterogeneous measures which cannot be readily compared to determine which type is most prevalent in any given industry. The usefulness of these measures is only in comparing the application of any given type of machine tool across different industries.
9. For a complete description of the machine tool data see Acs, Audretsch and Carlsson (1988).
10. Acs and Audretsch (1988a) found that in industries where skilled labor plays a relatively important role, small firms tend to have the innovative advantage. In such industries the evolution of knowledge is more likely to emanate from high levels of human capital, resulting in a firm-size distribution more favorable to small firms. We expect skill to exert a negative effect on changes in plant size.
11. The measure used in this paper to estimate economies of scale is time series data on plant size. If one wished to hold the state of the art constant the best method would have been to use engineering estimates of scale. However, if changes in technology are not held constant, this method distinguishes the effect of technological improvements and efficiency which occur over time, and are independent of scale (Pratten 1987, p. 25).

References

Abernathy, William J., Clark, Kim B. and Katrow, Alan M., 1983, *Industrial Renaissance*, New York: Basic Books.

Acs, Zoltan J., 1984, *The changing Structure of the U.S. Economy*, New York: Praeger.

Acs, Zoltan J. and Audretsch, David B., 1988(a) "Innovation in Large and Small Firms," *American Economic Review*, 78, September, 678–690.

Acs, Zoltan J. and Audretsch, David B., 1988(b) "Testing the Schumpeterian Hypotheses," *Eastern Economic Journal*, XIV, April June, 129–140.

Acs, Zoltan J. and Audretsch, David B., 1989, "Small-Firm Entry in U.S. Manufacturing," *Economica*, 56, May, 255–266.

Acs, Zoltan J., Audretsch, David B., and Carlsson Bo, 1988, "Flexible Technology and Firm Size," RPIE Working Paper, xx, Case Western Reserve University.

Acs, Zoltan J. and Audretsch, David B., 1990, *Innovaton and Small Firms*, Cambridge, MA. The MIT Press.

Audretsch, David B., Sleuwaegen Leo, and Yamawaki, Hideki, eds., 1989, *The Convergence of Domestic and International Markets,* Amsterdam: North-Holland.

Bain, Joe, 1956, *Barriers to New Competition*, Cambridge, MA: Harvard University Press.

Barnett, Donald D. and Schorsch, Louis, 1983, *Steel: Upheaval in a Basic Industry*, Boston, Ballinger.

Berle, Adolf and Means, Gardiner, 1932, *The Modern Corporation and Private Property*, New York: Mcmillan.

Blair, John, 1972, *Economic Concentration*, New York: Harcourt, Brace, and Jovanovich.

Carlsson, Bo, 1984, "The Development and Use of Machine Tools in Historical Perspective," *Journal of Economic Behavior and Organization*, 5, 91–114.

Carlsson, Bo, 1989(a), "The Evolution of Manufacturing Technology and Its Impact on Industrial Structure: An International Study," *Small Business Economics*, 1(1), 21–38.

Carlsson, Bo, 1989(b), "Flexibility and the Theory of the Firm," *International Journal of Industrial Organization*, 7(2), 179–204.

Carlsson, Bo, 1990, "Small-Scale Industry at a Crossroads: U.S. Machine Tools in Global Perspective," this volume, pp. 171–193.

Dodgson, Mark, 1985, *Advanced Manufacturing Technology in the Small Firm*, London: Technical Change Center.

Dosi, Giovanni, 1988, "Sources, Procedures and Microeconomic Effects of Innovation," *Journal of Economic Literature*, 26, September, 1120–1171.

Dasgupta, Partha and Stiglitz, Joseph, 1980, "Industrial Structure and the Nature of Innovative Activity," *The Economic Journal*, 80, June, 266–293.

Galbraith, John K., 1957, *The New Industrial State*; Boston: Houghton Mifflin Co.

Geroski, P.A. and Pomroy, R., 1987, "Innovation and the Evolution of Market Structure," Working Paper Series, 36, London Business School.

Globerman, Steven, 1975, "Technological Diffusion in the Canadian Tool and Die Industry," *Review of Economics and Statistics* 57(2), May, 428–434.

Koning, Cees and Poutsma, Frederick, 1988, "Automatisierung und die Qualität der Arbeit in Klein- und Mittelbetrieben," *Internationales Gewerbearchive* 36(4), 238–250.

Lazerson, Mark H., 1990, "Transactional Calculus and Small Business Strategy," this volume, pp. 25–41.

Mansfield, Edwin, et al., 1971, *Research and Innovation in the Modern Corporation*, New York: W.W. Norton.

Mills, David E., and Schumann, Laurence, 1985, "Industry Structure with Fluctuating Demand," *American Economic Review*, 75, September 758–767.

Nabseth, Lars and Ray, G.F., eds., 1974, The Diffusion of New Industrial Processes: An International Study, Cambridge: Cambridge University Press.

Northcott, J. and Rogers, P., 1984, Microelectronics in British Industry: The Pattern of Change, Policy Studies Institute, London.

Piore, Michael J., 1986, "The Decline of Mass Production and Union Survival in the USA," *Industrial Relations Journal*, 17, Autumn, 207–213.

Piore, Michael J. and Sabel, Charles F., 1983, "Italian Small Business Development: Lessons for U.S. Industrial Policy," in: John Zysman and Laura Tyson, (eds.), *American Industry in International Competition*, Ithaca, NY: Cornell University.

Piore, Michael J. and Sabel, Charles F., 1984, *The Second Industrial Divide: Possibilities for Prosperity*, New York, NY: Basic Books.

Poutsma, Erik and Zwaard, Aad, 1989. "The Effects of Automation in Small Industrial Enterprises," *International Small Business Journal*, 7(2), January/March, 35–43.

Pratten, Cliff, 1987, Final Report on "A Survey of the Economies of Scale," Department of Applied Economics, University of Cambridge, September.

Romeo, Anthony A., 1975, "Interindustry and Interfirm Differences in the Rate of Diffusion of an Innovation," *Review of Economics and Statistics* 57(2), May, 311–319.

Sands, Saul S., 1961, "Changes in Scale of Production in United States Manufacturing Industry," *Review of Economics and Statistics*, 43, November, 365–68.

Scherer, F.M., *Industrial Market Structure and Economic Performancs*, Chicago: Rand McNally, 1980.

Schwartzman, David, 1963, "Uncertainty and the Size of the Firm," *Economica*, 30, August, 287–296.

Shepherd, William G., 1985, *Public Policies Toward Business*, 7th edition, Homewook, IL: Richard D. Irwin.

Shepherd, William G., 1982, "Causes of Increased Competition in the Economy, 1939–1980," *Review of Economics and Statistics*, 64, November, 613–626.

Silberston, Aubrey, 1972. "Economies of Scale in Theory and Practice," *Economic Journal*, 82, March, 369–91.

Wheelwright, Steven C., 1985, "Restoring Competitiveness in U.S. Manufacturing," *California Management Review*, 27(32), 26–42.

White, Lawrence J., 1982, "The Determinants of the Relative Importance of Small Business," *Review of Economics and Statistics*, 64, February, 42–49.

Winter, Sidney G., 1984, "Schumpeterian Competition in Alternative Technological Regimes," *Journal of Economic Behavior and Organization*, 5, 287–320.

Comment on "Flexibility, Plant Size, and Industrial Restructuring" by Zoltan J. Acs, David B. Audretsch and Bo Carlsson

Joachim Schwalbach

The paper by Acs, Audretsch, and Carlsson is an extension of their 1988 paper in which they found support for the hypothesis that flexible production will tend to promote the relative viability of small firms. For plants, the authors find the same result which suggests that the influence of technological flexibility on corporate organizations seems to be robust and favour the viability of small businesses. This result is very interesting and will influence the "new learning" in industrial organization (*IO*) in various respects:

(1) Previous work on the analysis of scale economies influenced theoretical and empirical *IO* to a great extent, and still does. This work pointed towards a minimum efficient scale (*MES*) which businesses should have to be cost efficient. What we just learned points toward the opposite direction: flexible production technologies enable businesses to react flexibly to customers' needs. As a consequence, production lot sizes will decrease as the extent of product variety increases and *MES* will, therefore, decrease as the new technologies become more flexible due to technological advance. The flexible technologies seem to favor small businesses since they enter traditional market niches and pursue product differentiation strategies. On the other hand, large businesses are committed to a great extent to mass production strategies, and, therefore, are less flexible to adjust quickly to flexible production techniques.

(2) The traditionally assumed division of labor between small and large businesses will diminish the more important that flexible technologies are for the industry. Since product differentiation will become more important, small and large businesses will compete increasingly in the same market. In many instances, small businesses will outperform their large counterparts due to a higher degree of flexibility.

(3) The adaption of flexible technologies will lower technological entry barriers. Consequently, new businesses enter those markets, which partly explains the observed shift of the size distribution.

(4) Flexible technologies might influence the extent of multi-plant operation. Traditionally, it has been argued that *MES* and transportation cost determined the spread of production facilities across the market. As the *MES* becomes smaller, we expect a larger extent of multi-plant operation. This might also be reflected in the shift of the plant size distribution.

Although, Acs, Audretsch, and Carlsson argue that their results "... should be interpreted with caution" (p. 151), it will certainly stimulate the discussion on the dynamics of size distribution of businesses. Their statistical results in Table 9.2 show that basically all of the 20 percent of the explained variance is attributed to the selected technological variables, leaving one curious to know to what extent the remaining 80 percent can be explained by additional technological factors.

Z.J. Acs and D.B. Audretsch (eds.), The Economics of Small Firms: A European Challenge. 155.

10. Technology Strategy in Small and Medium-Sized Firms*

MARK DODGSON

I. Introduction

There is a wide literature on the role small and medium-sized firms (SMFs) play in technological development. Rothwell (1988) argues that SMFs are increasingly important in the process of technological innovation. Pavitt (1988) also argues that SMFs are significant contributors to innovation. He shows that although business-funded Research and Development (R&D) in most OECD countries is concentrated in a few large firms, SMFs are important innovators. In the U.K. Pavitt found that whereas firms with fewer than 1000 employees account for only 3% of business firms' R&D expenditure, they are responsible for 30% or more of significant innovations. In certain sectors – machinery, instruments, and R&D laboratories – firms employing below 1000 account for more than 45% of all innovations in the sector. Furthermore, firms employing less than 500 have increased in innovation intensity (innovations/share of employment) between 1956 and 1983 (Pavitt, Robson and Townsend, 1987).

This paper is based on the assumption that a population of SMFs exists which possesses the technological competence and excellence to enable them to be considered important contributors to the process of technological advance. There is evidence to suggest such firms do exist; in a recent review of Britain's high-tech "stars" – adjudged by a panel of experts – one-third of the 33 selected companies had a market capitalisation of below £ 100 million (*Management Today*, April 1987). A review of the best 20 U.S. small firms – according to growth in sales and earnings and return on invested capital – 15 were found to be high-tech based firms (*Business Week*, May 25, 1987). Examples of these firms – which have capitalised on their technological mastery, and grown into world-leading corporations – can be found throughout the industrialised world. DEC in the U.S. for example, employed only three people 30 years ago, it now employs over 110,000. The Japanese Sony corporation – that archetypal Schumpetarian entrepreneurial firm – has enjoyed phenomenal success around the world. The Italian Benetton company, has in the last twenty years transformed itself from a small clothing manufacturer employing 60, to the world's largest woollen knitwear maker with 12 factories and 4500 retail outfits.

However, there is very limited systematic information on the population and nature of such firms, and given their potential contributions this is a serious shortcoming. Various factors have been considered by researchers to account for the number and success of these firms. These range from the source and supply of entrepreneurs and venture capital to the specifics of industrial and sectoral structure and the technology in question. This paper will consider one particular facet of innovative SMFs, and will hypothesise and examine it as an important factor underlying their growth and success.

Z.J. Acs and D.B. Audretsch (eds.), The Economics of Small Firms: A European Challenge. 157–167.

It suggests that a significant factor underlying the success of such firms is a coherent strategy for organisational growth, which includes an important component addressing the strategic management of technology. As such, it will argue that highly innovative SMFs exhibit a level of strategic behaviour more commonly associated with large firms. Its focus will be, therefore, on the behavioural aspects of management, and on qualitative analysis of some of the important factors influencing the internal organisation of the firm.

II. Technology and Strategy in SMFs

There are those that argue that the opportunity for, and necessity of, strategy formulation are considerably greater in large rather than small firms (Birley, 1982). However, there appears to be a convergence in the strategic direction of large and small firms (Friar and Horwitch, 1986). Large firms, they argue, increasingly are attempting to emulate the conditions of organisational flexibility and entrepreneurial stimuli of small firms, and small firms are improving "professional" managerial practices for, for example, accessing technology from external sources.

All technology-based firms depend on technological novelty in their products or services to provide them with advantages over their competitors in price and/or quality and/or speed of delivery. After defining technology strategy, I shall suggest a number of reasons why technology should be considered strategically and present a number of hypotheses related to the contraints and stimuli affecting the propensity of technology-based SMFs to develop an effective technology strategy.

A technology strategy involves an understanding within a firm – manifest amongst senior management, but diffused throughout the organisation – of the importance and potential of technology for its competitive position, how in the future that potential is to be realised, and how this complements other aspects of strategy: growth, finance, marketing, personnel etc.

Technological Uncertainty and Complexity

Established markets are facing severe turbulence caused by rapid technological advances in microelectronics, information technology, biotechnology and new materials. Technological development is increasingly discontinuous, and product life cycles are shortening (Foster 1985, Link and Tassey 1987). To deal with this technological turbulence it is necessary to dedicate significant resources to R&D, and nurture appropriate technological competences and skills.

Advanced technologies are enormously complex. Complexity results from the convergence of technologies between, for example, electronics and mechanics to create "mechatronics". Few firms possess internally the range of skills required to merge previously discrete technologies, and technological collaboration is increasingly common between firms, and between firms and R&D undertaking organisations (Mowery 1987, Hladik 1985).

Given the high cost of R&D investment, and the potentially long time scale before returns are forthcoming from such investment, technology needs to be considered strategically. To share the costs and risk of technological development, to attain technological convergence and to deal with complexity, firms often have to collaborate in their technological activities. This may require the merging of previously discrete business interests; through acquisition, joint venture or technological alliance. Decisions on acquisition and collaboration as a means of dealing with technological complexity are an important part of technology strategy (Dodgson 1989).

Pavitt, Robson and Townsend (1987) argue that SMFs are specialised in their technological activities, and are dependent upon external sources of technology. However, those SMFs which attempt to become and remain technological leaders need to overcome the constraints of specialisation and reliance on large firms. Therefore:

Hypothesis 1. To cope with the uncertainty engendered by rapid technological change, and to deal with technological complexity, SMFs concerned with achieving technological leadership need to dedicate considerable resources to R&D and to the accessing of complementary technological competences through collaboration.

Complementarities

Technology strategy is important for firms as it needs to complement overall company strategy: encompassing business, marketing, manufacturing, personnel, investment and finance strategy. Project SAPPHO in the early 1970s showed successful innovative firms matched their tehnological developments with complementary marketing, advertising and manufacturing efforts (Rothwell et al. 1974). SAPPHO also showed successful innovators made use of external technology and scientific advice. Teece (1987) similarly refers to the importance of "complementary assets" (marketing expertise, distribution networks etc.) in realising full returns from technological innovation. He also highlights the importance of accessing external technological expertise.

Functional integration is, prima facie, an obvious target of corporate strategy. Nevertheless, attaining and retaining integration through periods of growth is problematic. The history of the small U.K. computer company, Acorn, illustrates how easy it is for corporate management to lose sight of the need for internal complementarity between functions. In this case, the technological excellence of the company, which had stimulated its extraordinarily rapid growth, was not matched by the requisite financial control and marketing skills, and this led directly to its collapse (Fleck and Garnsey, 1988). The case of Benetton, however, emphasises the importance of complementary innovative activities for its rapid growth from a small firm to a major world player. In this firm, product innovations were matched with process and organisational innovations, and information technology is utilised to facilitate financial and marketing control to great effect (Belussi 1987).

External complementarities are also required. Joint ventures and "strategic alliances" are increasingly commonplace in a number of industries such as consumer electronics, semiconductors, automobiles, pharmaceuticals and the aircraft industries. The accessing of external and complementary sources of knowledge are a feature of technologically-advanced SMFs. In the biotechnology industry in the U.S., Hamilton (1986) found widespread use of external technological linkages between small and large firms, and that these links were a significant part of the firms' technology strategies.

Rothwell and Beesley (1988), in a study of a sample of 103 innovative SMFs in the U.K., found a high external orientation. Eighty-nine percent of these firms enjoyed some form of collaboration with another firm for the purpose of know-how transfer. A study of twelve of Europe's highest technology SMFs, found that external technological linkages were an extremely important factor underlying those firms' technological advantage (Dodgson and Rothwell 1987). Such collaboration, particularly in its international forms, is an extraordinarily difficult process to manage. This is especially so in SMFs where the opportunity costs in terms of valuable key managers' time are very high. The outcomes from technological collaboration depend to a great extent on the skills and experience of managers.

Hypothesis 2. Factors conducive to a successful technology strategy include a high level of integration between a firm's functions, and between its activities and the activities of firms in complementary areas. In SMFs the size of the organisation is conducive to high levels of internal integration, but successful external liaison requires a potentially prohibitive high level of management input.

Global Markets and International Technological Development

The development of "new" technologies is a worldwide phenomenon, and the markets for 'high-tech' goods are commonly international. Firms producing for technologically advanced market niches will often find national markets too small to provide adequate returns on investment; international markets therefore need to be addressed. International marketing involves a heavy financial commitment, and attaining return from such efforts can be a lengthy process. Successful Japanese firms, in for example, consumer electronics, have taken great care in selecting those foreign markets to be targeted, and in ensuring that their product and service contains sufficient technological novelty to attract international customers. In doing so they have shown a considerable awareness of both their own and their competitors' technological competitiveness.

For many technologically-advanced firms, the need to access complementary technical know-how from external sources may involve international collaboration. Firms of sufficent calibre may not exist within national boundaries, it becomes necessary, therefore, for them to engage in the expensive process of creating, managing and attaining benefit from foreign partnerships. Although this may prove problematic for SMFs, there is some evidence to suggest that they are not unduly overawed by the prospect of such collaboration. Of the 240 firms involved in the European Community's ESPRIT Programme – designed to encourage cross-national collaboration in advanced information technology – 57% employed below 500 (Sharp 1989).

Hypothesis 3. Technologically advanced SMFs need to operate internationally in their R&D and marketing activities. This is likely to be high cost with long time-scale returns, and these factors, accompanied by their time-consuming nature for senior managers pose serious constraints.

III. Case Studies: Strategy in Practice

Having described some of the reasons why technology strategy is important for firms, and suggested a number of hypotheses regarding technology strategy in SMFs, I shall now describe the technology strategies of two "exemplar" companies, highlighting their significance for the firms' development and growth. These companies are selected from a series of studies into technology strategies in highly technologically advanced European SMFs (Dodgson and Rothwell 1987). The companies are well known to the author, who has conducted numerous interviews with their directors, managers and engineers, in one case since 1982, in the other since 1986. Both firms were included in a European Community-wide study, conducted in 1987, into the patterns of growth and R&D activities of 37 of the EC's most highly technologically advanced SMFs. The two firms are selected as they ideally exhibit the tendencies revealed by the larger sample.

The firms will be disguised to protect confidentiality. Numerical data and details of strategy are factually reported.

Company A: Seaford Ltd.

Origins: Seaford Ltd was formed in the early 1960s by a highly talented engineer, disaffected by a) his high ranking managerial position in a large chemicals firm (he had little opportunity to exercise his engineering skills), and b) the stifling bureaucracy and risk-aversion of the large firm. He was particularly annoyed at the large firm's lack of support for his "pet" project, which he blamed on short-term horizons. Starting work with a local technician in his garage, and self-funded, in six months he produced a novel product for use in the broadcasting industry. It readily found acceptance within the industry (which only possessed a limited number of customers), and it was succeeded by improved versions over the next few years, which maintained cash flow and a solid rate of growth.

Growth: Following a number of product improvements, and an increased number of potential applications, the company experienced remarkably rapid growth. In 1970, it employed 30, and by 1977 it employed 200. The company currently employs 500. Seaford has enjoyed fast sales growth throughout the 1970s and 1980s. During the 1970s turnover increased an average of 30 percent a year. Annual turnover doubled between 1983 and 1986 from £ 20 million to £ 40 million.

Profitability: Over the last three years, profits as a percentage of sales have averaged around 25 percent. One of the company's major products enjoys 100 percent of the world market.

Strategy: The aversion to the large company coloured the attitudes of this entrepreneur towards what he wished his company to be. From the beginning he wanted the company to produce state-of-the-art technology, and not to become a "manufacturing" company. Considerable funds have, however, been dedicated to sophisticated flexible manufacturing systems, and great care has been taken in ensuring the company possesses advanced manufacturing facilities. Technological leadership, based on R&D, has been the dominant strategy directing this firm's development, and this has influenced all aspects of the company.

Throughout the 1970s Seaford dedicated around 15 percent of annual turnover to R&D. Over the last five years this figure has varied from 10–12 percent. Twenty-six percent of the company employees work in R&D. While the primary source of technological know-how for the company is its internal R&D organisation, this is occasionally supplemented by joint projects with universities and by participation in European collaborative research programmes. Seaford also has particularly strong links with the manufacturers of the semiconductors used in its products. In this way advances in semiconductors can quickly be integrated into improved products.

The technology strategy is complemented exactly by marketing strategy. The broadcasting industry is noted for its demand for technological novelty, and there are few major European customers for the equipment Seaford produces. The company has therefore targeted leading users in worldwide markets (most particularly, the U.S. and Japan). This strategy has been extremely successful: at present 75 percent of production is exported. The high premium that the products can command (being so novel in such an innovation conscious industry, the products are in immediate demand, and once one broadcaster utilises the product, the others often feel compelled to follow), enables the continual high commitment to R&D. The size of the market also limits the growth of the firm's manufacturing, marketing and distribution efforts, in line with the company's strategy.

At a very early stage, Seaford's founder recognised the importance of attracting two very important skills into the firm. The first involved detailed knowledge of the broadcasting industry, the second involved "professional" management skills in financial control, personnel etc. He was fortunate to find these incumbent in one person, who was appointed managing director. This person has overseen the development of Seaford to its present position. Possessing this extremely talented manager has enabled the founder to create and acquire a number of other firms, also with a strong technological bias.

The managing director attributes the company's success to the skills and motivation of its employees. He pays particular attention to personnel matters, and has succeeded in recruiting and retaining a number of highly skilled software engineers in what is a very strong sellers' market. Seaford's managing director considers the major constraint facing the company's future growth is shortage of managers with marketing and entrepreneurial skills.

Company B: Newhaven Ltd.

Origins: Newhaven Ltd began its life in the late 1950s as a spin-off from a university laboratory. It was, if anything, a reluctant spin-off, the founder – an academic – began manufacturing a specific piece of scientific equipment, primarily because no-one else would make it. He began in the shed at the bottom of his garden. Industry lagged some way behind science, and for some years the only customers were a limited number of laboratories. However, a major scientific discovery opened a new demand for an application of the product, and the firm found as it possessed a considerable technological lead it was in a position to expand production considerably. Profits and employment grew accordingly.

Growth: Newhaven currently employs 350. Most of the increase in employees occurred during the late 1970s and 1980s. Unlike Seaford's relatively untroubled pattern of growth, Newhaven Ltd faced a potentially drastic period when it nearly collapsed. The company was run by an academic, with a technology strategy based on scientific curiosity rather than potential market need. Desperately short of cash flow, an experienced commercial manager was appointed. His first priority was to improve cash flow, and he identified a relatively simple product for the company to manufacture in quantity. This turned the company around, and it returned to profitability. Turnover has grown rapidly throughout the 1980s: it increased from £ 16 million in 1983 to £ 48 million in 1986. The managing director's next priority was to develop a strategy for the company.

Profitability: over the last three years, profitability as a percentage of sales has averaged around 19 percent. One of the company's main products enjoys 85 percent of the world's market.

Strategy: The strategy developed by the new managing director involved three main facets: first, utilising the very considerable scientific and technical expertise within the firm, and the very good links between these people and world leading laboratories and users of its equipment; second, diversifying away from the core competence based on the original technology (which had spurned a new industry with a number of huge conglomerates competing in the market place); third, maintaining cash flow through a number of relatively simple products.

The company has maintained its technological lead in the applications for its main product. It has been careful, however, of not competing directly with many of the conglomerates attracted to this fast growth industry. It has adopted a strategy of addressing market niches with a potential size of between £ 10 million and £ 100 million sales. The majority of Newhaven's sales are overseas, its current export ratio is 93 percent.

The technological lead has been maintained by a continued high commitment of resources to R&D. Around 17 percent of employees work in R&D, and over the last three years 10–11 percent of turnover is dedicated to R&D. The company has also paid particular attention to building and maintaining technological links with lead laboratories and key users of its equipment.

The process of diversification has been overseen by a new managing director. He has targeted a major new product and dedicated considerable resources to its development; created a number of spin-off companies; and has acquired a number of small firms possessing complementary expertise.

The entrepreunerial ethic has been stimulated by new product champions being awarded the managing directorship of the new spin-offs. In this way a number of new, and related companies have been created. The new managing director pays considerable attention to personnel matters; managers and senior scientists and engineers are well paid and have share option schemes.

IV. Lessons From the Case Studies

Both firms have to be considered successful by any measure. They have grown very rapidly in sales and employment, enjoy high levels of profitability, and have very high export ratios. The strategic management of technology has been a factor influencing their success, and the two case studies provide a certain amount of support for the earlier hypotheses concerning the significance of technology strategy for SMFs, and for the nature of such strategy.

Concerning Hypothesis 1, we find:

- Technological excellence is achieved by a high commitment to building core competences within the firms. This is attained through the dedication of considerable resources, both financial and personnel, to the R&D process. It is through such commitment that the cumulative skills are developed within the firms to enable them to maintain comparative technological advantage.
- To cope with technological complexity, and to improve new product lead times (which are so important when product life cycles are often so short), the firms established strong technological links with actors in vertically integrated activities. Thus, the case studies highlighted the importance of links with suppliers and users to facilitate every opportunity for product improvement, and of considering collaboration with leading infrastructural laboratories and other firms to access complementary knowledge and skills.

Concerning Hypothesis 2, we find:

- A high level of integration existed amongst the firms' activities. The case studies reveal the advantages derived from integrating, and dedicating significant resources to, marketing, R&D and manufacturing.
- The advantages of managing technology within the context of an overall company strategy which addresses all of the major activities of the firm. The case study companies possessed a strategy that encompassed growth through concentration on international market niches, high financial risk and high financial returns, and technological excellence based on cumulative core skills, complemented by external sources of knowledge, and informed by activities in vertically related firms.
- A particularly important facet of company strategy addressed personnel and, particularly the role to be played by senior management and scientists and engineers. Great emphasis was placed on developing a strategy for attracting, retaining, and providing incentives for key personnel.

Concerning Hypothesis 3, we find:

- The firms placed very considerable emphasis on export markets. One firm in particular made every effort to integrate technical feedback from advanced users in major overseas markets. Both firms felt that the ability to fund and attract additional international marketing capacity would determine future competitiveness.

V. Conclusions

We have seen that the concept of technology strategy can be meaningful for SMFs. Our two "exemplar" companies exhibited strategic behaviour in relation to dealing with technological turbulence and complexity, achieving internal and external complementarities, and functioning in international markets. Both companies had strategies of technological leadership in worldwide niche markets. Both had achieved predominance in their highly complex technologies through significant dedication to R&D. This involved high commitment of resources, both financial and in personnel. While such high financial expenditure is a significant burden, it followed a strategy of providing the means: first, to attract leading scientists and engineers into the firm; and second, to provide the products novel enough to warrant near monopoly rents.

In both companies internal technological expertise was complemented by external sources of knowledge. Newhaven cultivated extensive links with important sources of scientific knowledge and with leading users of its equipment. Seaford maintained good links with major suppliers of components, and was prepared to work collaboratively on particular project developments. In both firms we see a complementarity in the various facets of strategy. Both addressed international niche markets with a competitive position based on non-price (i.e. technological leadership) factors. The niches were selected on the basis of a number of criteria: including, potential size (Newhaven's avoidance of direct competition with large, financially powerful conglomerates), and its ability to sustain a technological lead over competitors for sufficient time to ensure return on the considerable outlay on R&D and international marketing.

Only two case studies have been described, selected from a series of studies into technology strategies. These particular firms were chosen as they in many ways represent "ideal types" of effective technology strategy in SMFs. Certainly the case study firms are exceptional, and it is unwise to generalise from case study material. Nevertheless, the firms do reveal the potential significance of coherent and cogent strategies for the success of SMFs. Obviously more research needs to be done: the hypotheses need to be developed further and to be tested systematically. The reported research does raise a number of questions germane to the study of the importance of high-technology SMFs. I shall conclude by referring to a number of issues worthy of future research.

- There is very little empirical evidence available on the population of such technologically advanced SMFs. More needs to be known about the number and sectoral distribution of these firms.
- The chapter focuses upon an important aspect of the contemporary managerial process within firms. Technological accumulation and use to attain comparative competitive advantage are processes highly dependent on the strategies and skills of managers. In Seaford and Newhaven great emphasis was placed on attracting and rewarding (and hence retaining) key personnel. Foremost amongst these appointments were those of the managing directors made by the founders of the companies. In Seaford, unlike Newhaven, the critical skills possessed by these managing directors – such as market awareness, and financial control – were recognised early in the company's history. Newhaven learnt the hard way. Both firms attempt to retain the entrepreneurial stimuli within their organisations, and both are aware that the major

potential constraint on future growth is the availability of key management skills. Much more research into the "management" factors which determine success and failure in advanced technology SMFs.

- There are few industrialised nations which do not possess public policies designed to encourage the formation and growth of small firms. Few of these policies attempt to deal with the thorny problem of selectivity: how do you pick potential winners? This is important as it is only a very small proportion of the population of SMFs which make important contributions to employment creation (Storey et al. 1987), and contribute to a similar extent as the case study firms to a nation's technology base and exports. Research examining the existence of a coherent and plausible strategy for growth as a defining factor underlying the identification of "special cases" for public policy support certainly warrants attention (Dodgson and Rothwell 1988).
- Policy makers, industrialists and academics need to understand better the dynamics of SMFs. Firms do not respond uniformly to changes in markets, capital markets and technologies. One of the major factors accounting for variability in performance is the quality of management. The success of firms of the type described above- clearly derived from the way technology was managed – should lead to greater emphasis being placed by researchers (and economists in particular) on developing research methods designed to incorporate micro-economic behaviour, and in particular qualitative factors such as management skills and flair.

Note

* The paper on which this chapter is based was presented at the *International Conference on Small Business Economics*, Berlin, November 17–18, 1988. The author would like to thank Chris Hull, Roy Rothwell and Keith Pavitt for their helpful comments on the paper.

References

Belussi, F., 1987, *Benetton: Information Technology in Production and Distribution – A Case Study of the Innovation Potential of Traditional Sectors,* Occasional Paper No. 25, Science Policy Research Unit, Sussex.

Birley, S., 1982, "Corporate Strategy in the Small Firm", *Journal of General Management,* 8(2), 82–86.

Dodgson, M., 1989, *Technology Strategy and the Firm: Management and Public Policy,* Harlow, Longman.

Dodgson, M. and Rothwell, R., 1987, *Patterns of Growth and R&D Activities in a Sample of Small and Medium-Sized, High Technology Firms in the U.K., Denmark, Netherlands and Ireland,* Research Report, IRDAC, Brussels.

Dodgson, M. and Rothwell, R., 1988, "Small Firm Policy in the U.K.", *Technovation,* 7(3), 231–247.

Fleck, V. and Garnsey, E., 1988, "Managing Growth at Acorn Computers", *Journal of General Management,* 3(3), 4–23.

Foster, R., 1987, *The Attacker's Advantage,* London, Pan Books.

Friar, J. and Horwitch, M., 1986, "The Emergence of Technology Strategy", in Horwitch, M. (ed.), *Technology in the Modern Corporation,* New York, Pergamon Press.

Hamilton, W., 1986, "Corporate Strategies for Managing Emerging Technologies" in Horwitch, M. (ed.) *Technology in the Modern Corporation,* New York, Pergamon Press.

Link, A. and Tassey, G., 1987, *Strategies for Technology-Based Competition,* Lexington, DC Heath.

Pavitt, K., 1988, "The Size and Structure of British Technological Activities: What We Know and Do Not Know", *Scientometrics,* 14(3–4), 329–346.

Pavitt, K., Robson, M. and Townsend, J., 1987, "The Size Distribution of Innovating Firms in the U.K.: 1945–1983", *Journal of Industrial Economics,* 35(3), 297–317.

Rothwell, R., 1988, "Small Firms, Innovation and Industrial Change", *Small Business Economics*, 1(1), 51–64.

Rothwell, R. et al., 1974, "SAPPHO updated – project SAPPHO phase II", *Research Policy*, 3(3), 258–291.

Rothwell, R. and Beesley, M., 1988, "Patterns of External Linkages of Innovative Small and Medium-Sized Firms in the United Kingdom", *Piccola Impressa*, 2.

Sharp, M., 1989, "Corporate Strategies and Collaboration – the Case of ESPRIT and European Electronics" in Dodgson, M. (ed.) *Technology Strategy and the Firm*, op. cit.

Storey, D., et al., 1987, *The Performance of Small Firms*, London, Croom Helm.

Teece, D., 1987, "Profiting from Technological Innovation: Integration, Strategic Partnering, and Licensing Decisions", in Teece, D. (ed.), *The Competitive Challenge*, Cambridge, Mass, Ballinger.

Comment on "Technology Strategy in Small and Medium-Sized Firms" by Mark Dodgson

Christopher J. Hull

Dodgson's paper continues more than a decade of research at the Science Policy Research Unit (SPRU) which has shown that small firms are significant innovators (cf. Dodgson's references to Pavitt and Rothwell). This and similar work elsewhere has successfully challenged the old notion that it takes a big R&D budget to be a successful innovator. *The key to innovativeness is not so much knowledge as the exploitation of knowledge.*

This paper focuses on the management of technology in small and medium-sized firms (SMFs). Dodgson believes that there is a significant population of technology-based SMFs making an important contribution to innovation, although how many there are is unclear. Indeed, we know little about them and need to know more so as to be able properly to understand and encourage their role.

It is implict in the paper that the problems or requirements of technology management in SMFs are in some way different from those in large firms. The nature of this difference is not discussed, however, and seems an important omission. Much of the difference may be related to the origins and scale of SMFs.

We know that many, if not most, technology-based SMFs are set up by scientists or engineers who have acquired an expertise for which they think there is a commercial application. Dodgson's two cases illustrate the phenomenon. One firm was set up by an engineer from a major industrial company, the other by a university scientist. Both individuals had pet projects which they had not been able to see realised in their original organisation.

This kind of background suggests two possible characteristics of technology-based SMFs: a relatively narrow technology base (deep but highly specific knowledge) and an already acquired competence at the time of launch.

Already acquired competence at the time of launch may suggest, in its turn, that many technology-based SMFs are technology users rather than technology developers. They may engage, even heavily, in R&D, but the emphasis is perhaps more on the D than the R.

The narrowness of their technology base may also suggest that they tend to be incremental rather than fundamental innovators. More precisely, at the time of their launch they may produce a fundamental innovation, but thereafter the narrowness of their technology base and their limited resources as small or medium-sized firms may constrain them to pursue the incremental route.

The techological specificity of SMFs is both a strength and a weakness. It is a strength as long as they can maintain leadership, and Dodgson is clearly right to emphasise the importance of continuous links with research centres and suppliers of production inputs as a means of staying state-of-the-art. He is also right to emphasise the most careful attention to the requirements of actual and potential customers.

Z.J. Acs and D.B. Audretsch (eds.), The Economics of Small Firms: A European Challenge. 168–170.

Marketing is one of the key "complementary assets" (see Dodgson's reference to Teece) which the technology-based SMF needs to develop. I wonder whether it does not deserve a primary ranking rather than the coequal status suggested by the term complementarity. Certainly, it would seem that the principal cause of failure among demised technology-based SMFs is precisely inattention to market demand. The original technological orientation of the founder risks obscuring commercial imperatives.

The threat to the technology-based SMF is, of course, that it will develop its target market so successfully that the big players are moved to enter the field. It would seem that a technologically specialised SMF can best maintain leadership in a clearly circumscribed niche market, but perhaps only as long as it stays a niche market. The problem is that a narrow technology base limits the scope for diversification into other markets once the going gets tough in the original market.

Another potentially substantial threat to the technology-based SMF is that the technological base of its product market may shift, what Dodgson refers to as technological uncertainty or turbulence.

When technology does shift, a firm in principle has two options: to stay with the old technology or to go with the new. Staying with the old technology implies finding new products (possibly new territorial markets) to which the old technology can be applied with advantage. The alternative is to try to master the new technology in order to be able to maintain position in an existing product market.

What puts the technology-based SMF particularly at risk in such circumstances is that its very specialisation may mean that it has no expertise in the new technology from which to maintain product leadership. Large firms with a portfolio of technologies will tend to be less at risk. Moreover, even when large firms have no base in the new technology their large resources, compared with SMFs, will make it easier for them to make good the deficit. Empirical research to ascertain how firms (of different size) weather the uncertainties of technical change would seem worthwhile.

It may also be, however, that we over-dramatise the uncertainty of technological advance. The First, Second, Third, etc. Industrial Revolutions – and the disjunctures which they represent – are essentially artefactual periodicisations based on hindsight. Viewing the evolution of technology from past to present, and in the flow of time rather than through snap-shot comparisons between one decade or half-century and the next, would suggest that there are more regularities than ruptures. Even admitting an accelerating pace of technological change towards the present day, the technological bases of product classes perhaps change more gradually than we sometimes suppose, and gradually enough to allow the open-eared and -eyed to prepare for the change. Nonetheless, the investment required to meet a shift in technology may still be such as to defeat the SMF with a narrow technology base and limited financial resources.

Technology-based SMFs are usually characterised as corresponding to a "technology-to-market" model. In other words, their origin lies in a technological competence, which is then converted into a marketed product. But there seem to be some SMFs which pursue almost a reverse "market-to-technology" logic. These are firms whose prime focus are market opportunities, for which they then try to mobilise the necessary technological skills.

Amstrad, the U.K. consumer electronics company, may be an example. It has very little manufacturing capacity of its own and is perhaps best described as a marketing company. The strategy is to identify potential demand for new or improved products and then to use the most competitive manufacturers, often located in Asia, to produce the goods under specification and the Amstrad label. A company of this kind still needs technological expertise, but it does not need to sink capital in manufacturing or R&D investment to anything like the same extent, and so guards a certain flexibility.

Benetton, which Dodgson cites as an exemplary technology-based SMF, may be another instance of a firm which mobilised technology to suit its market. My understanding of its rise is that it grafted production and information technology onto an already established organisational structure of production and marketing.

There appears to be a trend towards the buying and selling of technology which could increase the scope for "technology entrepreneurs" of this kind: more and more universities are trying, not least because of dwindling budgets, to commercialise their R&D output and technological know-how; there seems to be a growing population of private contract-research organisations; industrial research associations in many sectors and countries are adopting a more commercial posture; the number of technology brokers is growing... A trend in this direction could provide technology-based SMFs (but also large firms) with increased opportunities for external technology supply which could help them lessen the dangers inherent in a narrow technology base.

Dodgson closes his paper with some suggestions for further research, and I shall do likewise. One of the dangers in discussions about the relative merits or roles of large as against small firms – a discussion which has resurfaced with vigour during the past decade – is that the complementarity between large and small often disappears from view. For example, many of the innovations launched by large firms originate outside the firm, often in small organisations (firms or laboratories). Conversely, as already noted, the origins of many technology-based SMFs lie in large organisations. These interrelationships are often ignored because analysis is cross-sectional, or snap-shot, rather than evolutionary. We could surely learn a great deal from research which tracked the genealogy of innovations.

A second suggestion is that we may learn more about the problems and requirements of technology strategy in SMFs by studying not just cases of success but also cases of failure. The successful are, by definition, unusual and studying them alone may give no clue as to typical management errors or oversights which can cause failure.

11. Small-Scale Industry at a Crossroads: U.S. Machine Tools in Global Perspective*

BO CARLSSON

I. Introduction

In 1975, the United States was the world's largest producer of machine tools, the second largest exporter, and had the lowest degree of dependence on imports of all major machine tool producing countries. By 1987, the U.S. had slipped into fourth place as producer of machine tools (behind Japan, F.R.G., and the USSR), into sixth place in exports (behind Switzerland, G.D.R., and Italy), and relied on imports for more than half of its supply of machine tools.

This dramatic turn of events reflects the upheaval in the machine tool industry worldwide in the last decade. Until the early 1970s, the machine tool industry could be characterized as a mature industry with highly stable product technology, market structure, and competitive environment, although the demand for machine tools has always been extremely cyclical. As a result, it was not unusual to find 30- to 40-year-old products as major "breadwinners" even in leading machine tool companies (Rendeiro 1984, p. 62). But after the mid-1970s, all that changed. The machine tool industry is now in a profound state of flux and disequilibrium, in the United States as well as in several West European countries.

Given that the machine tool industry is often considered to be strategically important – illustrated e. g. by the fact that there is no major industrial country without a domestic machine tool industry and by the importance attached to that industry in the newly industrialized countries (NICs) – this development is clearly of grave concern.

It is the object of this paper (1) to explain what happened globally in the machine tool industry since the mid-1970s, (2) to examine the arguments concerning the strategic role of the industry in industrial development, and (3) to analyze the implications for the future and to recommend courses of action.

The plan of the paper is as follows. The basic characteristics of the machine tool industry, the recent development of output and international trade, and recent changes in technology are described in the next three sections. These are followed by an analysis of the current restructuring of the industry in the United States and Western Europe, and of the causes of the observed development. The strategic role of the industry and the implications for the future are discussed in the final sections of the paper.

II. Industry Characteristics

The machine tool industry is one of the smallest sectors of manufacturing industry in most industrial countries. In the United States, it represented only three-tenths of one percent of the value of shipments of manufactured goods at the end of the 1970s. This

Z.J. Acs and D.B. Audretsch (eds.), The Economics of Small Firms: A European Challenge. 171–193.

means that General Motors alone is about 40 times larger in terms of shipments than the entire U.S. machine tool industry! (*Industry Week* 1984, p. 70.) Even in the F.R.G., traditionally one of the world's largest producers of machine tools per capita, the share of machine tools in manufacturing employment does not exceed 1.5 percent (Commission of the European Communities 1983, p. 9).

The machine tool industry is extremely heterogeneous. It has been estimated that there are some 3,000 different types and sizes of machine tools in the market, ranging from less than one ton to over sixty tons and ranging in price from about $ 1,500 to over $ 600,000 (MTTA 1983, p. 2, cited in Jacobsson 1988, p. 2). The industry is made up of numerous small firms. In 1977, there were 1343 establishments in the United States machine tool industry, with an average of 62 employees per establishment. For comparison, the average firm size in the F.R.G. was about 225 employees in 1980, while it was only 21 employees in Japan (but around 300 if only members of the Japan Machine Tool Builders' Association are considered). There were 12 plants in the F.G.R. with more than 1000 employees, while there were 10 in the United States, 7 in the United Kingdom, 6 in Japan, 2 in France, and none in Sweden (CEC 1983, p. 11 and USITC 1983, p. 48).

Despite the miniscule size and heterogeneity of the industry and the smallness of its firms, the machine tool industry is far more important than its share of industrial value added or employment would indicate. Machine tools are usually defined as power-driven machines (not hand held) that are used to cut, form, or shape metal. Thus, machine tools represent the core of production machinery in the whole metalworking industry – a sector which contributes about 40% of value added in manufacturing in developed industrial countries and which is also generally expected to provide a major share of real growth in manufacturing in the coming decades. However, the role of machine tools is not confined to hardware alone; the whole "software," i.e., the organization and control of production machinery, in the metalworking industries is closely linked to the characteristics and use of machine tools. Thus, the machine tool industry may be regarded as a "node" for supplying both hardware and software to all metalworking industries, thus playing a crucial role in determining the performance of large sectors of manufacturing in terms of both productivity and international competitiveness.

In spite of this role, the machine tool industry has not been heavily research-oriented. It has relied on help from both customers (for applications and product development) and suppliers (e.g. for control equipment) – and in the U.S. case, on prime defense contractors for systems design – rather than on internal R&D efforts. Over the last decade or so, the U.S. machine tool industry's R&D expenditures ranged only between 1.6% and 2.6% of sales (USITC 1983, p. 32). A few firms have spent considerably more, however. Ex-Cell-O claims to have spent 4% of sales on R&D in 1985, and Giddings & Lewis 5% over practically the company's entire history (Sprow 1985, p. 47). But in a shrinking industry with depressed profitability, the smaller companies often lack the resources to keep up with technology.

Another characteristic is a high capital intensity, resulting primarily from large requirements of working capital: goods-in- process inventories are usually large, given a large variety of products, small batches, and a low degree of automation of the manufacturing process.

Even though international trade has traditionally played an important role in the industry, foreign direct investment has not. The small size of most firms in the industry is one reason; the widespread practice of selling machine tools primarily through distributors is another: it reduces the need to locate production close to the customers. According to a survey made in 1983, 54% of U.S. machine tool builders sell only through distributors, while 44% sell either directly or through distributors and only 2% sell only directly (ABC Group 1983).

III. Recent Developments in the Machine Tool Industry

Changing Distribution of World Output and Trade

The development of machine tool consumption in the 20 largest machine tool producing countries over the period 1975 to 1987 is shown in Table 11.1.[1] While the combined total consumption in all these countries doubled between 1975 and 1980, it grew by only 15 percent between 1980 and 1987 – having first fallen by about 30 percent during 1981–83. This development reflects two important characteristics of the consumption of machine tools: it is highly cyclical, and its long-term growth is fairly slow. The cyclical nature of demand becomes even more apparent when one examines the development in individual countries. For instance, the U.S. share of world consumption went from 20.4% in 1982 to 14.8% in 1983 and then increased to 18.8% in 1984. Similarly, Brazil's share dropped from 3.2% in 1977 to 0.7% in 1983 and then rose to 1.3% in 1985. Such an analysis also reveals that growth rates differ substantially among countries. While the consumption more than doubled during 1980–1987 in Taiwan and Spain, it was cut in half in Romania and the U.K. Since machine tools are used almost exclusively in the metalworking (engineering) industries, these differences in growth rates reflect the development in these industries in the various countries. Developing countries such as Taiwan, South Korea and India have extremely high growth rates, while among the highly developed industrial countries, higher than average consumption growth rates are found only in the F.R.G., Sweden, Japan, Switzerland, and Italy. The U.S. and U.K. show a declining trend after 1980, as do all of the communist countries except the U.S.S.R.

On the production side (see Table 11.2), all the countries with consumption growth rates higher than average also have production growth rates higher than average. The only exception is Sweden, where the consumption and production growth rates for 1980–1987 were 52 percent and 9 percent, respectively. The highest production growth rates during that period were in South Korea, Yugoslavia, and Taiwan. Among the developed non-communist countries, Japan, Switzerland, the F.R.G., and Italy were the only ones exhibiting higher than average production growth rates. Machine tool production actually declined in the U.S., U.K., and France, as well as in Romania and the People's Republic of China.

Historically, the United States has been by far the largest producer of machine tools, with Germany in second place. In 1955, about 40% of the world's machine tools were produced in the United States; by 1980, that share had been reduced to less than 20% and by 1987, to less than 8%. At the same time, in the F.R.G. machine tool production

Table 11.1. Shares of apparent consumption of machine tools in the 20 largest producing nations, 1975–1987. Percent.

	1987	1986	1985	1984	1983	1982	1981	1980	1979	1078	1977	1976	1975
Brazil	1.4	1.4	1.3	0.7	0.7	1.1	1.4	1.7	2.3	2.6	3.2	3.1	1.7
Czechoslovakia	0.6	0.6	0.7	1.0	1.1	0.8	0.9	0.9	1.2	1.6	1.8	2.1	2.0
France	4.0	3.7	3.1	2.4	3.4	3.8	3.9	4.0	3.7	3.6	4.4	5.9	5.[illegible]
F.R.G.	14.6	12.2	8.8	8.2	9.5	8.4	8.4	10.2	9.9	10.0	11.8	7.4	6.6
G.D.R.	1.1	1.8	0.3	0.9	1.0	1.8	1.5	1.8	1.8	2.1	1.6	2.4	2.2
Hungary	0.5	0.5	0.6	0.7	0.9	0.7	0.6	0.7	0.7	0.8	0.9	0.8	0.4
India	1.4	1.5	1.8	1.6	1.9	1.2	1.0	0.9	0.7	0.8	0.9	1.0	1.0
Italy	5.3	3.8	2.9	3.5	3.5	3.3	4.3	5.0	4.3	3.8	4.6	4.4	5.4
Japan	13.1	15.5	15.9	16.2	13.7	12.9	13.2	10.1	8.6	8.3	7.8	6.5	6.8
P.R.C.	1.6	1.8	2.6	3.3	3.3	2.7	2.1	2.1	2.1	2.6	2.9	2.9	2.9
Rumania	1.3	1.2	1.6	2.1	2.5	3.1	3.2	3.1	3.3	3.1	1.7	1.3	0.9
South Korea	3.0	2.5	1.8	1.5	0.6	0.9	1.9	1.8	2.6	1.4	1.3	0.8	...
Spain	1.7	1.2	0.8	0.9	1.3	1.4	1.0	0.9	0.9	1.0	1.3	1.2	2.[illegible]
Sweden	1.2	1.1	1.1	0.8	1.0	0.9	0.9	0.9	0.8	0.8	0.9	1.7	1.[illegible]
Switzerland	1.7	1.8	1.4	1.1	1.2	1.2	1.2	1.4	1.4	1.4	1.2	1.1	1.[illegible]
Taiwan	1.5	0.7	0.7	1.1	1.0	0.7	0.7	0.8	0.7	0.5	0.3	0.3	0.[illegible]
U.K.	2.6	0.7	3.9	2.5	3.1	3.4	2.3	5.4	5.3	4.6	3.8	4.7	5.1
U.S.A.	13.3	16.7	19.0	18.8	14.8	20.4	22.2	21.3	21.0	18.1	17.3	15.7	18.[illegible]
U.S.S.R.	18.4	18.6	20.0	21.6	23.9	18.3	14.5	15.0	15.6	17.9	20.4	20.2	18.[illegible]
Yugoslavia	1.4	1.2	0.8	1.3	1.3	1.4	1.4	1.3	1.5	1.6	1.5	1.4	1.[illegible]
Total	100.0	100.0	100.0	100.0	100.0	100.0	100.0	100.0	100.0	100.0	100.0	100.0	100.0

Note: "Total" refers to totals given in the *American Machinist* for all machine tool producing countries, not the 20 largest producing countries only.
Source: *American Machinist*, various issues.

Table 11.2. Machine tool production indexes in the 20 largest producing nations, 1975–1987 (1980 = 100).

	1987	1986	1985	1984	1983	1982	1981	1980	1979	1078	1977	1976	1975
Brazil	127.1	117.5	84.2	33.3	31.2	54.8	96.9	100.0	122.9	81.1	89.9	70.7	43.[illegible]
Czechoslovakia	122.2	115.5	102.0	106.2	113.0	93.0	107.9	100.0	107.9	109.6	93.2	101.9	92.[illegible]
France	75.0	68.9	52.3	39.5	58.8	65.1	84.9	100.0	92.0	75.8	61.9	68.9	71.[illegible]
F.R.G.	132.6	110.1	67.7	59.6	67.8	74.5	84.0	100.0	85.1	72.1	56.0	51.2	51.[illegible]
G.D.R.	146.1	159.7	81.9	88.5	93.0	92.1	92.8	100.0	90.4	78.4	71.9	63.8	65
Hyngary	178.7	148.6	144.7	122.1	111.3	105.7	105.3	100.0	92.6	90.1	86.4	48.6	41.[illegible]
India	168.0	163.2	148.3	99.4	131.5	112.9	111.7	100.0	76.9	67.6	54.3	58.1	56.[illegible]
Italy	122.8	93.9	64.6	57.6	60.0	65.9	89.1	100.0	78.4	61.4	50.8	43.5	50.[illegible]
Japan	167.6	179.6	138.9	116.8	92.5	99.2	125.4	100.0	75.6	61.4	41.9	29.5	27.[illegible]
P.R.C.	81.4	86.6	81.2	114.7	113.2	111.9	104.8	100.0	100.0	96.4	84.5	75.0	71.[illegible]
Rumania	60.2	52.0	54.9	59.8	74.4	104.3	105.9	100.0	77.8	49.9	20.3	20.3	18.[illegible]
South Korea	374.4	247.0	129.6	109.0	88.3	117.0	131.9	100.0	121.3	70.4	42.2	7.4	...
Spain	144.5	112.3	71.7	59.9	65.5	83.7	90.7	100.0	89.5	65.8	54.1	51.3	63
Sweden	109.1	92.5	92.8	61.3	67.6	77.6	91.0	100.0	95.3	71.0	63.1	75.5	63.[illegible]
Switzerland	148.4	143.2	96.1	65.7	77.1	82.1	85.1	100.0	93.6	77.3	58.4	53.9	53.[illegible]
Taiwan	236.1	149.6	113.5	99.6	83.6	75.7	101.8	100.0	80.8	51.4	23.8	14.3	8
U.K.	63.0	26.3	39.4	27.1	41.1	55.9	51.6	100.0	71.7	58.8	42.1	46.2	52.[illegible]
U.S.A.	50.6	57.1	56.5	50.4	43.8	77.9	106.2	100.0	84.3	62.4	50.7	45.1	50
U.S.S.R.	129.7	119.8	99.0	90.6	100.4	96.3	95.7	100.0	90.1	86.5	71.8	65.6	64
Yugoslavia	247.5	168.4	103.2	97.5	99.7	122.7	119.4	100.0	81.6	74.8	61.0	54.3	29
Total	117.2	108.0	82.1	72.0	73.0	83.6	98.0	100.0	85.7	71.3	56.6	50.6	51

Note: "Total" refers to totals given in the *American Machinist* for all machine tool producing countries, not the 20 large producing countries only.
Source: *American Machinist*, various issues.

increased so that it exceeded the U.S. level during most of the 1970s. By 1982, Japan reached the position as the world's leading machine tool producer, having been only half as large as the U.S. and the F.R.G. in 1975. See Table 11.3 and Fig. 11.1.

The changing international distribution of world production of machine tools is reflected also in changing trade shares. As shown in Table 11.4, the traditional dominance of the F.R.G. has been reduced in recent years, particularly by Japan. But at the same time, an internationalization process has taken place; the combined world market share of the F.R.G., the U.S., U.K., and Japan has been reduced from 90% before World War II to around 50% in the 1980s. Whereas in the mid-1960s about 25% of world production of machine tools was exported, by 1980 that share had increased to 43%. In the United States, the share of exports in total shipments remained constant at 12% between the periods 1956–60 and 1976–80, while imports rose from 6% of U.S. machine tool consumption in 1958 to about 24% in 1980 and 53% in 1987. Thus, the United States went from a position of a strong net exporter to one of a substantial importer.

New Technology

Another important development was the emergence of new technology in the form of numerical control (NC), i.e., the application of computers instead of manual labor to

ble 11.3. Shares of machine tool production in the 20 largest producing nations, 1975–1987. Percent.

	1987	1986	1985	1984	1983	1982	1981	1980	1979	1078	1977	1976	1975
azil	1.3	1.3	1.2	0.5	0.5	0.8	1.2	1.2	1.7	1.3	1.9	1.6	1.0
echoslovakia	1.3	1.3	1.5	1.8	1.9	1.4	1.4	1.2	1.6	1.9	2.0	2.5	2.2
ance	2.3	2.3	2.3	2.0	2.9	2.8	3.1	3.6	3.8	3.8	3.9	4.9	5.0
R.G.	19.9	17.9	14.5	14.6	16.4	15.7	15.1	17.6	17.5	17.8	17.4	17.8	17.6
D.R.	4.2	4.9	3.3	4.1	4.2	3.7	3.2	3.3	3.5	3.7	4.2	4.2	4.3
ngary	0.7	0.6	0.8	0.8	0.7	0.6	0.5	0.5	0.5	0.6	0.7	0.4	0.4
lia	0.9	0.9	1.1	0.9	1.1	0.8	0.7	0.6	0.6	0.6	0.6	0.7	0.7
ly	6.8	5.6	5.1	5.2	5.3	5.1	5.9	6.5	5.9	5.6	5.8	5.5	6.4
an	20.5	23.8	24.2	23.2	18.1	17.0	18.3	14.3	12.6	12.3	10.6	8.3	7.8
.C.	1.1	1.3	1.6	2.5	2.4	2.1	1.7	1.6	1.8	2.1	2.3	2.3	2.2
mania	1.1	1.1	1.5	1.8	2.2	2.8	2.4	2.2	2.0	1.5	0.8	0.9	0.8
uth Korea	1.6	1.2	0.8	0.8	0.6	0.7	0.7	0.5	0.7	0.5	0.4	0.1	...
ain	1.6	1.4	1.2	1.1	1.2	1.3	1.2	1.3	1.4	1.2	1.3	1.3	1.7
eden	0.8	0.7	1.0	0.7	0.8	0.8	0.8	0.9	1.0	0.9	1.0	1.3	1.1
itzerland	4.7	4.9	4.3	3.4	3.9	3.6	3.2	3.7	4.1	4.0	3.8	4.0	3.9
wan	1.8	1.3	1.3	1.3	1.0	0.8	1.0	0.9	0.9	0.7	0.4	0.3	0.2
K.	2.8	1.3	2.5	2.0	2.9	3.5	2.7	5.2	4.4	4.3	3.9	4.8	5.3
S.A.	7.8	9.5	12.4	12.6	10.8	16.8	19.5	18.0	17.7	15.8	16.1	16.0	18.0
S.S.R.	12.7	12.7	13.8	14.4	15.8	13.2	11.2	11.5	12.1	13.9	14.6	14.8	14.5
goslavia	1.8	1.4	1.1	1.2	1.2	1.3	1.1	0.9	0.8	0.9	0.9	0.9	0.5
al	100.0	100.0	100.0	100.0	100.0	100.0	100.0	100.0	100.0	100.0	100.0	100.0	100.0

e: "Total" refers to totals given in the *American Machinist* for all machine tool producing countries, not the 20 largest ducing countries only.

rce: *American Machinist*, various issues.

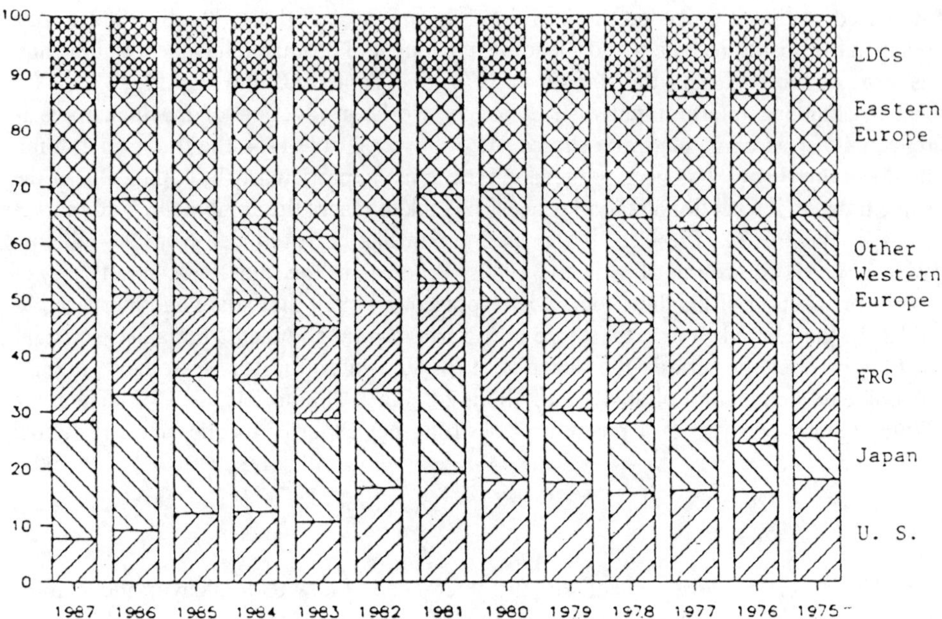

Fig. 11.1. Distribution of machine tool production among the largest producing nations, 1975–1987. Percent.
Source: *American Machinist*, various issues.

Table 11.4. Share of world exports of machine tools: F.R.G., United States, United Kingdom and Japan, 1913–1987. Percent.

Year	F.R.G.	U.S.	U.K.	Japan
1913	48	33	12	N.A.
1924	30	35	14	N.A.
1937	48	35	7	N.A.
1955	35	30	12	N.A.
1965	28	17	13	3
1975	32	10	6	6
1980	26	7	6	13
1987	23	4	3	20

Sources: 1913–1955: Daly and Jones, p. 53; 1965–1980: NMTBA, *Economic Handbook*, various issues.

guide the operations of machine tools. While the technological breakthrough of numerical control came during the late 1950s (see Carlsson 1984, for an account of the historical circumstances), the commercial breakthrough was delayed until the late 1960s. The United States had taken an early lead, followed by Sweden and Great Britain, with the F.R.G. somewhat behind (Nabseth and Ray 1974, p. 55). By the late 1960s, NC machine tools represented about 20% of the total production of machine tools in the United States (See Table 11.5). Then the share actually fell during the first half of the 1970s (in connection with a sharp decline in total machine tool production) and did not exceed 20% again until the late 1970s. But until the latter half of the 1970s, the United States was unquestionably the leading producer of NC machine tools. The NC shares of the value of machine tool output were significantly lower elsewhere. But as Japan, the F.R.G. and France surged ahead in the 1980s, the U.S. and U.K. were unable to respond.

The widespread diffusion of NC machine tools did not start until after 1975 when the microcomputer began to be used as the basis for the numerical control unit, i.e. as

Table 11.5. Share of NC machine tools in total machine tool production in various countries, 1968–1987. Percent.

Year	United States	Japan	F.R.G.	United Kingdom	France	Taiwan	South Korea
1968	20.5			7.8			
1969	17.4			8.5			
1970	13.5			7.9			
1971	14.5			9.6			
1972	13.4			6.0			
1973	15.2			6.5			
1974	17.5	12.2		6.3			
1975	20.6	12.6		7.0	11.1		
1976	23.1	15.2		8.0	12.2		
1977	20.4	18.7	10.0	8.0	16.5		
1978	21.6	24.2	11.0	10.0	22.6		
1979	25.0	32.4	12.1	12.0	22.4		
1980	28.5	39.1	14.3	15.0	19.8		
1981	28.7	41.0	15.1	19.0	25.7		4.8
1982	30.1	44.4	23.4	23.0	31.0		12.6
1983	32.1	50.7	29.6	25.0	45.4	7.0	13.3
1984	31.5	55.6	34.2	32.0	59.9	13.4	16.9
1985	30.2	55.4	38.2	32.0	54.3	15.0	21.7
1986			43.9	33.0		20.4	
1987			44.7	35.0		17.8	

Sources: U.S., France and Japan: NMTBA, *Economic Handbook*, various issues; F.R.G.: VDMA; U.K.: *Metalworking Engineering and Marketing*, March 1988; Taiwan: Metalworking Engineering and Marketing, July 1988; South Korea: *Metalworking Engineering and Marketing*, November 1988.

hard-wired NC units were replaced by CNC (computer numerical control). This change has led to a decline in the market for conventional (non-NC) machine tools: it is shrinking in the industrialized countries and growing only slowly, at best, in the newly industrializing countries (NICs). Hence it has become strategically important for producers even in the NICs to enter into the production of CNC machine tools (Jacobsson 1986, pp. 28–30).

As shown in Table 11.6, the share of NC machine tools in total investment in machine tools has increased sharply in recent years. It reached about 60% in the U.K. and Sweden in 1984, with somewhat more modest shares reported for Japan and the United States.

The replacement of conventional by NC machine tools is driven by cost considerations: "It is generally acknowledged that one NC lathe can displace four con-

Table 11.6. Share of NC machine tools in total machine tool investment in the U.S., Japan, U.K. and Sweden, 1978–84. (Percent, in value terms.)

Year	U.S.	Japan	United Kingdom	Sweden
1978	n.a.	15.6	19.0	26.0
1979	n.a.	27.2	22.5	31.1
1980	27.8	28.3	30.9	28.6
1981	30.2	29.3	44.9	30.6
1982	38.1	38.8	40.8	31.4
1983	43.8	47.5	54.6	55.0
1984	40.1	54.3	62.4	59.4

Source: Edquist and Jacobsson (1988, p. 25).

ventional machines; or one NC machining center, three conventional. First cost may be multiplied by about three, but the number of operators is significantly reduced; so, overall, the gain is likely to more than justify the preference for NC" (*The Engineer* 1984, p. 26). Furthermore, the market for special purpose machine tools (conventional machine tools built to order for individual customers) is shrinking. They are more expensive than general purpose NC machines, and the industries using special purpose machines are not growing. Also, users such as the aerospace and motor vehicle industries are replacing metal parts with plastics, composites, and ceramics, further reducing the demand for metalworking machine tools (*Engineering* 1987, p. 581). In certain types of machine tools, such as lathes, CNC machines have now become dominant. In 1975, the share of CNC lathes in the total production of lathes was 23 percent globally. By 1984 it had reached 73 percent. The value of output of conventional lathes fell by two-thirds between 1981 and 1984. (Jacobsson, 1986, p. 16).

The Japanese were the first to capitalize on the new CNC technology. In the mid-1970s they began to phase out conventional machine tools and moved instead into NC and CNC machine tools. Already by 1977 the number of NC machine tools produced in Japan surpassed that in the United States. While traditionally their machine tool production had been oriented almost entirely toward the domestic market, it now became much more export oriented. Already by 1979, 43 percent of the total Japanese production of NC machines was exported (Sunaga 1981, p. 6); by 1980, the number of NC machine tools produced in Japan was nearly three times as great as that in the U.S., and the value of NC shipments also exceeded that in the U.S. The high degree of product specialization of Japanese production, in combination with the strong Japanese export orientation, meant that close to 50% (by value) of the NC lathes and machining centers sold in the United States in 1980 were Japanese; the Japanese shares of the market in the European Economic Community were 19% in NC lathes and 13% in machining centers (CEC, p. 24). According to calculations for 1984, the Japanese share of the world market (excluding Japan) for CNC lathes "grew, in terms of units, from 12.6 percent in 1975 to nearly 50 percent in 1984. Thus, every other CNC lathe sold in the West in 1984 was made in Japan. In terms of value, the Japanese share rose from less than 6 percent in 1975 to around 35 percent in 1984." (Jacobsson 1986, p. 34.) Whereas in 1975, the main trade flows in CNC lathes went from the EEC to socialist and developing countries, in the 1980s the main trade flows consist of Japanese exports to the US and Europe (ibid., pp. 35–37).

In addition, the pace of technological change is increasing. "According to one of the leading Japanese CNC lathe builders, a design made in 1974–75 had a lifetime of eight years; while a design introduced in 1978 was being phased out in early 1983 and the expected lifetime of a design put on the market in 1983 was around three years" (Jacobsson 1986, p. 89). It has been reported that 80% of the machine processes displayed at the 1986 national machine tool show in Chicago did not exist in 1982 (Schor 1986, p. 14).

Structural Change

As one might expect, the market development just described has resulted in vast structural change within the industry in most countries. In the United States, where employment in the machine tool industry has fluctuated widely with the business cycles over the years, the number of employees was reduced from approximately 100,000 in 1980 to 58,000 in 1983, increasing slightly after that year. In the F.R.G., employment was reduced gradually from 122,500 in 1971 to 83,000 in 1984, while in Britain it declined from around 60,000 in the early 1970s to about 30,000 in the mid-1980s. Interestingly, employment in the Japanese machine tool industry declined as well: from about 50,000 in 1970 to 28,000 in 1978. After that time, however, employment has again increased, to about 35,000 in 1985. See Table 11.7.

It is noteworthy that even though Japan is now the largest producer of machine tools, it has less than half as many people in the industry workforce as the second largest producer, West Germany. This reflects differences in productivity as well as degree of

Table 11.7. Number of employees in the machine tool industry in various countries, 1970–1987.

Year	U.S.A.	F.R.G.	Japan	U.K.	Spain	France	Sweden
1970	102.2		49.2	65.1			
1971	78.4	122.5	50.6	59.0			
1972	76.6	117.6	46.7	50.1			
1973	86.9	115.5	45.2	48.4	12.1		
1974	94.0	115.8	45.3	50.0	12.2		
1975	88.8	109.3	40.9	49.1	11.6		
1976	81.0	101.4	34.5	47.1	11.0		
1977	83.1	95.9	32.2	47.7	10.5		
1978	89.5	94.8	28.2	48.5	10.3		
1979	96.1	95.0	31.1	48.4	10.0		
1980	99.7	98.0	33.7	46.4	9.5		4.0
1981	98.3	97.0	33.4	40.5	8.8	19.0	3.7
1982	77.8	93.0	34.2	37.0	8.5	17.7	3.2
1983	58.3	83.7	33.7	30.4	7.6	15.5	3.0
1984	63.0	83.0	33.6	29.5	7.4	13.4	3.0
1985		88.0	34.6	30.4	7.3	12.1	3.1
1986							
1987							

Note: Japanese data includes only those companies affiliated with JMTBA.
Source: National Machine Tool Builders' Association, *Economic Handbook of the Machine Tool Industry*, various issues.

vertical integration similar to those observed in other industries, such as the automobile industry. As shown in Table 11.8, the largest Japanese machine tool firms (in terms of machine tool sales) were considerably smaller in terms of number of employees than their largest foreign competitors. It is likely that most of the differences were attributable to a substantially higher degree of specialization by process (primarily involving assembly) in Japan, and more extensive outsourcing of components (especially CNC units, i.e. a much lower degree of vertical integration. Networking with suppliers seems to be the rule, not the exception.

United States. Between 1977 and 1982, there were at least 64 mergers, acquisitions, and purchases of corporate assets in the U.S. machine tool industry. These mergers and acquisitions involved primarily larger companies (some of which were foreign owned) acquiring smaller firms. This, in combination with other factors, led to the elimination of about 200 establishments. The total number was reduced from 1343 in 1977 to approximately 1140 in 1982. (USITC, 1983, p. 18). But that was only the beginning; in retrospect we know that 1981 and 1982 were really peak years, with orders exceeding $ 5 billion dollars. In 1986, machine tool orders were only $ 2 billion. It has been estimated that between 1981 and 1986, the number of firms in the U.S. machine tool industry was reduced from 700–750 to about 400 (Farnum 1986, pp. 57–58). The National Machine Tool Builders' Association estimated that some 25 percent of U.S. machine tool companies went broke or were absorbed by larger firms between 1984 and 1986 (Schor 1986, p. 14). Whereas at the end of the 1970s the major machine tool companies in the U.S. were independent firms, most of them were bought up by conglomerates by the mid-1980s (*The Engineer* 1985, p. 37). "Over two-thirds of this industry has already merged to survive, and some feel only a dozen or so companies will survive the decade" (Sprow 1985, p. 35).

But being part of a conglomerate does not guarantee survival; given the traditionally low profitability of the industry even during good years, "[a] lot of US machine tool

Table 11.8. World's largest machine tool companies.

No.	Company	Country	MT sales 1987	Tot. sales 1987	No. of Empl.
1	Yamazaki Mazak Corp	Japan	675.0	675.0	3000
2	Fanuc Ltd	Japan	650.9	693.1	1700
3	Litton Industries	U.S.A.	556.7	4735.6	54200
4	Amada Co Ltd	Japan	553.1	608.8	1560
5	Cross & Trecker Corp	U.S.A.	422.2	422.2	4100
6	Comau SpA	Italy	400.0	697.0	4971
7	Okuma Machinery Works	Japan	388.1	426.5	1782
8	Cincinnati Milacron	U.S.A.	374.0	828.0	9253
9	Mori Seiki Co Ltd	Japan	320.2	320.2	1537
10	Toyoda Machine Works	Japan	315.3	731.1	4367
11	Ingersoll Milling	U.S.A.	310.0	390.0	4500
12	Komatsu Ltd	Japan	298.1	3726.8	15801
13	Makino Milling Machine	Japan	242.7	242.7	951
14	Gildemeister Konzern	F.R.G.	234.0	234.0	2082
15	Aida Engineering Ltd	Japan	211.3	236.1	684

Source: *American Machinist*, August, 48.

companies will either be sold or closed because they are in the hands of conglomerates who traditionally are pretty cold-hearted concerning their bottom line and their stock prices" (ibid., p. 60). Indeed, some of the largest machine tool firms have already been sold off and some closed by the conglomerates which recently bought them. Even the largest privately held firms are having trouble: Cincinnati Milacron, until recently the largest U.S. machine tool firm, reduced its workforce from 14,000 to 9,000 during the period 1980–86 (O'Brien 1987, p. 32). Of the top 20 U.S. machine tool firms in 1966, only two remain; the others have disappeared from either merger, liquidation, or abandonment of particular product lines (*American Machinist* 1988, p. 48).

In view of these developments, it is not difficult to understand why protectionist sentiments have increased. Towards the end of 1986, the United States demanded the introduction of voluntary export restraints (VER) by Japan at levels 20% below 1985 sales. It also imposed quotas on NC lathes, machining centers, punching and shearing tools from the F.R.G., Switzerland, and Taiwan. Moreover, the UK and other countries have agreed not to take advantage of the vacuum created in the U.S. market by the reduction in imports resulting from these quotas (O'Brien 1987, p. 29, and *Engineering* 1987, p. 582).

Europe. The situation in the British machine tool industry is similar to that in the United States. As pointed out earlier, employment has dropped from 60,000 at the beginning of the 1970s to about 30,000 in the mid-1980s. Since 1966, Britain's share of the world machine tool market has fallen by a third, to just 2.8% of the world market in 1987 (compared with over 20 percent for Japan). In 1981–82, the Japanese market penetration reached 60% for machining centers and 50% for lathes in the UK, with total imports of these machines having an 80% market share. Due largely to a successful campaign by UK manufacturers to get the Japanese to restrict the number of CNC lathes and machining centers they ship to the UK, the share of Japanese imports in the total market dropped to around 30% for both CNC lathes and machining centers (*The Engineer* 1985, p. 35). But at least part of this decline is probably attributable to production of CNC machine tools by Japanese subsidiaries in the UK. Market penetration by German firms may also have contributed to the decline in market share of Japanese imports. The strategies pursued by UK manufacturers of CNC lathes and machining centers, specializing on advanced stand-alone machines and machines that come ready to be linked together into flexible machining cells, seem to have been no more successful than similar strategies in other Western countries.

In France, following the election of President Mitterrand's socialist government, almost the whole machine tool industry was brought under state control, either directly or via shares held by nationalized banks (*The Engineer* 1985, p. 37). The industry was merged into three giant firms (Renault, CGMO, and MFL) which now account for about 50% of output and 60% of exports. The rationale for this intervention was to achieve scale economies (Rendeiro, p. 66). Thus far, the reorganization appears to have yielded disappointing results. Although the NC share of output has increased sharply, French exports of machine tools have continued to decline, and the import dependency has continued to climb. This is in spite of the fact that over half the industry's customers are state controlled as well and are under pressure to "buy French", and that capital purchases in the public sector companies require trade union approval which is unlikely to be obtained for imported machines if domestic machines are available (*The Engineer* 1985, p. 37).

Apart from Japan, the only country that seems to have come through the 1980s relatively unscathed is the F.R.G. Its domestic market held up fairly well, and its share of the world market remained steady at about the 15% level where it had been since the mid-1960s, rising above that level in 1986 and 1987.

> West Germany remained less vulnerable to the effects of Japanese imports because in the early days at least, its machines were not so heavily slanted towards CNC. Indeed, until [1984], Germany maintained a positive balance of trade in machine tools with Japan.
>
> But the industry's reputation for building high quality, high reliability machines to high precision has been overtaken by advances in computer controls that can compensate for lack of precision in the machine. German machines were generally over-engineered and overpriced compared with their Japanese counterparts. There are signs now that that trend is being reversed and sales of German machining centers and CNC lathes to the UK, for example, seem to be on the increase (*The Engineer* 1985, p. 37).

Summary of Recent Developments

In summary, what happened in the machine tool industry in the late 1970s and in the 1980s is the following. (1) As in many other industries, there was a shift during the 1980s in the distribution of world output from the traditional suppliers in the United States and Western Europe to firms in Japan. During the late 1970s, the Japanese gains were mainly at the expense of the F.R.G. and the East European countries. Over the period as a whole, the shares of the developing countries and Eastern Europe (including the USSR) have been remarkably stable. (2) This shift in the locus of production was associated with increased international trade and specialization. (3) There was a shift from traditional products to a new "technological paradigm" as conventional machine tools began to be replaced on a large scale by numerically controlled machine tools. After the mid-1970s, Japan was in the forefront of this development. Thus, there was a strong connection between the shift in production and the emphasis on numerical control. (4) As a result of these changes, there were dramatic declines and structural changes in the machine tool industries in most Western countries, often triggering protectionist policy responses.

IV. Causes of the Observed Development

There are three features of the observed development which need to be explained: (1) Why did it take almost two decades for NC machine tools to become widely accepted? (2 Why were the Japanese able to move so rapidly into production of numerically controlled (NC) machine tools on a large scale; and (3) why were other countries slow to respond to the Japanese challenge? Each of these questions will be dealt with in turn.

Why Did It Take 20 Years for NC to Become Widely Accepted?

As regards the first question, there were both technical and market reasons. The main technical reasons were the following:

> First, the logic in the control units of these first numerically controlled machine tools was made of hardwired circuitry and, if new functions were to be performed, a change in the hardware had to be made. Secondly, the components were very unreliable and, thirdly, very costly. It was not until around 1970, when these relatively inflexible numerical control units were replaced by softwired minicomputers, that the diffusion of numerically controlled machine tools took place on a larger scale.
>
> A still more significant change in the technology, which indeed could be looked upon as a great qualitative change as opposed to a change in degree, was the use of microcomputers for the numerical control unit. This technology began to be incorporated in the numerically controlled machine tools in 1975–76, only a few years after the development of the micro chip. Indeed, Dr. Inaba, President of the very successful Japanese firm Fanuc, which pioneered this development, stated: "We applied the technical innovations in the semiconductor field to machine tools earlier than the computer industry did" (Jacobsson 1986, p. 9).

The shift to computer-based, and particularly to microcomputer-based, NC units has had several important implications for the NC machine tools:

1) The versatility and flexibility of the machine tools have been enhanced;
2) Programming has been simplified.
3) More functions can be controlled automatically (Jacobsson 1986, pp. 10–13).

It was only after these technical changes in the NC machine tools themselves in the mid-1970s that diffusion became widespread.

Another important reason why numerically controlled machine tools failed for almost two decades to be diffused on a wide scale is the traditional orientation of most major machine tool builders, both in the U.S. and Western Europe, towards the largest, most sophisticated users of machine tools. During the first half of the 20th century, the automobile industry provided the main impetus for technological change in machine tools, while from the 1940s on the aircraft and later the aerospace industries have dominated (Carlsson, 1984). Therefore, machine tool development was geared primarily to high-performance special-purpose machines, built to the specification provided by the user.

This tendency was reinforced in connection with the development of numerical control, which originated in the production of military aircraft in the U.S.

> The firms engaged in this effort found that the cost of the equipment mattered less than its capabilities, since the air force was paying for developing the tools and soon became the most important customer. At the same time, U.S. military and space agencies were administering their contracts with companies essentially on a "cost-plus" basis. Robert McNamara, while secretary of defense under Kennedy, introduced 'historical costing' into weapons procurement, whereby costs were allowed to increase at a steady rate based on past increases, rather than being tied to actual engineering estimates...

> The close connection between the military and the machine tool industry has had unfortunate results. In developing advanced machine tools, firms were able to avoid the hard work of keeping costs down through efficient design and production... Heavily influenced by military sponsorship, advanced numerically controlled machine tools have been so expensive as to be out of reach of most U.S. metalworking firms. In 1979, after the technology had been available for more than 20 years and had been heavily promoted in the trade press, only 2 percent of all the machine tools in use in this country were numerically controlled (Melman, pp. 58–60).[2]

Although West European machine tool firms have not been oriented particularly toward military applications in their machine tool development, they share with American firms a heavy emphasis on complex special-purpose machines for sophisticated users. It was this orientation towards a sophisticated and therefore limited market, in combination with the technical problems mentioned earlier, which kept NC machine tools from broader diffusion throughout metalworking industry until the mid-1970s. It was the Japanese who first broke through these barriers, i.e. they redefined the market and introduced computerized rather than hardwired controllers; this explains a great deal of their success. This is the subject to which we now turn.

What Did the Japanese Do Differently?

To some extent, the market was perceived differently in Japan, due to a difference in the source of demand pull. In the United States, and to some extent also in Western Europe, the aircraft industry has been a major user in the postwar period. This resulted in the orientation toward relatively large and sophisticated machines just mentioned, with more emphasis on the engineering built into the machines than on price. In Japan, by contrast, where the aircraft industry is small, the demand from the automotive industry has been relatively more important; the automobile producers and their subcontractors absorb one-half of all machine tool output (O'Brien 1987, p. 24). The competitive pressure in Japan (as reflected e.g. in the "just-in-time" delivery system) has led to stiff price competition and product standardization. Thus, in Japan there was more pressure for highly productive, reliable standard machines, whereas in the U.S. in particular there was relatively more demand for low-volume, high-precision, highly versatile machines.

It is not surprising, therefore, that in the mid-1970s several Japanese firms began to look at the limited application of NC machine tools as an opportunity rather than as a parameter. By simplifying the product, making it more general-purpose, and aiming it for small and medium-size firms, they completely changed the market.[3] The potential number of customers now suddenly numbered in the thousands, rather than the hundreds. This allowed these Japanese machine tool firms sharply to increase the volume of output, take advantage of scale economies to an extent not possible with the small batches prevailing before, and thereby significantly to lower costs.

There are potential economies of scale in virtually all operations within the machine tool industry. Jacobsson has calculated that prices on components vary substantially with the bargaining strength of the buyer, ranging from 10% reduction on raw materials to 40% reduction on control units. Combined with 35–40% cost reductions in machining and assembly and 50% in marketing, sales, and after-sales costs as output increases from 100 NC machines per year to the minimum efficient scale of 800–1000 units per year, the overall cost reduction amounts to about 40% (Jacobsson 1986, p. 98).

Thus, by virtue of their orientation to smaller, standardized machines and by increasing their output sharply, the Japanese were able to take advantage of scale economies to an extent never seen before in the machine tool industry. Thus they were able to emphasize price as a competitive tool to an extent not known before. The simplification and standardization of the product allowed an increased proportion of sales via distributors rather than direct sales to customers; the sharply increased output volume required this change in marketing approach (Jacobsson 1986, p. 50). Suddenly, Western machine tool firms found themselves faced with competition from Japanese CNC lathes and machining centers costing only one-third of the cost of their own.

Why Did It Happen in Japan First?

There were several factors which put Japanese machine tool firms in a particularly advantageous position to undertake this redefinition of the product and its market. As indicated already, the leading Japanese machine tool firms are large by international standards. When it is also taken into consideration that Japanese machine tool firms are basically assemblers (buying over 70% of their components from outside specialized firms) (Sprow 1985, p. 48), it becomes apparent that by measuring firm size in terms of employment, we are underestimating the size difference between Japanese and Western firms. This is illustrated by the following example: "one of the smaller Japanese firms, employing only 100 workers, disclosed that it was producing numerically controlled machine tools at the remarkably high rate of 30 units a month. With steady production... it is possible to buy components from suppliers on a predictable schedule at good prices... Japanese firms can produce advanced machining centers at prices averaging 40 percent below comparable U.S.-produced equipment" (Melman 1983, p. 62). A U.S. or West European firm of that size would more likely produce 30 NC machines per year.

Also, the broadening of the technological base of the industry creates problems for small firms. The introduction and integration of electronics into an industry previously dominated by mechanical technologies requires new technical skills which smaller firms often find it difficult to obtain: "[L]athes are no longer designed by an inventive mechanical engineer alone, but require a team with a multidisciplinary background. The market leaders' design teams have 30–50 percent electronic engineers, out of a total of 150–275 designers" (Jacobsson 1986, p. 99).

In addition, some of the leading Japanese machine tool firms are members of large industrial groups. Of the ten largest machine tool firms in Japan, at least four belong to such groups. An example is the Toyoda Machine Works, which is owned by the Toyota group. But given the important role played by "Network Industrial Organization" in Japan (see Imai, 1989) – i.e. informal (not via ownership), long-term close relations between suppliers and users in networks throughout Japanese industry – the benefits of close collaboration with certain customers are probably not restricted to those machine tool firms actually owned by industrial groups. One suspects that close links to large industrial users have been helpful in developing the technology. Being able to share detailed technical information with a machine tool firm as an in-house supplier rather than as an outside vendor changes the nature of the relationship and the information shared, and therefore most likely the resulting production system as well.

While there are a few examples of similar arrangements in Europe (e.g. within Volvo, Fiat, and BMW), they seem to be virtually nonexistent in the United States. Although many U.S. machine tool firms have recently been taken over by large, diversified firms (conglomerates), the acquisitions of machine tool firms appear to be motivated more by financial and diversification considerations than by vertical integration. Thus, it is not at all certain that being taken over by such firms makes greater financial resources available to the machine tool firms. In fact, the truth may be rather the opposite, as a number of U.S. firms have discovered: it is difficult for typically low-yielding machine tool firms to compete for funds with firms in more "glamorous" businesses.

In addition, in Japan there have also been strong links historically between producers of the numerical controllers and the machine tool builders. For example, Fujitsu Fanuc, the world's largest manufacturer of CNC units, began its collaboration with machine tool firms as early as 1958 when it developed the first Japanese NC machine tools in collaboration with Makino Milling Machine Company. It also appears that Japanese suppliers of CNC units, especially Fanuc, initiated the development of simpler and cheaper CNC units which could be applied advantageously to smaller machine tools than those manufactured in Western countries (Jacobsson 1986, pp. 56–57). Furthermore, virtually all Japanese machine tool firms have relied on Fanuc as supplier of their numerical controllers. This has given Fanuc the advantage of very large production volume (the primary reason why Fanuc is the world leader in numerical control today), at the same time as it has freed the machine tool firms to use their limited research and development resources in other areas.

By contrast, Western machine tool firms have often been fiercely independent in terms of both technical development and ownership. They have remained small and, until recently, have remained outside industrial groups. Many of them have chosen to develop their own numerical controllers, claiming that successful integration of electronic and mechanical components in the machine tools requires in-house development of both. But the result up until now appears to be that the Japanese approach involving closer integration between users and suppliers (in the form of informal networks rather than vertical relationships via ownership) and a more concentrated effort to develop numerical controllers has yielded a substantial lead over their Western competitors in the form of a more generic, powerful, and high-level technology. According to a study by the U.S. International Trade Commission in 1983, Japanese machine tools

> are generally perceived to be better designed than U.S.-made machine tools, have higher productivity, and require less maintenance. This appears to be especially applicable to standardized machines such as lathes and machining centers... The quality of after-sales service is reflected in providing spare parts in a timely manner, implementing warranties and product servicing, communicating product changes to the customer, and customer training. According to the Commission's survey of machine tool purchasers, in the U.S. marketplace, after-sales service for foreign-made standard machine tools, such as NC lathes and machining centers, appears to be superior to that for comparable U.S.-made machine tools. After-sales service for

U.S.-made specialty machine tools, however, received a higher rating from U.S. purchasers than the comparable foreign-made products...

The U.S. industry is regarded in world markets as the leader in high-technology machine tools that are designed for highly specialized operations. Such operations include aircraft component machining, military equipment machining, special health care equipment machining, and long assembly line operations such as those found in the automobile industry. In the standard-type machine tools, such as lathes and machine centers typically ordered by independent job shops, the U.S. equipment is perceived to be of lesser quality than that of major foreign producers, especially Japanese producers (USITC 1983, pp. xii–xv).

Summary of the Observed Development

While U.S. and European producers of NC machine tools were strongly oriented towards large, complex machines for few but sophisticated users, the Japanese revolutionized the industry by producing small, standardized machines for a much broader category of users. They were thus able to take advantage of economies of scale in purchasing of components, in machining and assembly, and in marketing and distribution, giving them a substantial cost advantage over their Western competitors. Thus, price competition and economies of scale have entered the competitive picture to an extent not know in this industry before. The nature of industrial organization in Japan is seen as giving Japanese machine tool firms a further advantage over their Western rivals.

V. Strategic Role of the Machine Tool Industry

In spite of its small size in terms of employment and value added, it is generally accepted that the machine tool industry plays an important role in industrial development. Its importance stems from the fact that metalworking machine tools constitute the production equipment in all metalworking industries. To the extent these industries have any competitive advantage at all in production techniques vis-à-vis their counterparts in other countries, it involves machine tools and their use. It is in its role as supplier of production equipment that the machine tool industry can be considered "leading" or "strategic."[4]

Following this line of reasoning, it is frequently argued that a domestic machine tool industry is necessary for user industries successfully to assimilate new technologies developed and diffused by machine tool suppliers. According to this argument, a strong machine tool industry can give the user industries a technological advantage over foreign competitors. If they have to rely on imported tools instead, they will, in effect, have to export a wide range of their manufacturing knowhow, thereby giving up a potential competitive advantage. Further, a domestic tool industry is better positioned than overseas builders to identify the needs of users and to work with them to solve problems. The more complicated and sophisticated the machine tools get, i.e., the more highly engineering intensive they are, the closer is the required collaboration between the supplier and the user, and the more crucial the geographical proximity between them becomes. In addition, it is also important to ensure compatibility of new machine tools with tools and production systems already in place, as well as availability of replacement parts over the life of the machine. For these reasons, many customers prefer to place orders with large domestic suppliers who may be expected to survive in the long run, rather than with foreign companies or small domestic ones (*Industry Week* 1984, p. 70).

In order to analyze the question whether the machine tool industry is strategic or not, it is necessary to distinguish between the supply of the technology and its practical application. A competitive advantage can be derived from using a machine tool in three ways:

a) standard use of a superior machine;
b) superior use of a standard tool; and
c) superior use of a superior machine.

When the claim is made that the machine tool industry is strategic, differences among customers in the way they use machine tools are usually ignored. The implicit assumption is that the use is identical in all applications. If that is true, competitive advantage does indeed depend on access to superior technology.

But while U.S. machine tool firms had a technological lead in NC machine tools for a couple of decades, that is true only of special-purpose NC machines today – where the competitive edge lies in the application rather than in the basic technology. It is well known that new machine tool technologies spread rapidly. Technical information diffuses through frequent trade shows, reverse engineering, and copying. If a machine tool builder has a superior technology, he wants to make it known and sell it as widely as possible. As shown earlier, the share of machine tool output which is traded internationally has been increasing. Reduced trade barriers, reduced cost and increased frequency of travel, and vastly improved communications have combined to reduce geographical distances greatly in the last few decades, thus eliminating some basic advantages previously enjoyed by local suppliers. The market today is becoming truly global rather than national or regional.

One implication of a global market is that new technology becomes available to potential users everywhere at the same time, or with only a short time lag.[5] It does not mean that certain suppliers cannot have a technological lead – the firms which are on the technological frontier – but it does mean that the use of their products is not restricted to any particular (home) market. If this is true, Japanese machine tools are available not only to Japanese users but also to users everywhere (except the planned economies, for well-known reasons).

There have been numerous studies of Japanese as compared with American and West European manufacturing techniques in the last decade. Even though most of the reports have found superior Japanese performance in several respects (productivity, reliability, quality, etc.), none of them have indicated Japanese superiority as far as the actual machinery and equipment are concerned. This indicates that the Japanese superiority lies in better use of the machine tools. A particularly striking example is the study by Jaikumar which showed that identical machines in similar production were used with an order of magnitude greater flexibility in Japan than in the United States (Jaikumar 1986, p. 70).

Thus, there is substantial evidence that whatever competitive advantage the Japanese may have in the manufacture of engineering products derives primarily not from superior machine tools but rather from superior use of standard tools. A highly educated and motivated labor force, a high degree of engineering competence, and a systematic approach to manufacturing have been combined to yield a Japanese technological lead in many areas.

Where does this leave us with respect to the argument that the machine tool industry is strategic, and that therefore a strong domestic machine tool industry is necessary for successful industrial development? The answer to the first part of the question depends on how fast new technology is diffused internationally. If new machine tool technology spreads rapidly across national boundaries, as the evidence suggests it does, it is difficult to sustain the argument that the machine tool industry is strategic. While there is ample evidence that the industry was strategically important in the past, its strategic position has been undermined by all the technological, political, and cultural changes which have made the world smaller in recent decades.

If this argument is correct, it is difficult to accept the notion that a domestic machine tool industry is necessary. Of course, if there already is a successful machine tool industry, so much the better for the balance of payments of the nation. What is of strategic importance is that there be technologically advanced, highly competent users of machine tool technology within the country.

It is of grave concern in this connection that many U.S. manufacturing firms, forced into financial and organizational restructuring, trimming of overhead, reduction of staff, and elimination of middle-level managers, have also sharply reduced their engineering staffs in the last decade. The reduction of engineering personnel may have been due partly to the fact that the complexity of the manufacturing systems was increasing and the existing staff did not have the required skills, particularly in the area of electronics. The result is that these firms are no longer competent buyers of complex manufacturing systems. Whereas ten years ago they designed their own systems, relying on machine tool firms only for bids on equipment specified by the buyer, now they often ask the machine tool firms to design the whole system. Thus, machine tool firms are being asked to perform tasks which they never had before, and this at a time when they are weakened by foreign competition, slow or declining sales, and when they are themselves struggling to keep up with the technology.

The magnitude of the task facing a machine tool firm can be illustrated by the following example: if a large company like General Motors requests a machine tool firm to design a new plant or process, chances are that there are more engineers on the floor of that plant than there are in the whole machine tool company.

This also raises the issue of who should pay for the system development. Traditionally, the buyer has requested bids from several machine tool firms for each project; only the eventual winner of the contract has been able to get paid for its efforts. But this is now changing, since systems proposals are often too costly for machine tool builders. Companies like GM are beginning to share some proposal costs. They may not narrow the competition to a single firm, but they select only a few for proposal projects, and they may share the costs of developing the system (Sprow 1985, p. 66).

The implications of the weakening of engineering competence on the part of many U.S. machine tool buyers are twofold: these firms are more dependent on outside engineering expertise than are many of their foreign competitors, particularly in Japan; and few machine tool firms (in the U.S. or elsewhere) are prepared to take up the challenge. The further implications of this "vacuum" in the market will be discussed below.

It is only to the extent that there exist barriers to international trade and technology transfer that the machine tool industry can be viewed as strategic. If such barriers exist, there may indeed be some positive effects of domestic availability of machine tools, for the following reasons: For small users, the search for appropriate machinery and for large users, the joint development and design activities, may be less costly if they are carried out with nearby domestic firms rather than with distant or foreign firms. There may also be external economies involved in regional concentration of machine tool users and producers. Local labor mobility, in combination with learning on the shop floor, may be an effective instrument for diffusion of manufacturing techniques.

Both of these hypotheses need to be tested empirically. Preliminary evidence gathered by the author in interviews with machine tool producers and users in both the United States and Sweden suggests that geographic proximity is a positive factor for successful collaboration between customer and vendor, but also that other factors are much more important. The most important criterion is that the supplier is on the technological frontier. Another important aspect is the existence of a common approach or "philosophy." For example, Swedish users reported that they would prefer to work with Swedish machine tool firms, but in the absence of domestic firms with competence in the relevant areas, they were often forced to rely on foreign suppliers. The search for technological leaders often led to Japanese, German and American firms. In choosing between these, the Swedish users found themselves most often selecting Japanese suppliers because of a commonality of approach to manufacturing which they did not find in American suppliers. (Cost arguments also entered in, particularly when the value of the U.S. dollar rose sharply in the mid-1980s.)

Similarly, American users clearly prefer to work with domestic American suppliers, provided they are on the technological frontier. If they are not, there is no alternative but to turn to foreign suppliers. Considering the leading position Sweden has in the application of NC machine tools as well as flexible manufacturing systems (FMS), the lack of a strong, broad-based domestic machine tool industry does not seem to have constituted an obstacle. By the same token, the early existence in the United States of strong, even unique, capability in these technologies does not seem to have generated a strong manufacturing base. The conclusion has to be that the existence of competent, sophisticated users is much more important for industrial development than the existence of a strong domestic machine tool industry. This is corroborated by the fact that the history of machine tool development is one of demand pull, not technology push. The role of the U.S. Air Force in the development of numerically controlled machine tools and of the automobile industry in developing transfer machines are two illustrative examples. (See further Carlsson 1984.)

VI. Implications for the Future

Business Strategy

The machine tool industry is at a crossroads today. The product standardization which was brought about via the introduction by Japanese producers of high-volume, mass-produced, low-cost, yet highly reliable and versatile CNC machines has completely changed the rules of the game. The rate of technological progress has increased dramatically; economies of scale have begun to become much more important than earlier; the flexibility and low price of the machines have opened up vast new markets, but at the same time the commodity-like nature of the machines has led to an increasing supply from newly industrialized countries. Through all these changes, the previous strategies of Western machine tool firms of supplying customized, special-purpose machines to few but sophisticated producers have become difficult to sustain.

One option in dealing with this challenge is to adopt a "Japanese" strategy of utilizing economies of scale and becoming the low-cost producer of sophisticated but standardized CNC machine tools. Scale economies can be obtained by specializing in only a few key components, outsourcing other components, and sharply increasing the volume of output of finished goods up to the levels of the top Japanese firms. This involves head-on competition with the Japanese in an area where they already have a substantial lead and where entry may also be expected by existing Western firms and by new competitors in the NICs. This is likely to be a battleground with a lot more losers than winners.

Another option is to move towards systems integration capability to meet the needs of many Western machine tool users, large and small. This is an area where the Japanese have been conspicuously absent, at least as far as Western markets are concerned. However, as suggested earlier, this competence seems to reside within the large industrial groups and informal networks in Japan. The problem with a strategy of this sort is that it requires technical skills which few, if any, machine tool firms currently possess. It also requires much closer collaboration with users than has been customary in the industry.

From the point of view of users, there is no question that the latter strategy would be the most desirable. However, there is an inherent problem in relying on outside suppliers for systems capability: a significant amount of manufacturing know-how has to be shared with the supplier, with possible leakage to competitors as a result. Also, the maintenance of the system once it is in place, and after the supplier has left the premises, is problematic. Thus, many users may be reluctant to engage in such ventures, unless the supplier can truly be regarded as an in-house operation. It therefore seems likely that many machine tool firms will either be bought up by large industrial firms to serve as captive sources of systems technology or be integrated in Japanese-like networks of suppliers and users working closely together in long-term relationships but without formal ownership.

In the final analysis, the problems of the machine tool industry in the Western countries (with the exception of the F.R.G.), and particularly in the United States, stem at least as much from the failure of users to think through their long-term manufacturing strategies and to make specific demands on machine tool suppliers, or to work with them in generating new technology, as from failures on the part of the machine tool firms themselves.

Public Policy

Under these circumstances, what is the appropriate role for public policy? Erecting trade barriers to protect domestic machine tool manufacturers is likely to be the worst of all possible policies. Such a policy would protect a few hundred machine tool firms, some competent to survive on their own without government intervention, others not, while raising machine tool prices for thousands, if not millions, of domestic users, thus making it more difficult for them to compete in world markets.

Another policy which might have appeal at first glance is so-called Strategic Trade Policy (STP), the idea of which is via government intervention to give domestic companies an advantage over their foreign competitors by enabling them to expand their capacity, or by making the threat of such a move more credible, thus preempting similar moves by foreign competitors. However, the first U.S. attempt to carry out such a policy in the semiconductor industry does not bode well: even in a case where the producers are few and the product well defined, it is difficult in a democracy to arrive at a consensus in a timely fashion such that effective policy can be made. In the machine tool industry, with hundreds of producers and thousands of products, such a policy would be simply impossible to carry out.

A policy more likely to succeed would involve government procurement or sponsorship of new machine tool technology. The U.S. Department of Defense has a long history of doing precisely this; the development of numerical control is a perfect example. But if machine tools are strategic not only in a military sense but also more broadly as conveyors of new production techniques, a technology procurement policy beyond military applications would be justified. Such a policy could take the form of subsidization of private procurement of new machine tools. Its object would be to provide greater incentives for development of new technology, to reduce the risks inherent in such projects, and to encourage more extensive cooperation between users and suppliers of machine tools.

Another policy option, which could be pursued parallel with the previous one, would be to encourage more and better engineering education.

Notes

* I would like to thank Staffan Jacobsson, Jürgen Müller and Nils-Olov Stålhammar, as well as the participants of the International Conference on Small Business Economics, for helpful comments on earlier versions of this paper, and Erol Taymaz for valuable research assistance.

1. Several of the tables presented here are based on national data in current prices converted into U.S. dollars using official exchange rates. Because of the volatility of exchange rates in recent years, caution must be exercised in interpreting the numbers.
2. Similar views have been expressed by David Noble: "The point of this story is that the same thing that made NC possible, massive Air Force support, also quite possibly determined the shape the technology would take. Criteria for design of machinery normally include cost to the user. Here cost was hardly a major consideration; machine tool builders were simply competing to meet performance specifications for government funded users in the aircraft industry. They had little concern with cost effectiveness and absolutely no incentive to produce less expensive machinery for the commercial market" (Noble 1978, p. 329, quoted in Jacobsson 1986, p. 55).
3. The different approach taken by the Japanese with respect to the design of the CNC lathe is illustrated in a Japanese journal article of 1977:

   – At the first stage, these low cost NC lathes could not be introduced smoothly due to the prejudice that NC lathes should be machine tools of high quality equipped with luxurious functions. Though NC lathes of high grade with luxurious functions were really required for some turning operations, it is also true that all the valuable functions are not required for all the turning operations. In many fields, NC lathes of simplified functions can sufficiently turn the parts, and many low-cost NC lathes are now accepted positively (*Today's Machine Tool Industry* 1977, pp. 70-2, quoted in Jacobsson 1986, p. 49).

4. It is also often argued that the machine tool industry is strategic from a national security point of view. This argument is not examined here, since our focus is on industrial, not military, capability.

5. This argument is subjected to critical analysis in Carlsson & Jacobsson (1990), where it is found that in certain types of machine tools, particularly involving flexible manufacturing systems, supply restrictions may apply, hindering transfer of new technology, sometimes for substantial periods.

References

ABC Group, 1983, "Marketing Machine Tools in the United States." Unpubl. mimeo.

American Machinist, 1988, "Machine-Tool Scorecard," *American Machinist*, August, p. 48.

Carlsson, Bo, 1984, "The Development and Use of Machine Tools in Historical Perspective," Journal of Economic Behavior and Organization, 5(1), 91–114.

Carlsson, Bo and Staffan Jacobsson, 1990, "What Makes the Automation Industry Strategic?" Working paper, Case Western Reserve University and Chalmers University of Technology (mimeo.).

Commission of the European Communities (CEC), 1983, "The European Machine Tool Industry. Commission Statement. Situation and Prospects," SEC (83) 151 final. Brussels, February.

Edquist, Charles and Jacobsson, Staffan, 1988, *Flexible Automation: The Global Diffusion of New Technology in the Engineering Industry*, Basil Blackwell, Oxford.

The Engineer, 1984, "Switching the Focus to the Buyer," 17 May, 24–26.

The Engineer, 1985, "Machine Tools: The View over Europe," 12 September, 35–37.

The Engineer, 1986, "Machine Tool Survivors Fight Back," 21/28 August, 47–49.

The Engineer, 1986, "Suppliers Seek More Integration," 21/28 August, 57.

The Engineer, 1986, "Good, Bad – and Unavoidable," 21/28 August, 87–92.

The Engineer, 1987, "Machine Tools: Facing the Future," October, 581–582.

Farnum, Gregory T., 1986, "The Machine Tool Industry – A Look Ahead," *Manufacturing Engineering*, November-December, 57–62.

Imai, Ken-ichi, 1989, "Evolution of Japan's Corporate and Industrial Networks," in B. Carlsson (ed.), *Industrial Dynamics: New Issues in Industrial Economics*, Kluwer Academic Publishers, Boston (forthcoming).

Industry Week, 1984, "Machine Tools: Will the Cornerstone Erode?" *Industry Week*, April 30, 63–78.

Jacobsson, Staffan, 1986, *Electronics and Industrial Policy. The Case of Computer Controlled Lathes*, Allen & Unwin, London.

Jaikumar, Ramchandran, 1986, "Postindustrial Manufacturing," *Harvard Business Review*, Nov.-Dec., 69–76.

Melman, Seymour, 1983, "How the Yankees Lost Their Know-How," *Technology Review*, October, 56–64.

Nabseth, Lars and Ray, G.F. (eds.), 1974, *The Diffusion of New Industrial Processes: An International Study*, Cambridge University Press, Cambridge.

NMTBA (National Machine Tool Builders' Association), Economic Handbook of the Machine Tool Industry, various issues. NMTBA, McLean, VA.

Noble, David F., 1978, "Social Choice in Machine Design: The Case of Automatically Controlled Machine Tools and a Challenge for Labor," *Politics and Society*, 8, 3–4.

O'Brien, Peter, 1987, "Machine Tools: Growing Internationalisation in a Small Firm Industry," *Multinational Business*, No. 4 (Winter), 23–34.

Rendeiro, Joao, 1984, "How the Japanese Came to Dominate the Machine Tool Business," mimeo.

Schor, Adam, 1986, "Some Small Companies Sidestep the Falling Machine Tool Industry," *Cincinnati Business Courier*, Nov. 10, 14–15.

Sprow, Eugene, 1985, "Industry Report – Machine Tools," *Tooling & Production*, June, 35–72.

Sunaga, A., 1981, "The Machine Tool Industry in Japan," *Utlandsrapport från Sveriges Tekniska Attachéer*, Japan 8103.

United States International Trade Commission (USITC), 1983, Competitive Assessment of the U.S. Metalworking Machine Tool Industry. Report to the United States International Trade Commission on Investigation No. 332–149 Under Section 332 of the Tariff Act of 1930. USITC Publication 1428, September. Washington, D.C.: USITC.

Comment on "Small-Scale Industry at a Crossroads: U.S. Machine Tools in Global Perspective" by Bo Carlsson

Jürgen Müller

Bo Carlsson had provided us with an insightful piece of analytical research on the (no longer small scale) machine tool industry. Perhaps the picture is so complex, because the interaction of changes in technology, in economies of scale, in demand and geographic market size all take place at the same time.

First of all there is a change in technology, which involved the crossing of industry boundaries from mechanical to electronics in the product itself and the change from stand-alone machines to integrated transfer processes whithin the user sector. Especially this crossing of boundaries has severely challenged traditional mangement doctrines in the industry and favoured those firms that were more flexible in combining the virtues of quick process and product adoptions within and across sectors.

Secondly, the move to electronics (i.e. the introduction of special process computers for NC-machines) has increased the research and development costs and thereby changed, the ratio of fixed costs to variable cost (mainly because of set-up and software costs). Furthermore, the move towards an integrated systems approach by the users has required a larger assembly of intelligence within the investment goods producing industry rather than within the user sector. Both effects have tended to increase economies of scale as larger sales are required to distribute the fixed R&D costs.

The increased need to manage the system's know-how (both staying in touch with diverse customers and integrating this knowledge into several products has also raised the overhead costs. As a consequence of these scale effects we have seen a strong nationalization within the industry.

Thirdly, the markets for these products have become much more global. This has been helped by increasing intra-industry trade, a movement towards more standardized products (in line with a more global approach to marketing in the manufacturing sectors, where machine tools are especially important), and a standardization of manufacturing techniques around the world. These tendencies have meant that traditionally national or regional markets have been combined into a world market. These manufacturers that recognized this process early and move aggressively in their marketing effort have moved down the scale and learning curve very successfully, as demonstrated especially by the Japanese manufacturers. The Japanese have been helped in this process by a fairly large domestic market for machine tools that existed before electronically controlled NC-equipment was introduced. Their initial comparative advantage in exploiting scale with standardized products was thereby further enhanced by this extra change in product characteristics.

We see that these three factors lead to a change in comparative advantage and international specialization. Comparative advantage here refers much more to the relative endowment in human capital, technology know-how and the ability to have a close collaboration and networking relationship with users and the research and development establishment. Bo Carlsson has stressed the first link to final users, in which

Z.J. Acs and D.B. Audretsch (eds.), The Economics of Small Firms: A European Challenge. 194–195.

the Japanese seem especially well adapted. It might be useful to also explore the second link to research and development activities, a link which seems to have helped the West German industry to survive the initial onslaught of the Japanese.

What is missing in this part of the paper is an attempt at characterizing the eventual long term structural equilibrium and to analyse to what extent changes in the final demand for products, for which machine tools are used, influence this new structural equilibrium.

Also the issue of second sourcing and its influence on the long term structure is not discussed. Normally second sourcing leads to a reduction in the realization of economies of scale that can be exploited on the supplier's side. Given the fact that a close collaboration between producers and users is so important for both, we may observe a very different relationship between equipment suppliers and users than the one envisaged under the notion of second sourcing. This may then be better characterized by close collaboration in the sense that there exists a long term supplier relationship with one supplier only. This would give a supplier a chance to keep up with the technology race, and to maintain a fairly secure market position, which is much more difficult to dislodge, while the weakness of those who fall behind would be quickly exploited.

While I don't think a more formal model is necessary to exploit the consequences of this development, some ideas of how the long run structural evolution might look like would be useful. Against this background Bo raises quite correctly the strategic trade issue, but without giving us any answers or policy advice.

D. SMALL FIRMS, NEW ENTRY AND EMPLOYMENT

12. The Size of the Small-Firm Sector in Hungary

ZOLTÁN ROMÁN

I. Introduction

There currently exists an unprecedented enthusiasm for small business in virtually every country in the world. This applies not only to the developed nations, the so-called market economies, but also within the socialist bloc (Sato 1989). Traditionally there exist two reasons why centrally planned economies usually prefer larger plants and firms to smaller ones: (1) the belief that economies of scale are found in larger firms, and (2) a small number of firms are more conducive to central planning, and party control. Monopoly power will not be questioned since the party itself constitutes a monopoly. These motives prevailed for many years leading to highly centralized economies in Eastern Europe.

After a decade of "crisis" following the twin oil shocks it is widely recognized that strengthening the small-business sector is a prerequisite to revitalizing the Hungarian economy. The need for a shift in the firm-size distribution to increase efficiency is widely recognized, while more fundamental issues of private ownership are taking longer due to resistance and ideological uncertainty.[1]

Although the post-1973 period required a high degree of adjustment and mobility on the part of both companies and individuals, this was obstructed by the drive for stability and security. As in many other countries, the government allocated most of its resources to declining sectors of the economy instead of boosting promising fields that would contribute to future development. Structural adjustment was also delayed by the pressure to maintain full employment, as well as by strong export incentives irrespective of structural considerations. Strengthening the small-business sector should facilitate structural reforms needed to revitalize the Hungarian economy.[2] This process, as in the United States,[3] is hindered by the simple fact that comprehensive data on small business are not available. The purpose of this paper is to estimate the size of the small-firm sector in the Hungarian economy.

In the second section of this chapter we provide a brief overview of the Hungarian economy in the 1980s. In the third section we estimate the size of the small-firm sector in Hungary, while in the fourth section we examine the contribution of small firms in the Hungarian economy today. We find that small firms account for 35 percent of employment in the Hungarian economy.

II. The Hungarian Economy in the 1980s

In order to understand the condition of the Hungarian economy today, and to assess the actual and potential role of small business, a short overview of the last two decades

Z.J. Acs and D.B. Audretsch (eds.), The Economics of Small Firms: A European Challenge. 199–204.

is needed. Following the 1968 economic reforms the economy expanded rapidly, supply conditions improved, and some decision making was decentralized. However, when the reforms started to differentiate between profitable and unprofitable enterprises, opposition to the reforms stiffened. The next steps in implementing the reforms, organizational and institutional changes, and a greater reliance on the market as a coordinating mechanism did not materialize. After an initial period, centralization was again strengthened and enterprise autonomy was once again restricted.

In part, this reversal was motivated by changes in the world economy which seriously affected Hungary in the 1970s. These changes were judged to be of a transitory nature and their consequences thought to be countered with appropriate policy measures. As the changes proved to be more long lasting, i.e. more structural than cyclical, substantial losses were inflicted upon the terms-of-trade by rising energy and raw material prices. These losses could not be balanced by stronger economic growth. In order to maintain a rising standard of living, borrowing from the West increased significantly. By 1978 the deficit in the balance of foreign trade reached 59.8 billion Forint.

Economic growth slowed as policy makers focused on bringing about an equilibrium in the balance of trade. At this time the support for the economic reforms of 1968 were reaffirmed by the political leadership. After the second oil price explosion, depression, increasing protectionism, and a worsening political climate followed in Western Europe and the United States, making credit more difficult and expensive, creating a serious liquidity problem in Hungary. Maintaining international liquidity became the first priority of economic policy.

Between 1980 and 1988, the economy grew more slowly, averaging only 1–2 percent a year. While full employment was maintained, inflation averaged over 7 percent throughout the decade, and growth in real wages declined from 3.1 percent in 1978 to 1.3 percent in 1985. Gross domestic investment declined by between 2–5 percent a year for most of the decade. As a consequence the balance of trade recorded a surplus and the net foreign debt (in convertible currencies) decreased from 8 billion dollars in 1978 to 6 billion dollars in 1983. Based on the performance of the economy in the mid 1980s growth was expanded, as well as easing curbs on consumption and investment. However, the euphoria was short lived. The foreign exchange surplus needed to service the debt stagnated in 1984 and decreased the following year, turning into substantial deficits in 1986 and 1987.

Twenty years after the introduction of promising economic reforms, in 1988 the Hungarian economy is in a crisis-situation. The convertible currency debt (gross) as a percentage of GDP increased to 80 percent, and the debt service ratio as a percentage of exports in convertible currency increased to 50 percent. Inflation is near 20 percent, job security is vanishing, real wages are declining and the next five years do not offer much hope for visible improvement. In September 1987 Parliament approved a program for stabilization of the economy with more emphasis on *long-term reforms*, providing for an expanded role for market coordination and expansion of the small-firm sector. This is to be carried out in conjunction within the political sphere (more decentralization and democratic participation). The hope is to regain the confidence and support of the population, but recent developments do not meet this expectation.

III. The Size of the Small-Business Sector

Comprehensive data on the small-business sector are not available from official data for the Hungarian economy. To estimate the size of the small-firm sector, we must first distinguish three types of activities: (1) the formal economy; (2) the shadow or underground economy; and (3) the second economy. In Hungary, according to different estimates, between 25–30 percent of total hours will be in the second economy, accounting for about 20 percent of GDP. While these activities often have close ties to large firms, all of these activities are at least in some sense private activities and should be counted as small firms.

In the industrial sector large state-owned enterprises dominate. Between 1950 and 1980 the number of state-owned enterprises declined from 1,425 to 700. Since then the number has increased by 50 percent. Table 12.1 shows that in 1987 1,043 state-owned enterprises employed 1,258,000 workers and produced 80.3 percent of industrial output. There are 1,392 industrial co-operatives accounting for 6.1 percent of industrial output. The majority of their 3,973 establishments had less than 500 employees accounting for 95.7 percent of employment. Non-industrial organizations employ 218,000 workers and operate 13,667 establishments. Although these organizations are only semi-autonomous, under the special Hungarian circumstances they function like small businesses.

Before giving an estimate of the share of small business in Hungarian manufacturing we have to decide how to deal with the Working Communities and Groups, and semi-autonomous industrial sub-units of the Non-Industrial Organizations. I suggest to exclude the former and include the latter. On this basis 31 percent of industrial employment and 34 percent of manufacturing employment can be considered as small i.e. less than 500 employees. At least in terms of employment, Table 12.2 shows that no other country has a smaller percentage of employment in manufacturing than Hungary. The U.S. and the U.K. are the only countries that come close to this level of concentration in manufacturing. Countries similar to Hungary, for example Belgium, Austria and Ireland, have at least 50 percent of manufacturing employment in small firms.

Table 12.1. Industrial activities in Hungary by type of organization, 1987.

Type of organization	Number of enterprises or other units	Employment thousands	Percentage share in the value of total industrial output
State-owned enterprises	1043	1258	80.3
Industrial cooperatives	1392	196	6.1
Working communitites and groups	12484	193	0.6
Private industry	47691	81[a]	1.8
Non-industrial organizations	2492	218[b]	11.2
Total	–	–	100.0

Source: *Statistical Yearbook 1987*, pp. 90–91; *Industrial Statistical Yearbook 1987*, pp. 309–310.

[a] Without the employees of the partnerships.

[b] Workers only.

Table 12.2. The percentage share of employees in the small and small-and-medium-sized enterprises in the manufacturing sector.

Country	Small Enterprises (less than 100)	Small-and-medium-sized enterprises (less than 500)
Italy (1981)	58.9	80.2
Japan (1980)	57.8	73.4[a]
Ireland (1980)	38.1	79.6
Portugal (1985)	43.8	77.5
Denmark (1982)	39.8	74.4
France (1980)	44.1	72.9
Spain (1978)	43.4	65.2
Austria (1976)	39.0	62.7
Netherlands (1980)	38.8	–
Belgium (1985)	32.8	58.7
Luxembourg (1980)	19.2	45.0
Finland (1984)[b]	25.5	43.8
F.R.G. (1983)[c]	(16.0)	(40.8)
U.K. (1983)	22.0	36.4
U.S.A. (1986)	23.7	37.4
Hungary (1987)	23.0	34.0

Sources:
For EEC countries: Johnson, S. and Storey, D.J., *Small and Medium Sized Enterprises and Employment Creation in the EEC Countries – Summary Report*, 1988, p. 7.
Japan: Small Business Agency, *Small Business in Japan 1984*, MITI, 1984, 92.
Austria: Aiginger, A. and Tichy, S., *Die Größe der Kleinen*, Signum Verlag, 1985, 43.
Finland: *Statistisk arsbok for Finland*, 1987, p. 195.
U.S.A.: *The State of Small Business.* A Report of the President, Washington, DC, 1988, p. 49.

[a] Enterprises with less than 300 employees, estimate for the 500 category: 78 percent.
[b] Industry.
[c] Only enterprises with more than 20 employees, estimate including these firms also: 22 percent and 47 percent, respectively.

In 1987 two-thirds of total agricultural output was produced on 130 state farms and 1,392 co-operatives. The other one-third was produced by 1,400,000 small producers mostly as part of the second economy. Almost all of the small farms are members of the co-operatives. While only 7.5 percent of employment on state farms is on establishments of less than 500 employees, the co-operatives have over half of their members working on units with less than 500 employees. The small business share of agricultural output can be estimated at between 60–70 percent.

The construction sector is dominated by 351 state-owned enterprises and 909 co-operatives. However, 50 percent of the employees are engaged in non-construction activities. Of the state-owned enterprises only about 20 percent had less than 500 employees. All other construction activities are performed by small-business units. In spite of the high concentration in the state-owned sector, about 70 percent of construction activity is carried out by small firms. While state-owned enterprises and co-operatives dominate in retail trade and catering, the private sector is growing. The share of small business in this sector accounts for about 30 percent of employment. It should be mentioned that about two-thirds of the retail trade and catering units of the state enterprises are working with a high degree of autonomy.

Telecommunications, transport and foreign trade are all concentrated in large state-owned monopolies. However, some decentralization is taking place in the foreign trade sector.

Accepting the author's interpretation of small business in Hungary, the share of small-firm employment is about 20 percent for firms with less than 100 employees and 35 percent for firms with less than 500 employees. This estimate included employment in the second economy.These firms contribute about 25 percent and 35 percent to GDP, respectively. New studies, estimates, and calculations are in progress which should fill in the gaps. Even if these figures are "rough", it is interesting to note that small firms accounted for 44 percent of total U.S. employment in 1986!

IV. Small Business in the 1980s

Small business already fulfills an important role in the Hungarian economy. In the area of market competition the recent expansion of the small-firm sector has brought improvements in some segments of the economy. Still many conditions of market competition are lacking and an expansion in the number of firms is needed. Small firms have been innovative in finding market niches. This potential of the small-business sector is seriously underutilized.

Because of the lack of small firms in the Hungarian economy, the role of small firms as suppliers to larger enterprises, as found in Japan for example, is lacking. As the centralized administration of large firms is reduced, a greater role for small firms will emerge. Small business because of its greater flexibility and stronger market orientation fulfills an important role providing a wider assortment of consumer goods. At the present time this is an important source of support for small firms.

While investment into the small-business sector is increasing, its share of total investment is still very low. However, before investment in small business can be increased, the general climate for investment should be improved. For example, a stable price level, lower real interest rates, lower taxes and government spending. Given a stable environment institutional lending for small firms should increase.

Small business as an entrepreneurial sector of the Hungarian economy is still small, lacks dynamism, and is far from being innovative enough to have a significant impact on structural adjustment. In this respect the decentralization of large multiplant firms should accelerate this process. A wider network of small firms as sub-contractors could facilitate changes in the pattern of production of large firms. It should be noted that the behavior of small firms often mimics the behavior of larger firms in Hungary. In order to modify this pattern of behavior, better management is needed.

V. Conclusion

One of the most striking conclusions of this paper is that the small-business sector in the Hungarian economy is smaller than that of any other industrialized country. In fact, small firms account for only 34 percent of employment in the manufacturing sector. As the Hungarian economy evolves from a "centrally planned" to a market ("socialist market") economy, and as political developments move from a one-party system to a multi-party system, strengthening the small-business sector is a prerequisite for the transformation and revitalization of the Hungarian economy. A successful small-business development program should be threefold: create a favorable environment for entrepreneurship: eliminate political and administrative barriers for new start-ups; and create a network of institutions to promote, finance, and facilitate small business. Today we are closer to a consensus on these issues. More communication, better understanding, and cooperation between governments, small-business associations and research should help to implement this program.

Notes

1. For example, see Falusné (1985), Gábor (1985), Kornai (1986), Laky (1984), Nyers (1985), Révész (1986), Román (1981, 1984,, 1985, and 1988), Kovács (1986).
2. Small firms in the U.S. have been the key to revitalizing the entire structure of the economy. For a review of this literature see Acs and Audretsch (1989) and Brock and Evans (1989).
3. The United States has recently constructed an excellent small business data base (Phillips and Kirchhoff 1989).

References

Acs, Zoltan J., and Audretsch, David B., "Job Creation and Firm Size in the U.S. and West-Germany," *International Small Business Journal*, 2 (3), 1989.

Brock, William A. and Evans, David S., "Small Business Economics," *Small Business Economics*, 1 (1), 1989, 7–20.

Falusné Szirikra, Katalin, "Small Enterprises in Private Ownership in Hungary," *Acta Oeconomica*; 34 (1-2), 1985, 13–26.

Gábor, István, and Galasi, Péter, "Second Economy, State and Labour Market," in P. Galasi and Gy. Sziráczki (eds.), *Labour Market and Second Economy in Hungary*, Frankfurt-New-York: Campus Verlag, 1985, 122–132.

Kovács, Géza József, "Job-Creating Capacity of the Private Sector in Hungary Between 1981–1985," *Acta Oeconomica*, 37 (3-4), 1986, 341–354.

Kornai, János, "The Hungarian Reform Process: Visions, Hopes, and Reality," *Journal of Economic Literature*, 24 (4), 1986, 1687–1737.

Laky, Teréz, "Small Enterprises in Hungary – Myth and Reality," *Acta Oeconomica*, 32 (1-2), 1984, 39–63.

Nyers, Rezsó, "National Economic Objectives and the Reform Process in Hungary in the Eighties," *Acta Oeconomica*, 35 (1-2), 1985, 1–16.

Révész, Gábor, "On the Expansion and Functioning of the Direct Market Sector of the Hungarian Economy," *Acta Oeconomica*, 36 (1-2), 1986, 105–121.

Román, Zoltán, "Industrial Organization in Hungary," in *Economics, Planning and Management*, Papers of the Fourth Hungarian-Indian Round-Table of Economists, Budapest, 12–15 October 1981, New Dehli, 26–50.

Román, Zoltán, "Productivity, Entrepreneurship and Intrapreneurship in the Hungarian Economy," *EPI* (Europe Productivity Ideas), January, 1984.

Román, Zoltán, "The Conditions of Market Competition in the Hungarian Industry," *Acta Oeconomica*, 34 (1-2), 1985, 79–97.

Román, Zoltán, "Productivity and Performance in the Hungarian Economy," in *Managing for Productivity*, EPI (Europe Productivity Ideas) Special Issue, 1988, 6–20.

Sato, Yashio, "Small Business in Japan: A Historical Perspective," *Small Business Economics*, 1 (2), 1989, 121–128.

Storey, David J., Johnson, S. and Steven *Job Generation and Labour Market Change*, London: Macmillan, 1987.

Comment on "The Size of the Small-Firm Sector in Hungary" by Zoltán Román

István R. Gábor

Professor Román's paper is an extremely informative and insightful analysis of the controversial role of small business in Hungary.

His central thesis is that, as a result of economic reforms implemented by the country's political and economic leadership since 1968, the Hungarian economy – a "centrally planned economy" at the outset – is undergoing, although reluctantly and interrupted by reversals, a process of transformation towards a "socialist market economy". As long as this final goal has not been achieved, the country must face social and economic conflicts. Because of these conflicts, exacerbated by the economic recession and the over-indebtedness of the country, the Hungarian leadership should accelerate the implementation of the reforms.

The predominance of market coordination as the final goal of the reforms will be attained through measures taken to decentralize economic power. By decentralization, Professor Román means, (1) a reallocation of economic power within the industrial and large-scale cooperative sector, i.e. a higher degree of autonomy of firms operating there; and (2) a more favourable attitude by the state towards private entrepreneurship, i.e. adoption of less restrictive economic and legal regulatory practices.

It is hoped that such a process of decentralization would bring about an increase in the number of competing firms clearly an indispensible precondition for the market to function effectively. On the other hand, since the obvious controversies that now exist on the role of the – mostly private – small business sector, and the chronic malfunctioning of the large-scale sector, are closely interrelated, they could only be eliminated simultaneously through a consistent implementation of the reform principles.

As a matter of fact, these ideas are largely accepted by the majority of leading Hungarian reformers, who like Professor Román (and unlike myself) are not influenced by the disappointing experience of the last two decades. They insist that social and economic conflicts arising from the extensive presence of the second economy are characteristic of a longer than anticipated transition. They also maintain that these conflicts would almost automatically be resolved by further reforms within the first economy if both state enterprises and large-scale cooperatives would operate as profit-seeking, market-sensitive, and cost-sensitive undertakings. In this view, the dominantly bureacratic coordination of the first economy could be replaced by market mechanisms, as the dominant mode of coordination, making regulatory principles of the two sub-economies more or less uniform, and the boundary between them less marked.

Recently, however, we have seen an erosion of confidence in the practicality of reforms which intend to promote market coordination by decentralizing economic power without altering the predominance of state ownership. Such scepticism – seemingly not shared by Professor Román – questions the unproven assertion that publicly owned firms can successfully resist systematic short-run pressures and adopt goals of long-term profitability. With the bureaucratic coordination renounced and

Z.J. Acs and D.B. Audretsch (eds.), The Economics of Small Firms: A European Challenge. 205–206.

market coordination unattainable, the pursuance of the intended policy of decentralization could result in a coordination vacuum which would soon prove to be a self-defeating course of action. Thus, rather than pursuing the goal of reforming the first economy, a markedly different view points to the emergence of a socialist mixed economy in which the antagonism and interdependence of multiple modes of coordination are explicitly acknowledged.

Whether one shares Professor Román' faith in the compatibility of state ownership and market coordination, or favours, as I do, the latter scenario, or even regards both as fictitious, is clearly an important determinant of what lessons one draws from the Hungarian experience. All parties seem to have come to agree on at least one important point. Namely that "strengthening the small business sector is a prerequisite to revitalizing the Hungarian economy". Opinions only differ in the pace and means of relaxing discriminatory constraints. Personally, I doubt if events will accelerate to bear out Professor Román's optimistic expectations in the next few years.

Professor Román's optimism for some of his short-term economic policy recommendations are disturbing. Anticipating increasing unemployment he suggests a reduction of full-time employment in the state sector with a simultaneous wage increase. Higher wages should reduce participation of employees in the second economy allowing state firms to extract greater efforts from their work force. The unemployed would be encouraged to become self-employed.

These propositions are not supported by empirical evidence: in spite of the lasting economic stagnation of the 1980s, demand for labour still exceeds supply, and the unemployment rate rests below one percent. In addition, unemployment is confined almost exclusively to minority groups and the unskilled, with negligible, if any, overall impact on job security and job performance of other segments of the labour force. Second, these anticipations are seemingly inconsistent even with Professor Román's own "mixed economy" concept, in which chronic excess demand for labour, as well as for all other factors of production, is regarded as a systematic characteristic, and is treated as a factor of high explanatory power in his analysis of the controversial role and postition of small business in contemporary Hungary.

Optimism against all odds might be understandable. However, we should free ourselves from overly optimistic expectations which contradict both theoretical considerations and empirical facts, giving unsound policy recommendations to politicians.

List of Contributors

Zoltan J. Acs
Research Fellow
Merrick School of Business
University of Baltimore
USA-Baltimore, MD 21201-5779
and
Wissenschaftszentrum Berlin für Sozialforschung
Reichpietschufer 50
D – 1000 Berlin 30

David B. Audretsch
Research Fellow
Wissenschaftszentrum Berlin für Sozialforschung
Reichpieterschufer 50
D – 1000 Berlin 30

Bo Carlsson
William E. Umstattd Professor of Industrial Economics
Department of Economics
Case Western Reserve University
USA – Cleveland, OH 44106

Bruno Contini
University of Torino
R.&P. s.c.r.l.
Via Eusebio Bava, 6
I – 10124 Torino

Arnold C. Cooper
Louis A. Weil Jr. Professor of Management
Department of Management
Purdue University
USA – West Lafayette, IN 47907

Mark Dodgson
Science Policy Research Unit
University of Sussex
Mantell Building
Falmer, Brighton
GB – East Sussex BN1 9RF

William C. Dunkelberg
Dean School of Business and Management
111 Speakman Hall
Temple University
USA - Philadelphia, PA 19122

David S. Evans
National Economic Research Associates, Inc.
123 Main Street
USA - White Plains, NY 10601

Felix R. FitzRoy
Research Fellow
Wissenschaftszentrum Berlin für Sozialforschung
Reichpietschufer 50
D - 1000 Berlin 30

István R. Gábor
Department of Economics, Labour and Education
Karl Marx University of Economics
H - 1828 Budapest 489 Pf. 5.

Christopher J. Hull
Assistant Secretary General
TII - European Association for
Technology Transfer Innovation
3, rue des Capucins
L - 1313 Luxembourg

Bruce A. Kirchhoff
Rothman Institute of Entrepreneurship
Fairleigh Dickinson University
Madison, NJ 07940

Mark H. Lazerson
European University Institute
Via Boccaccio 121
I - 50183 Firenze

Linda S. Leighton
Department of Economics
Fordham University
USA - Bronx, NY 10469

Jürgen Müller
Deutsches Institut für Wirtschaftsforschung
Königin-Luise-Str. 5
D – 1000 Berlin 33

Riccardo Revelli
University of Torino
R.&P. s.c.r.l.
Via Eusebio Bava, 6
I – 10124 Torino

Zoltán Román
Institute of Industrial Economics
Hungarian Academy of Sciences
Budaörsi ut 45
H – 1502 Budapest, Pf. 132 XI.

Joachim Schwalbach
Wissenschaftszentrum Berlin für Sozialforschung
Reichpietschufer 50
D – 1000 Berlin 30

David J. Storey
Small Business Centre
School of Industrial & Business Studies
University of Warwick
GB – Coventry CV4 7AL

A.R. Thurik
Small Business Economics
Erasmus University Rotterdam
Burg Oudlaan 50
NL – 3062 PA Rotterdam

Hideki Yamawaki
Research Fellow
Wissenschaftszentrum Berlin für Sozialforschung
Reichpietschufer 50
D – 1000 Berlin 30

Index

Studies in Industrial Organization

Series Editors:
H. W. de Jong, *University of Amsterdam, The Netherlands*
W. G. Shepherd, *University of Massachusetts, Amherst, U.S.A.*

Publications:

1. H. W. de Jong (ed.): *The Structure of European Industry.*
   Revised edition, 1988: see below under Volume 8
2. M. Fennema: *International Networks of Banks and Industry* (1970–1976). 1982
   ISBN 90–247–2620–4
3. P. Bianchi: *Public and Private Control in Mass Product Industry.* The Cement Industry Cases. 1982 ISBN 90–247–2603–4
4. W. Kingston: *The Political Economy of Innovation.* (1984) 1989 2nd printing
   ISBN 90–247–2621–2
5. J. Pelkmans: *Market Integration in the European Community.* 1984
   ISBN Hb: 90–247–2978–5; Pb: 90–247–2988–2
6. H. W. de Jong and W. G. Shepherd (eds.): *Mainstreams in Industrial Organization.* 1986
   Book I: *Theory and International Aspects.* ISBN 90–247–3461–4
   Book II: *Policies: Antitrust, Deregulation and Industrial.* ISBN 90–247–3462–2
   Set ISBN Book I + II: 90–247–3363–4
7. S. Faltas: *Arms Markets and Armament Policy.* The Changing Structure of Naval Industries in Western Europe. 1986 ISBN 90–247–3406–1
8. H. W. de Jong (ed.): *The Structure of European Industry.* 2nd revised ed. (of Volume 1). 1988 ISBN Hb: 90–247–3689–7; Pb: ISBN 90–247–3690–0
9. I. L. O. Schmidt and J. B. Rittaler: *A Critical Evaluation of the Chicago School of Antitrust Analysis.* 1989 ISBN 90–247–3792–3
10. W. Kingston: *Innovation, Creativity and Law.* 1990 ISBN 0–7923–0348–2
11. Z. J. Acs and D. B. Audretsch (eds.): *The Economics of Small Firms.* A European Challenge. 1990 ISBN 0–7923–0484–5

